Britain's maritime

MEMORIALS & MEMENTOES

Other books by the same author:
Rare Birds of the British Isles

As part of our ongoing market research, we are always pleased to receive comments about our books, suggestions for new titles, or requests for catalogues. Please write to: The Editorial Director, Patrick Stephens Limited, Sparkford, Nr Yeovil, Somerset BA22 7JJ.

Britain's maritime
MEMORIALS &
MEMENTOES

David Saunders

Patrick Stephens Limited

For all of those whose only memorial is the sea

© David Saunders 1996

First published 1996

British Library Cataloguing-in-Publication Data:
A catalogue record for this book is
available from the British Library.

ISBN: 1 85260 466 2

Library of Congress catalog card no. 96-075166

Patrick Stephens Limited is an imprint of
Haynes Publishing, Sparkford, Nr Yeovil,
Somerset, BA22 7JJ.

Designed & Typeset by G&M, Raunds, Northamptonshire
Printed and bound in Great Britain by
Butler & Tanner Ltd, London and Frome

Contents

Acknowledgements

To supplement my own investigations, I was pleased during the course of writing this book to enlist the help and support of many kind people who have drawn my attention to memorials, and in some cases provided outstanding amounts of information concerning them. Without them my work would be that much poorer.

I would like to pay a special tribute to Jim Armes of the Coastal Forces Association; Marion Bayliss, whose husband was chief officer on board the ill-fated *Derbyshire* and who kindly provided details concerning both the loss of the ship and the memorials to her crew; Stan Bond of the St Andrew's Arts Centre, formerly St Andrew's Waterside Church, Gravesend; Brookwood Cemetery Society for providing much from their records concerning maritime memorials in the cemetery; David Burrell; Jim Cook of the HMS *Stevenstone* Association; the late Hugh Cowley, who ensured the brig *Lily* at Kitterland on the Isle of Man is properly remembered; John David, who as a young coastguard witnessed the *Samtampa* tragedy, and Mrs Cynthia Richmond, whose first husband was lost in the disaster; David Dawson; George Donnison, without whom my knowledge of Liverpool and the Wirral would be very much poorer; Fred Dooley who tracked down an elusive memorial in Norfolk; Fred Duxbury DSM, for information on memorials to the Dieppe Raid in which he participated, and much else besides; Peter Everard, who gave me so much on the *Athina B* at Brighton, having served on the Shoreham lifeboat during the rescue; Maurice Fairall for the Isle of Wight; Reg Foster and Stan Lawrence of the HMS *Warspite* Association; Ron French; Reverend Leonard Griffiths, who kindly provided information on Christopher Tanner GC; Ted Goddard, a mine of ready information on Nelson; Tony Grimmer of the HMS *Ganges* Association; Commander Ian Hamilton RN, who provided so much help; Fred Hortop, who has single-handedly recorded the merchant seamen of Barry lost in two world wars; Richard Hunter, for much on ships' figureheads; Debbie Laws, whose grandfather was lost on HMS *Picotee*; Colin McIntyre; Mac and Brenda MacKay, for much on the *Dasher* memorial and for efforts elsewhere in the west of Scotland; Captain Roddy McKinnon regarding the memorials on Barra and Vatersay; Donald MacLeod, who ensured I had every bit of information concerning the *Iolaire* disaster; George Monk, who has done so much to ensure radio operators are properly remembered; June Pledger for her poems; Norman Pollitt with help on Charles Frohman and other memorials; Gavin Richardson; Mark Roberts, who kindly loaned a number of lifeboat memorial photographs; Doug Rose; Phil Rowett, for numerous contributions for north-east England and the Borders; Victor Sheppard; Jennifer Stringer, who scoured Portsmouth and Southampton and nearby locations and also provided much information from reference libraries not easily accessible to me; Helen Tarrant, whose husband was lost while flying from HMS *Avenger*; Brian Taylor of the Jack Cornwell VC National Memorial; Ann Thompson, bibliographer for the Public Monuments and Sculpture Association; Barbara Tomlinson of the National Maritime Museum; John Vigar; Clive Vinson; Margery Weston, for so much about the Isle of Man; Lionel Whebble of the Maritime Royal Artillery Old Comrades' Association; Jack Williams, founder of the Algerines Association; Roger Williams, who provided so much relating to Newport, Monmouthshire; and Ronald Wren of the Arctic Campaign Memorial Trust.

Generous thanks are also due to the editors of a number of maritime journals and magazines, together with those from the diocesan and church magazines who published my requests for information and thereby put me in contact with many other contributors, including Andrew Abbott; Alan Adamson; Richard Alexander, archivist of the Furnace Withy Group; David Alle; Dr D.A.R. Anderson; Michael Anyan; T.S. Atkins; Howard Atkinson; Stewart Atkinson, Stranraer District Council; Peter Bailey, Newhaven Historical Society; Roger Baker; Vera Barber; Reverend John Barnett; Margaret Barton; Stephen Bates; Canon Walter Beasley; James Bell; John Bell, Mersey Mission to Seamen; H. Bench; Harold Bennett, Chatham Dockyard Historical Society; Friar Jerome Bertram; Commander D.G.F. Bird RN; H. Bird; Rosemary Boaler; G. Bracey; Marion Brassington; L.A. Bridge, Coastal Forces Veterans' Association; Geoff Bridger; Jack Brown, Bounty Boys' Association; Captain S.L. Bruce, Royal Marines; Commander Henry Brook RN; Janet Brown; Mike Bundock; Robin Butler; Rosslyn Buyers; John Caine; Derek Calderwood, Grace Darling Museum; Christopher Carlisle; Very Reverend Herbert Cassidy, Dean of Armagh; Lorna Cassidy; J.E. Chamberlain-Mole, Curator of the Arbuthnot Museum, Peterhead; Diane Chamberlain, Ramsgate Maritime Museum; Don Chewins; Reverend Clive Clapson; K.E. Clapson; Bobby Clarke; Hilary Claxton; E. Coates; T.Y. Cocks; Jennifer Cole; Patrick Collinson; W. Cookson; H.L. Cooper, information officer Trinity House Lighthouse Service; Jeffrey P. Cooper; R.F. Cooper; Canon Graham Corneck; Valerie Cox; Reverend Patrick Crean; Lieutenant-Commander Mike Critchley, director of the Warship Preservation Trust; Canon Walter Crooks; John Crowther; Constance Cuff; Jo Darke, Public Monuments and Sculpture Association; Derek Davidson; Leslie Davies, Coastal Forces Veterans' Association; Cecil Dawson; Captain William Dawson; Dr Nigel Daziel, Senior Keeper of Maritime History, Lancaster Museum; D. Dixon; Reverend N.S. Dixon; John Dore-Dennis; Paul Driscoll; Ian Dufferin; Reverend Alan Duke; Philip Dunne; Captain J.E. Dykes OBE, RN, Shipwrecked Fishermen & Mariners' Royal Benevolent Society; Reverend Tim Eady; Jeffrey Eaves; John Edwards, Aberdeen Museum; Reverend Rodney Elbourne; Ron Elliott; Iris Ellis; David Ellison; Michael Elsdon and Theo Stibbons, Spalding Shipwreck Society; John Elsworth; M.E. Emerson; Andrew England; Beryl Evans; David Evans; D. Handel Evans, Llangefni Library; Gwyn Evans, Fast Minelayers Association; Helen Evans, Whitstable Museum; Bill Ferguson Knight; Peter Field; David Forshaw; J.S. Forster; Elizabeth Foxall; A. Franklin, Manx Museum; Horace Gamble; May Garland; Reverend R.H. Gillies; Nick Gilman; Alice Goodman; Fiona Gorman, Isle of Arran Museum Trust; T. Govier; C.S. Guy; C. Haddington; John Hall; John G. Hall; A.G. Halliwell; J.R. Hamer-Harries; Barrie Hampton; George Hancock; Basil Harley; J.G. Harman; Cyril Hart; R.G. Hart; Charlotte Haviland of John Swire & Sons; W. Hay; Reverend Richard Hayes; Tony Hayward; Anthony Haywood; David Head; John Herrivan; Brenda Hibberd; Duncan Hill; Mary Hoban, Hartlepool Central Library; Peter Hoare; John Hobson; Reverend W.R. Hogg; Charlie Holder; Ken Horne; Alan House; E.C. Howarth; Reverend Andrew Huckett; Hull Tourist Information Office; A.G. Humphreys; E. Hyatt OBE; Reverend David Ineson; John Ross Ireland; Mike Isaacs; Robin Ivy; Reverend Hilary Jackson; David James, Scarborough Borough Council; Morrison James; Peter James; John Jeffries; W. Jenkins; P.D. John; John Jones,

Landing Craft Gun and Flak Association; Meurig Jones; Reverend Nicholas Jones; Reverend T.H. Kaye; R.G. Keen; Captain Reg Kelso, Boatsteerer Southampton Master Mariners' Club; L. King; Margaret King, curator Bell Rock Lighthouse Museum; William Laing; Roy Lane; Gillian Laughton; John Lawton; Mike Lawton; Alan Ledbury; Christopher Lee, Maritime Trust; Edward Lendrum; M. Little, Royal Marines' Museum; Ivor Lloyd; A. Overt Locke; Alan Lockett; J.M. Longstaff; Judith Lovell; Fiona Macoll, archivist National Westminster Bank; Canon J.I. McFie; Reverend Duncan MacGillivray; Kathleen McLaren; David McLean; Malcolm MacNaughton; Reverend John McNaughton; Jane Maingay; Harold Mann; John Marlow; Michael Martin; Major E.S.L. Mason; V. Mather; Reverend Peter May; Jim Merson, Buckie District Fishing Heritage Society; Patricia Midgley, North End Trust, King's Lynn; Reverend Robert Mighall; Eric Mills; Sheila Moreby; Catherine Moriarty, National Inventory of War Memorials, Imperial War Museum; John Moore; Roy Morgan; Judith Morgenstern; Margaret Morrison, Bowmore Information Centre; Captain R.B. Mortlock RN; Reverend Robin Murch; Mary-Rose Murphy; P.G. Newton; T.K. Norledge, Institute of Marine Engineers; John Norrington; Fred O'Brien; John Ockenden; Jonathan Orr; Steve Ottery, Isles of Scilly Museum Service; Harry Pack, a survivor from the *Lancastria*; the late Jimmy Page; Peter Parke, Southwold Sailors' Reading Room; Reverend Jack Patrick; J.M. Pead; Elizabeth Pearce; John Penfold; Dr Christopher Penn; Janet Pennington, archivist Lancing College; J.R. Philip; Dr E.H.D. Phillips; Reverend Michael Phillips; Tony Phillips Smith; Dr J.R. Piggott, head of archives Dulwich College; Tina Pittock, Gurkha Museum; the late Rear-Admiral Godfrey Place VC; the late P.C. Plumtree; Mary Poole; R.J. Pope; P. Prichard; M.D. Purgavie; Paul Raggett; Laureen Raine; Joan Rayment; Lieutenant-Commander J.H. Rees RN; John T. Rees; Brian Reynolds, Lancastria Association; C.D. Reynolds; Canon Stanley Reynolds; Reverend Nicholas Richards; M.D. Richardson, Fleet Air Arm Museum; W. H. Roberts; Hamish Robertson of the frigate HMS *Unicorn*; John Robson; L.A. Rogers; Reverend Trevor Rogers; W. Rolfe; Philip Roper; Lieutenant-Commander Brian Rowland RN; Oliver Ryan; Margaret Sadler; Graham Salter; Captain B.D. Salwey RN; Reverend Geoffrey Scott; Canon John Seymour; Reverend Michael Shears; Syd Shilling; John Simpson; Arthur Skelton, Royal Naval Patrol Service Association; Peter Slater of the Buckie Seamen's Memorial; J.E. Smith, Lowestoft and East Suffolk Maritime Society; John S. Smith, Centre for Scottish Studies, University of Aberdeen; John Soanes, Ton Class Association; E.W. Sockett; Canon Hall Speers; Margaret Stevens; G. Stoddart; Brian Stone; Fred Stitt; P.J. Stoffell; Jim Swaine; Canon Michael Swindlehurst; Doreen Tait, Northumberland and Durham Family History Society; R.C. Taylor; R.S. Taylor; Gloria Tengwall; David Thomas; Gabe Thomas, registrar of shipping; Keith Thomas; Captain J.D. Thomson, Trinity House of Leith; Ron Thomson; Brian Ticehurst; I. Tiller, Islay Museums Trust; John Tipton, Tenby Museum; J.M. Tomison; R.H. Trivett; Andrew Tulloch; Royston Varley; Gerald Vernon; Commodore J.F. Wacher CBE, Honourable Company of Master Mariners; J. Walker; Canon Heather Wallace; Elizabeth Walters; Penny Ward, heritage officer Margate Library; Captain R.W. Warwick; Dr Linda Washington, National Army Museum; J.S. Watson; S.W. Webb; Zoe White; Reverend Anthony Wibberley; Douglas Wiggins; H. Wilcock; Trevor Williams; Charlie Williamson; H.B.W. Williams-Wynne; Christopher Willis, Association of Old Worcesters; J. Wynne Lewis; Ron Wood; C. Woollcombe; Dennis Wright; Ron Wylde; John York; and Iain Young, Lichfield Library.

A special word of thanks to all those who in addition to sending written material also contributed photographs of memorials. These proved especially valuable and some enliven the text. To Mac Mackay, George Donnison, Catherine Saunders and D. Rose I am especially grateful for their photographs which grace the back of the jacket.

Last, but by no means least, my thanks to my family, who have helped in many ways: Robert and Ruth, who, when a problem arose at a critical moment, loaned their camera, with which I was able to obtain most of the photographs reproduced in the book and many others which were such an invaluable reference. Rachel, Jim, and Rhys, who tracked down an elusive model ship and visited and photographed in other churches; Catherine, for help in Cornwall, and most especially for the HMS *Warspite* photograph which graces the rear dust jacket; Norman and Heather, whose venture into the wilds' of Hertfordshire was memorable and will live long in the family annals; to my father, who tracked down George Archer-Shee; and finally my wife Shirley, without whom this book could not have been written. Companion, driver, navigator, researcher, and provider of sustenance, whose alertness in spotting that extra special memorial which might otherwise have been missed, enlivened many a journey, and contributed greatly to this book. I hope that they all agree the end result is worth it.

Introduction

Two quotations from Robert Louis Stevenson spring immediately to mind when one considers our wealth of maritime history and the many memorials to be found dedicated to those who served at sea, and especially to those lost at sea. Who would question his poignant words: 'I suppose no other nation has lost as many ships or sent as many brave fellows to the bottom'? While his observation that 'the best monument of the brave dead is the thought of them in the minds of their friends – their resting place is the love of their fellow countrymen', has a particularly eloquent ring, and a special meaning for those who have lost loved ones at sea. Numerous, indeed almost countless, maritime memorials help ensure that those who went to sea and did not return, as well as those who lived to peaceful and graceful retirement, are well remembered throughout our country.

One does not have to travel very far to find a maritime memorial in a church or town hall, on a village green or city square, a sea front esplanade or dockside wall, or

Unveiling of the memorial to HMS Dasher *at Ardrossan.* (John Hall)

PRESENTED BY THE P.S.P.S.
(SCOTTISH BRANCH)
IN MEMORY OF
CAPTAIN JOHN E. CAMERON, D.S.C., R.N.R.,
WHO COMMANDED H.M.S. WAVERLEY
SUNK AT DUNKIRK IN MAY 1940,
WAS THE FIRST MASTER OF THIS STEAMER
AND ADVOCATE OF HER PRESERVATION

Memorial plaque on board the paddle-steamer Waverley.

on a wave-dashed headland or a remote hillside, though, naturally, in coastal areas the density of memorials is much higher. Even at sea there can be memorials, like those to her gallant predecessor on board the last sea-going paddle-steamer, *Waverley*. Some of our large cities and coastal ports – places like Liverpool and Southampton – abound in maritime memorials. The great naval bases, in particular Portsmouth; with nearby Southsea, have so many that one cannot do them justice in the space available. There must be many more awaiting discovery.

The words of fiery Admiral of the Fleet Baron Fisher of Kilverstone are certainly almost correct for London, as far as monuments to great captains in public places are concerned:

'I see another General is to be deported into Trafalgar Square! [Lord Napier, from opposite the Athenaeum, to make way for King Edward's statue.] Why don't they pull down the Duke of York's, who sold commissions to haberdashers via Mrs Clarke (*quifacit per alium facit per se*.) When Nelson looks around London, he sees only one naval officer, Sir John Franklin, and he died from ice not war! Where are Hawke of Quiberon, Rodney, Cornwallis, Howe, Benbow, and all of Nelson's Captains? Was this country made by sailors or soldiers? If monuments are any guide then the sea had no victories for us.'

Since then another maritime statue has been added in Waterloo Place, to Captain Robert Falcon Scott, but he too 'died from ice not war'. There is also Captain Cook outside the Admiralty, and now Admiral Mountbatten in Whitehall. An absence of maritime statues in the London squares there may be, but this is more than recompensed by those in St Paul's Cathedral and Westminster Abbey, while elsewhere in London, as this book will demonstrate, numerous other maritime memorials await your visit, while many more await discovery. At the same time one is moved to ask why that to the Royal Naval Division, which formerly stood outside the Admiralty, was moved to the Royal Naval College, Greenwich, and so beyond the reach of most onlookers? Let us bring it back to an honoured place in central London.

What prompted my voyage of maritime discovery, for that is how I see my search for memorials? How did it all start? Here I hasten to add that I have never served at sea myself, nor do I recall ever particularly wishing to go to sea, though for virtually the whole of my adult life I have lived within sight or sound of it, and in rough weather there have always been good deposits of salt on my windows. From where I write I look west, through the entrance to Milford Haven, beyond which there is no land until one reaches Florida, some 5,000 miles away.

Was it listening with my mother to a programme on Children's Hour about the hunt for and subsequent sinking of the *Bismarck*? Was it the waterline model of a battleship – *Warspite*, as far as I was concerned – purchased in that heaven for small boys in the 1940s, the Bon Marche toy department in Gloucester? And two other childhood maritime influences remain clear in my mind. Briefly I was a Wolf Cub, and on the wall of the Scout hut where we met was a picture of Jack Cornwell VC, standing by the gun of HMS *Chester* at Jutland; and at school there was a picture of the *San Demetrio*, and I remember being told the gripping story of how she was brought back to port after having been set on fire by the *Admiral Scheer*.

The first memorial that I photographed, however, was military, not naval, being that of Lieutenant-Colonel Doughty Wylie VC at Thebberton Church in Suffolk, who fell at Sedd-el-Bahr during the Gallipoli landings in April 1915. This was in 1957, though it was some years more before I began to visit, collect if you like, maritime memorials, that little row on the seafront at Southsea, almost in the shadow of the great Royal Navy memorial, being my inspiration.

At every opportunity I have sought memorials, from Lerwick in the Shetlands to Mousehole in Cornwall, from St David's on the Welsh coast to Great Yarmouth in Norfolk, where a fine monument to Nelson looks out over the North Sea. Nevertheless, despite my own efforts, and those of a tireless band of contributors, I know that this book only scratches the surface. Space would not allow more, and numerous memorials await discovery. Hopefully others will be now be moved to take up the search, both for their own pleasure and also to contribute to the index of

Left *Royal Naval Division memorial, currently in the Royal Naval College, Greenwich.* (Royal Navy)

Below *Fast Minelayer Memorial at Milford Haven.*

pre-1914 maritime memorials maintained by the National Maritime Museum, and the National Inventory of War Memorials maintained by the Imperial War Museum.

Maritime memorials provide a marvellous insight into our history. They tell of high endeavour, of battles won, and sometimes battles lost, of great voyages and great ships, of discovery, fire, piracy, and even cannabilism, murder and mayhem at sea. They tell of lost lives and lost ships, of ships thrown on to rocky coasts and sandy bars and epic rescues, many doomed to failure and more tragedy.

As one reads the details, standing in a church, a town square, or on a windy esplanade, one has shed many a quiet tear as one has turned away, moved by the tragic story that unfolds. For here is written our great maritime history. No nation has one greater, and, as Rudyard Kipling said, 'if blood be the price of admiralty, Lord God, we ha' paid in full!'

There are frustrations, such as the discovery that so many inscriptions are now unreadable, some the result of erosion or the accumulation of many years' growth of lichen, but others the victims of wanton vandalism, especially in city cemeteries. However, the biggest frustration without question is locked churches, understandable though this is these days, when security is paramount and nothing is safe from vandalism or plain theft. A big plea, though, to those who administer them (and many manage it well enough): at the very least give details of where a key may be obtained, and thus allow access to be gained with proper safeguards. There is nothing worse for a weary researcher who has travelled far than to find a church firmly shut with no clue as to how he might gain access.

Such disappointments are, fortunately, generally far out-weighed by the friendliness and helpfulness of many incumbents and parishioners: such as the ladies of Audlem late one November afternoon, who could not have been more delighted to provide tea and cakes; the vicar of the Caernarvon Garrison Church on another November evening; the lady at Old Walls, who showed us round and remembered being at school with those whose names were recorded there; and the vicar of St Leonard's at Deal, whose grass-cutting we interrupted.

What a delight it is to find the name of the ship on a memorial, and what a tragedy they are not recorded on the great naval memorials at Chatham, Plymouth, and Portsmouth. One town in north-west England has a massive war memorial, on which, though the names of Army regiments are provided, there is not the name of a single ship. To me this is a lamentable omission, though, for those with access to the records of the Commonweath War Graves Commission, it can result in the need for further research, that most enjoyable of pastimes.

So to the book, divided into regional sections, and then arranged alphabetically by location, including the grid reference from the 1:50,000 scale Ordnance Survey map. The grid reference is omitted in respect of Central London, where the name should be sufficient for those seeking the location. Many entries are multiple, for example Liverpool, and in such cases I have given the grid reference for the first memorial referred to. However, it should not prove difficult, from the subesquent descriptions, to locate the others. Perhaps you will even make additional discoveries on the way: they are there to be made.

You may call me old-fashioned, but I have followed the old county names pre-dating the reorganization of administrative boundaries in 1972, some recently re-organized again. The old names are those which have stood the test of time, so let us stay with them.

Quite a number of incidents and individuals are commemorated at more than a single location, as a glance at the indexes will reveal. In the text I have by and large referred to subsequent entries in the first one, and then in each of these have cross-referenced to the intitial account.

I have, as far as possible, tried to provide background information concerning the individual, the vessel, or the incident commemorated. Space by and large precludes a great deal being said, but I hope that what I have provided is sufficient to inspire the reader to search for more. Each memorial will have its own particular story, and reading the inscription is just the beginning of one's search.

I have not touched upon the names of hotels and public houses, another rich field for the maritime historian (and lover of good food and drink) to explore. Street names could also prove worthy of investigation, as indeed could the 'Blue Plaques' which can now be found on many buildings in cities and towns.

More memorials are being added all the while. During the course of writing this book several new ones were unveiled, including a *Titanic* memorial garden at Greenwich, the first memorial in London to all those lost in this best-known of all maritime disasters. While on this very day I have attended the unveiling in Milford Haven of a memorial to those who served on the fast minelayers during the Second World War.

I would be delighted to hear from anyone with information on maritime memorials and mementoes, old or new, which they feel deserve to be recorded.

I know that other memorials are planned for the years ahead. These need our support and blessing. There is certainly no shortage of epic deeds and worthy individuals deserving our attention. For, to quote the words found at the memorial flagstaff at Northam, Devon: 'May these shores never be without brave and pious mariners who will count their lives as worthless in the cause of their Country, their Bible and their Queen. Amen.'

This book was written at Woosung, Milford Haven, the house of Captain William Griffiths (died 1944) who made 34 voyages around Cape Horn in great sailing ships, and was completed on 8 May 1995, Victory in Europe Day.

David Saunders

The Memorials

England

Addington, Kent
178/653588

An obelisk in the churchyard was erected in memory of Lucy Locker, 'the amiable and affectionate wife' of William Locker, who is also remembered here. He entered the Royal Navy in 1746 as a captain's servant on the 70-gun *Kent,* rising to become a post captain at the age of 38. Nelson, then a lieutenant, served under him in the *Lowestoft*, and in the West Indies received his first command, a schooner, which was named *Little Lucy* after Locker's daughter. William Locker died at Greenwich, aged 70, on Boxing Day 1800, Nelson recording that 'he left a character for honour and honesty which none can surpass and very few attain.'

Aldeburgh, Suffolk
156/464568

A lifeboat disaster is remembered by a tablet in the church and a memorial at the eastern edge of the churchyard. These record the names of the seven men lost, from the crew of 18, when the lifeboat *Aldeburgh* capsized on 7 December 1899 while being launched 'in the teeth of an easterly gale and a heavy rolling sea.'

Also in the church, a small tablet records that Ordinary Seaman George Taylor was drowned at sea from HMS *Dragon* in April 1932. The war memorial includes 18 Royal Navy names, including one Christine Jay, for the First World War, and nine for the Second World War plus one from the Merchant Navy.

Aldenham, Hertfordshire
166/140985

The last British destroyer to be sunk in the Second World War, HMS *Aldenham,* is remembered by a stained glass window in the church. This Hunt class destroyer took part in no fewer than 14 convoys to Malta, and the invasions of Sicily and Italy, before being mined off Yugoslavia on 14 December 1944 with the loss of 126 lives.

Alnwick, Northumberland
81/186134

The White Swan Hotel has a ballroom panelled with wood from the *Olympic,* the sister ship of the *Titanic*. She was scrapped at Wallsend on the Tyne after a career lasting from 1912 to 1936.

Alum Bay, Hampshire
196/305855

A small memorial records how Marconi erected the first permanent wireless station

Memorial to the fact that the first newspaper produced at sea was transmitted from Alum Bay. (Maurice Fairall)

here in 1897 and tells how, on 15 November 1898, the first newspaper ever produced at sea was transmitted and printed on the United States liner *St Paul* some 36 miles away.

Amble, Northumberland
81/267047

A plaque reminds passers by of Freddie the bottle-nosed dolphin which frequented the harbour for several years, much to the delight of all. There have been similar occurrences at other harbours around the coast.

Angmering, Sussex
197/066044

One of the most gallant actions of the Second World War is recalled by a tablet in the church, this to Lieutenant-Commander Gerald Molson RN, who, as second-in-command and gunnery officer on HMS *Rawalpindi*, lost his life during the action with the *Scharnhorst* and *Gneisenau,* 23 November 1939. The armed merchant cruiser *Rawalpindi* was patrolling between Iceland and the Faroes when she sighted the two battle-cruisers at dusk. Despite having only six-inch guns, Captain Edward Kennedy immediately engaged the *Scharnhorst,* scoring one hit before being overwhelmed by her more powerful adversary. In the words of the Admiralty Report: 'The *Rawalpindi* maintained the fight until every gun was put out of action and the whole ship ablaze.' The German battle-cruisers picked up 27 survivors, and the following day HMS *Chitral* found a further 11.

Anwick, Lincolnshire
121/115507

Few naval disasters of the nineteenth century stirred the emotions more than the loss of HMS *Captain*, remembered in the church here by a plaque to Midshipman Alfred Angelo Ashington, who, aged 18, was lost when she 'foundered off Cape Finisterre on the morning of 7 September 1870.'

The building of HMS *Captain* had been the result of a fierce argument which had raged between those, led by Captain Cowper Coles RN, who favoured a turret ironclad and those who still yearned for broadside armament. Coles had 'fought year after year to get a sea-going turret ship built – only to be subjected to departmental obstruction and frustration while suffering the handicap of constant illness, which prevented him from putting his views before the Committees called to consider them, and finally fated to have the ship of his dreams built overweight, so that under stress of weather she was to shatter the hope of success her achievements

seemed to justify before taking him down in the vortex of her foundering.'

HMS *Captain* was bound for Gibraltar on her maiden voyage when, shortly after midnight, she capsized in a full gale and heavy seas, turning completely over and sinking with the loss of 483 souls. There were just 18 survivors, the gunner James May and 17 ratings, who managed to scramble aboard the pinnace. (See *Bedstone*; *Boscastle*; *Chislehurst*; *London – St Paul's Cathedral*; *Lymington*; *Micheldever*.)

Appledore, Devon
180/464307

Twelve young men who had attended the Appledore Young Mens' Bible Class but who were subsequently lost at sea are listed in the church, together with their vessels, while a separate brass records another, Ernest Carter, drowned off the Cape of Good Hope from the barque *Abyssinia*. The First World War memorial fortunately includes the ships, while a White Ensign hanging here was from the nearby camp where men trained for the Normandy landings.

Arrow, Warwickshire
150/070560

A plaque in the church commemorates Vice-Admiral Lord Hugh Seymour. While in his twenties, leading 'an irregular and convivial life, he was admitted to the intimacy of the Prince of Wales; from this fate he was in great measure rescued by his marriage'. His youthful misdemeanours, however, did not impair his career, the inscription recording 'his skill and courage . . . in the relief of Gibraltar 1792, also in command of the *Leviathan* in the victory of 1 June 1794 and in the successful action off L'Orient in 1795 when the flag was in *Sans Pareil*.' He died in the West Indies of yellow fever in 1801 aged 42, 'closing prematurely a career of honour.'

There is also a white marble reclining figure of Admiral of the Fleet Sir George Francis Seymour, who died in 1870 aged 83, eldest son of Vice-Admiral Hugh Seymour and Lady Horatio, and a window in memory of Admiral Henry Meynell, who died in 1865 aged 74.

Aston Rowant, Oxfordshire
165/727990

An early loss in the First World War was the battleship HMS *Formidable*. A plaque in the church records the death of Commander J.F. Ballard RN on board when she was torpedoed by *U-24* in the English Channel in the early hours of 1 January 1915. The *Official*

History records that Captain A.N. Loxley remained 'standing with his terrier on the bridge till the last, giving his orders as coolly as though the ship were lying in harbour, cheering and steadying the men, praising the officers for each smart piece of work, and his reward was to see perfect discipline and alacrity maintained to the end.' Despite such courage he and 546 others were lost. Some 71 survivors were spotted by the three crew and a boy of the Brixham trawler *Provident*. In a brilliant piece of seamanship they came alongside and rescued all on board just before the launch sank. For this the *Provident* was awarded a gratuity of £550 and each of the crew a silver medal for gallantry at sea.

Aswarby, Lincolnshire
122/377702

A plaque in the church is in memory of George Bass, born in the village in 1771, who sailed as a naval surgeon with Matthew Flinders (see *Donnington*) on his voyage of discovery around Australia. It was he that, by sailing a small whaling-boat south along the coast of New South Wales and past Cape Howe in 1796, first revealed the existence of the stormy waters of the strait that bears his name. In the following year he circumnavigated Tasmania. Little more seems to be known, one possibility being that he died in South America in about 1800.

Audlem, Shropshire
118/660437

A marble wall-tablet includes a reference to Sub-Lieutenant Jack Hainsworth Maxwell, Drake Battalion, Royal Naval Division RNVR, who was killed in action on the outskirts of Beaucourt, France 'while bravely leading his Company, though wounded, 13th. Nov. 1916, aged 21 years.'

Bamburgh, Northumberland
75/178350

> *T'was on the Longstone lighthouse,*
> *There dwelt an English maid:*
> *Pure as the air around her,*
> *Of danger ne'er afraid.*
> *One morning just at daybreak.*
> *A storm toss'd wreck she spied;*
> *And tho' to try seemed madness,*
> *'I'll save the crew!' she cried.*

So runs the first verse of the Grace Darling song, just part of an outpouring of national pride in the part she played rescuing survivors from the steam packet *Forfarshire*, which had run aground on the Big Harcar, Farne Islands, in heavy weather on 7

September 1838. Grace was the 22-year-old daughter of William Darling, lighthouse keeper on the Longstone Light nearly half a mile away. Together they launched their coble and, on reaching the rocks, took on board five survivors and returned to the Longstone. Then William Darling and two of those rescued made the perilous voyage again, and brought back the remainder, making a total of nine in all.

The *Times* asked. 'Is there in the whole field of human history, or of fiction even, one instance of female heroism to compare for one moment with this?' Showered with tributes, donations, and awards, and in receipt of invitations to appear on the stage, and even in a circus, Grace Darling chose to remain with her parents at the Longstone Light. Alas, she succumbed to tuberculosis, and died just four years later. There is a large and ornate memorial at her grave in Bamburgh churchyard, and a memorial window in the church, which is just opposite the house where she was born. (See *Hull*; *Inner Farne*.)

Bampton, Oxfordshire
164/312034

A stone plaque in the church is to Lieutenant John Loveday, who died with 14 other officers and 173 ratings when HMS *Exmouth* was sunk, most probably by a torpedo, in the Moray Firth on 21 January 1940.

Banbury, Oxfordshire
151/454402

A superb window in the parish church is to Admiral Sir George Back, who died in June 1878 aged 81. The border is made up of snowflakes, while the exploration scenes, based on the Admiral's own sketch books, show reindeer, Polar bears, Arctic foxes, and Eskimos, as well as an ice-bound HMS *Terror*. His was as adventurous a life as one could wish for. He was captured by the French while on a cutting out expedition from the *Arethusa* when just 13, and was in the *Akbar* when she was dismasted during a hurricane. He was a member of the naval expedition which reached Spitzbergen in 1818, and later made epic journeys along the shores of Arctic Canada. He led a search expedition for Sir John Ross in 1833, and made one further voyage, aboard the *Terror*, when she was beset by ice in Fox Channel and only just survived the winter.

Bardney, Lincolnshire
121/120696

A memorial to IX Squadron RAF, which flew from here 1943–5, includes a stone brought from Kafjord, lair of the *Tirpitz*, which ship the squadron damaged during a raid.

Barking, Essex
177/440839

Standing in the grounds of the long-demolished Abbey, the parish church of St Margaret's contains a specially fine memorial to Captain John Bennett, who died in 1706. Alas, this was not accessible during my visit as a fire started by vandals had caused extensive damage to part of the church.

Barnstaple, Devon
180/558333

A recent memorial is the plaque in the Guildhall to those lost when the Hunt class destroyer HMS *Stevenstone* was badly damaged by a mine while patrolling off Walcheren on 30 November 1944. Fourteen of her crew were killed, to be remembered 50 years later in a moving ceremony when the plaque was unveiled in the presence of some of the survivors and relatives of those who did not return.

Barnston, Cheshire
108/280832

A grave in the churchyard records that Thomas Evans lost his life 'through the sinking of the *Lusitania*'. The 32,500-ton Cunard liner was torpedoed off the Old Head of Kinsale by *U-20* on the afternoon of 7 May 1915. Much controversy has raged since regarding her cargo and the circumstances of her sinking, in which 1,198 were lost and 761 saved, a tragedy 'still cited as a poignant example of how fatal bad faith, bad luck and bad judgement can be.' (See *Constantine*; *Grange-over-Sands; Marlow*.)

Barrow, Lancashire
96/198708

Commonwealth War Graves Commission headstones each have their own particular story. Here in the cemetery are the graves of four seamen from the HMCS *Saguenay*, pride of the Canadian Navy. On 1 December 1940, while escorting a homeward bound convoy, she was badly damaged by a torpedo which left 18 of her crew dead. With the vessel on fire, preparations were made to abandon ship, but eventually the blaze was brought under control and the crippled vessel slowly made her way to Barrow. The *Saguenay* subsequently returned to service, helping escort HMS *Prince of Wales* to Newfoundland with Winston Churchill on board to meet President Roosevelt.

Basing, Hampshire
185/666529

A memorial in the church is to Harry Paulet, last Duke of Bolton (1719–94), known as 'Captain Sternpost' as a result of an incident when in command of the 90-gun *Barfleur*, part of Admiral Hawke's fleet. Ordered to 'chase sail', he lost contact with the rest of the fleet on the night of 22 August 1755 and returned to Spithead, giving as a reason a loose sternpost. He was aquitted of the charge of returning to port without permission, while the ship's carpenter was dismissed for gross incompetence. It was popularly thought that Paulet was to blame, having forced the carpenter to falsify his report.

Bath, Somerset
172/740640

A number of naval officers are remembered in the Abbey, including Admiral Hargood, who died in December 1839 aged 79. His services had included being a lieutenant on board the *Magnificent* at the Battle of the Saintes, 12 April 1782, and commander of the *Bellisle* at Trafalgar. There is a plaque to Admiral Arthur Phillip, first Governor of New South Wales, who had lived nearby (see *Bathampton; London – Cheapside*). Another recalls Captain John Edgcumbe, who accompanied Captain Cook on his first two voyages of discovery. A fine carved monument is to Admiral Sir Richard Bickerton.

A poignant memorial is one to Cecillia, daughter of Edward P. Henslaw, storekeeper of HM Dockyard, Chatham, who died in 1802 aged nine months and three weeks. Another recalls the deaths of a father and two of his infant children on the voyage home from India in 1860.

Rear-Admiral Sir Edward Berry, who died in 1831, is remembered in Walcot Church. He was one of few men to have commanded a ship in three general actions – those of the Nile, Trafalgar, and San Domingo – while 'if we add St Vincent and the First of June, and the five actions in the East Indies between Hughes and Suffren, together with the loss of the *Leander* and the capture of the *Genereux* and the *Guillaume Tell*, it will be seen that the record of his war service is in the highest degree exceptional.'

Bathampton, Somerset
172/777665

The church is a place of pilgrimage for all those interested in the history of Australia, for here is buried Admiral Phillip, who commanded what has become known as the 'First Fleet', being the first which sailed to

Memorials in the Australia Chapel, Bathampton Church.

Australia, where he landed on 26 January 1788. The Admiral and his wife lie just inside the entrance, in front of a low wooden shrine erected by the Fellowship of the First Fleet in 1995. (See *London – Cheapside*; *Portsmouth*; *Ryde*.)

On another wall there is a plaque to members of the Sause family. Robert, a Royal Navy captain, who died 13 June 1827 aged 69, and his only son Richard, who 'was wounded in the Battle of Trafalgar and died on the 26 February 1807 in his twentieth year.'

Batheaston, Somerset
172/777679

In the church is a plaque to Lieutenant D. Sealy DSC RN, commander of HM Submarine *H-42*, lost with all hands off Europa Point, Gibraltar, 23 March 1922. While surfacing she was almost cut in two by HMS *Versatile*. There were no survivors. Lieutenant Sealy had been awarded the DSC in 1916 and a Bar in 1918 for his services in the Baltic.

Bayfordbury, Hertfordshire
166/318100

An obelisk, in woodland appropriately known as 'Sailors' Grove', is to members of the Baker family, including Henry who died while rescuing the crew of a Spanish schooner foundering off Jamaica in 1804, and Charles who was shipwrecked in 1822. Another is Admiral Sir Lewis Clinton Baker, who took part in the bombardment of Alexandria in 1882, and commanded the *Hercules* at Jutland.

Bearsted, Kent
178/801555

A window in the church recalls a casualty from HMS *Glorious*, which, while proceeding home from Norway in June 1940 with the destroyers *Ardent* and *Acasta*, was caught unawares by the *Scharnhorst* and *Gneisenau*. Unable to launch her torpedo bombers in defence she was quickly sunk. The destroyers, carrying the fight to the enemy, were also sunk, though not before a torpedo from *Acasta* severely damaged the *Scharnhorst*. Few survived that day, the *Official History* reporting 'the names of Glasfurd and Barker of the *Acasta* and *Ardent* . . . lost in unhesitatingly attacking heavy, even hopeless, odds should be remembered for ever in the Navy's long story of unquestioning devotion to duty.' (See *Boscastle*; *Gosforth*; *Martindale*.)

Beaulieu, Hampshire
196/388025

Some of the famous shipbuilders whose yards were situated downstream at Buckler's Hard are remembered at the church. Among several other maritime memorials is a bronze tablet in memory of Eleanor Thornton, who died on board the liner *Persia*, sunk off Crete with the loss of 334 persons in December 1915. (See *Berwick-upon-Tweed*.)

Beckingham, Nottinghamshire
112/779903

A brass plate to Mrs Marian Parkinson, who died on 17 November 1904, was erected by the 1st Battalion, The Queen's Regiment. As a four-year-old girl, the daughter of Drum Major John R. Darkin, Marian had been one of the survivors from the troopship *Birkenhead*. This auxiliary three-masted paddle-steamer had been carrying men for the Eighth Kaffir War when, at appropriately-named Danger Point east of Cape Town, she hit a previously uncharted rock on 25 February 1852. The troops were paraded on deck with 'order and regularity' as evacuation began. However, the *Birkenhead* quickly started to break up, and only three boats could be launched, carrying amongst others the seven women and 13 children aboard. As the ship began to settle some 40 men climbed the main mast, the only part to remain above water, while a further 68 managed to reach the shore, despite the shark-infested waters. (See *Bury St Edmunds*; *London – Chelsea*; *Edinburgh*.)

Bedstone, Shropshire
148/369758

A plaque in the church was erected 'as an expression of affectionate regret by the officers of HMS *Royal Oak*' to the memory of Midshipman Alfred Ripley, aged 18, who was lost in HMS *Captain*. He had served in the *Royal Oak* for two years, only leaving some four days before his death. (See *Anwick*.)

Belton, Lincolnshire
130/930395

A plaque in the church is to Sub-Lieutenant Arthur John Purey-Cust and his gallant comrades. He was serving on the destroyer *Strongbow* which, together with the *Mary Rose* and the armed trawlers *Elise* and *P. Fannon*, was engaged on North Sea convoy duties east of the Shetlands when, on 17 October 1917, she was attacked by the German minelaying cruisers *Bremse* and *Brummer*, sinking about 90 minutes later with the loss of 47 officers and ratings from her crew of 88.

A carved head at Biddenden, reputed to have come from an Armada ship.

Berwick-upon-Tweed, Northumberland
75/999532

Among several memorials in the parish church is one to John Maitland Foster, just 16, who fell while serving on HMS *Bellerophon* during the first bombardment of Sebastopol, October 1854. Another is to John Robertson, attached to the 2/3 Queen Alexandra's Own Gurkha Rifles, who was one of 334 lost when the liner *Persia* was torpedoed south of Crete in December 1915. (See *Beaulieu*.)

In the Guildhall are displayed the plaque and name-plate of the tenth *Berwick*, a cruiser (1928–48), together with details of her service which included action against the German cruiser *Hipper*, and at the Battle of Spartivento off Sardinia on 27 November 1940. The ensign flown that day now hangs in the nearby King's Own Scottish Borderers Museum.

Betteshanger, Kent
179/312525

An ornate memorial in the church by the Belgian artist Peter Scheemakers is to Admiral Morrice of the White Squadron, who died in 1740.

Biddenden, Kent
189/851384

Above the doorway of a shop on the south side of the High Street, formerly a wig-makers, is a carved head said to be from a wrecked Armada ship.

Bideford, Devon
180/454264

One of Devon's greatest sons is remembered by a large brass plaque in the parish church – Sir Richard Grenville, who had fought the Spaniards many times before being cornered at Flores in the Azores, where he was killed on board his ship the *Revenge* in 1591 facing an overwhelming force. The church register contains an entry concerning 'Raleigh', a Wyanditoian, who was the first Red Indian to land in Great Britain, having been brought from Virginia by Sir Richard.

There is a plaque to Thomas Browne Smith, killed while boarding a Turkish fire-ship, who 'was much esteemed in the service and no officer fell at Navarino more beloved and regretted.' We are told of John Strange, mayor four times, who died in 1646 of the plague, the plaque to his memory being erected by a sea-captain he had helped. A lengthy inscription tells of the life of Rear-

Admiral Bedford Pimm, who died in 1866, who made a lengthy sledge journey during the search for Franklin. (See *Spilsby*.)

Binton, Warwickshire
151/145540

There is a marvellous memorial window in the church to Captain Scott and his companions who together reached the South Pole on 17 January 1912. Scott's brother-in-law was at one time vicar here, hence the connection, and there is a bronze crucifix by Lady Scott on his grave in the churchyard. (See *Devonport, Exeter; London – Waterloo Place; Glen Prosen – Scotland; Cardiff – Wales*.)

Birkenhead, Cheshire
108/311903

HMS *Plymouth*, a Rothesay class Type 12 Frigate completed in 1961, is moored at West Float as a memorial to those who lost their lives during the Falklands Campaign of 1982. The chapel on board is a fine tribute to the 88 men of the Royal Navy, 27 of the Royal Marines, ten of the Royal Fleet Auxiliary and six of the Merchant Navy. The lectern was specially made at Walton Prison, Liverpool, for presentation to the *Plymouth*. At the dedication in October 1993 the words of Admiral Sandy Woodward, who had commanded the task force, were recalled: 'As I haul my South Atlantic flag down, I reflect sadly on the brave lives lost, and the good ships gone, in the short time of our trial. I thank wholeheartedly each and every one of you for your gallant support, tough determination and fierce perseverance under bloody conditions. Let us all, as we return severally to enjoy the blessings of our land, resolve that those left behind forever shall not be forgotten.'

John Laird (1805–74), pioneer shipbuilder, has a statue in the Hamilton Square Gardens. At Christ Church in Claughton there is a plaque to George Cochran, lost when the RMS *Leinster* was torpedoed on 10 October 1918. In the grounds of the Royal Naval Association in Park Road East there is a plaque on a boulder which reads: 'This stone once part Birkenhead Docklands Quay is dedicated to the memory of all seamen who sailed down the Mersey and passed over the Bar in war and peace.'

In June 1993 the rebuilt mizzen mast of the training ship *Conway* (1859–1974), formerly moored on the Mersey and later in the Menai Straits, was erected at the head of Egerton Dock as a memorial 'to the many thousands of Cadets trained to Command not forgetting those who lost their lives at sea.' Then follow the immortal words by John Masefield: 'I

must go down to the sea again to the lonely Sea and the Sky.'

St Saviour's Church at Oxton has a very beautiful memorial by Sir Giles Gilbert Scott to those who laid down their lives in the First World War. The names include two lost at sea, and two who died at Gallipoli in 1915.

Do not miss the Williamson Art Gallery and Museum with its fine models, and memorials to the No 1 pilot boats sunk in the world wars. The loss of the first, caused by a mine on 28 December 1917, resulted in 39 deaths of whom 19 were pilots. In the sinking of the second, on 26 November 1939, 23 lives were lost, including eight apprentice pilots. A *Thetis* plaque and a memorial to another pilot serve as a reminder that civilians were also lost when that submarine sank on 1 June 1939. (See *Wales – Holyhead*.)

In July 1974 HMS *Conway*, the boys' training school founded in 1857, closed. Three ships, all given the name *Conway*, successively served as accommodation on the Mersey until, because of the danger from air raids, the third, formerly HMS *Nile*, was taken to Anglesey in 1940. (See *Parkgate*.) Alas, she caught fire and the school was accommodated on shore for its remaining years. The memorials and Rolls of Honour, formerly at Plas Newydd, of boys who gave their lives in the two wars have recently been returned to Birkenhead, where it is hoped they will find a permanent home at the Priory. Individual plaques recall two who made the ultimate sacrifice: Geoffrey Dowding, lost on HMS *Good Hope* at Coronel (see *Gilling West*), and Lieutenant-Commander B.M. Skinner, killed in action on the Yangtze when commanding HMS *Amethyst* in 1949.

Birmingham, Warwickshire
139/069870

A White Ensign hanging in the Cathedral was flown during the First World War by HMS *Birmingham*, which claimed the first success against enemy submarines when she sank *U-15* some 120 miles ESE of the Orkneys on 9 August 1914. Later she was present at the Heligoland Bight, and then briefly skirmished with the German battle-cruisers of the redoubtable Admiral Hipper during his raid on the east coast. She was present at the Battle of the Dogger Bank, assisted in the hunt for the minelayer *Meteor*, and was part of Admiral Goodenough's Second Light Cruiser Squadron at the Battle of Jutland in 1916.

One of the finest memorials to Nelson stands in the Bull Ring at the city centre, being unveiled in 1809 on the fourth anniversary of the Battle of Trafalgar. (See Index under *Nelson* for the numerous other memorials.)

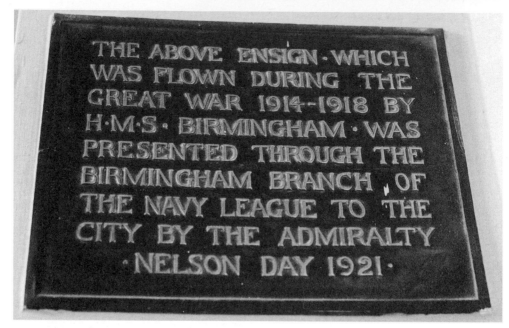

Plaque below the ensign of HMS Birmingham *in Birmingham Cathedral.*

Bishop Rock, Cornwall

203/807065

A memorial rarely seen is that at the lighthouse to the south-west of the Isles of Scilly. Here it is recorded on a plaque that the lowest stone was 'laid in a chasm of the rock at one foot below the level of low spring tides on 30 July 1852.' The building was completed and the light first used on 1 September 1858. A further plaque tells of the additional work needed in 1883 to strengthen the base and to raise the height, concluding: 'This additional undertaking was scarcely less difficult than the first and was marked by a continuance of the immunity from accident commemorated above.'

Bishop's Lydeard, Somerset

181/168297

A memorial in the church is to John Arundel 'who died for his country on board HMS *Britannia* sunk off Gibraltar on November 9th, 1918, aged 36 years.' The *Britannia*, a King Edward VII class battleship, one of eight built (known as the 'Wobbly Eight'), has the sorry distinction of being the last British warship to be sunk in the First World War. She was torpedoed by *UB-50*, with the loss of 40 of her crew.

Bishop's Sutton, Hampshire

185/606320

In the churchyard, at the base of a small cross

to the McNeile family, an inscription reads: 'Also of Ethel Rhoda his sister drowned at sea May 20th 1922 aged 46 while returning to missionary work in India.' The *Egypt*, on which she was a passenger, was rammed in thick fog off Ushant by the French steamship *Seine* and sank within 20 minutes, 71 of her crew and 17 passengers being lost.

Bishop's Waltham, Hampshire

185/555177

A plaque to the memory of Admiral of the Fleet Viscount Cunningham of Hyndhope (1863–1963) reminds us that he was Commander-in-Chief Mediterranean 1939–43 and then First Sea Lord until 1946. 'A man of florid and smiling countenance, with the blue eyes of the born sailor and the genial manner of one whose naval career had been passed chiefly in small ships, Cunningham was never one to insist on rigid formalities or precedents, and though he would excuse no failure in courage or seamanship, he would ever turn a blind eye to faults arising from dash or excess of zeal.'

Other plaques are to members of the Gifford family, several of whom served in the Royal Navy including a 17-year-old midshipman killed on board the *Invincible* at Jutland, 31 May 1916. Another is to Commander Henry Colpoys, who died aged 29 having 'sailed from Halifax in HM Packet *Calypso* which vessel is supposed to have foundered at sea. Never heard of again.'

Bishop's Wood, Staffordshire
127/841093

A plaque in the church tells of Chief Petty Officer Harry Onions who was Mentioned in Despatches for his services aboard HMS *Wigeon* at Washein on the Yangtze, 5 September 1926. His ship, together with HMS *Cockchafer*, was in action against a belligerent local war-lord who had seized two British merchant ships and was holding their officers hostage. He served in both world wars and was standard-bearer of his branch of the Royal Navy Old Comrades' Association.

Blackpool, Lancashire
102/305363

At the base of the massive war memorial on the sea front, where surrounds of bronze plaques list the fallen of two world wars, is a single name, that of F.M. Foulkes, Merchant Navy. Mechanic F. Foulkes of Great Plumpton was one of 12 men lost when the Cunard vessel *Atlantic Conveyor* was hit by an Exocet missile on 25 May 1982 during the Falklands conflict. (See *Liverpool*.)

Blakeney, Norfolk
133/033436

In the church, which has a beacon shining every night as a landmark for ships, hang the records of the Blakeney lifeboat station, including a plaque and portrait commemorating one of the coxswains, George Long, who on the night of 7 January 1918 took the lifeboat *Caroline* to the rescue of 30 men, the average age of his crew being 58. The clock in the tower was given in memory of Midshipman Christopher Gresham Cooke. A plaque records his services on HMS *Aboukir* when she was sunk on 22 September 1914, at Jutland, and then his death when HMS *Vanguard* exploded on 9 July 1917. (See *Scotland – Lyness*.) Two naval brothers, both warrant officers, feature on the war memorial plaque: William King, lost when HMS *Bulwark* exploded on 26 November 1914 (see *Hambledon*; *Little Marlow*), and George King, drowned from HMS *Crusader* while serving with the Dover Patrol in January 1917.

Blandford, Dorset
194/885064

A brass plate in the church was erected to the memory of Able Seaman George Vince of HMS *Discovery*, lost on Captain Scott's first Antarctic expedition (1901–4). He was one of a small party returning from Cape Crozier in strong winds and driving snow which found itself on the seaward slopes beyond Castle Rock. Here they became separated, and no trace of Able Seaman Vince was ever found; probably he slid into the sea.

Below a White Ensign a simple wooden plaque reads 'Hood Battalion Royal Naval Division, Antwerp, Gallipoli, France & Flanders, 1914–1918.' (See *Greater London – Crystal Palace Park, Greenwich*; *London – Covent Garden*; *Pimperne*.)

Bletchingley, Surrey
187/327508

The model of a Tristan da Cunha longboat in the church was given to the parish 'from the people of Tristan da Cunha in gratitude', a fine memento of the stay here by some evacuated islanders following the volcanic eruption in 1961. An ornate marble memorial is in remembrance of Sir William Bensley, died 1809, who 'in the early part of his life was an active and meritous officer in His Majesty's Navy.'

Lifeboat service boards in Blakeney Church.

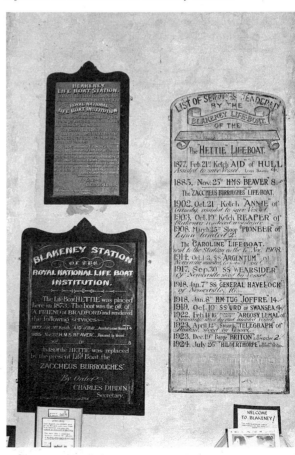

Blyth, Northumberland
81/309801

In the chapel of the Wellesley Nautical School are two wooden war memorial panels. That from 1914–18 lists 81 names, while that for 1939–45 – made from teak taken from the battleship *Iron Duke* when she was broken up – lists 26 names. In the cemetery just south of the town is a memorial pillar to four submariners.

Boldre, Hampshire
196/324994

The church is noted for its memorials to HMS *Hood*, pride of the Royal Navy, a mighty ship launched by the widow of Rear-Admiral Horace Hood, lost at Jutland on board HMS *Invincible*, from which there were but five survivors. (See *Brooksby*.) The *Hood* was to suffer a similar fate, for she was sunk by the *Bismarck* in the Denmark Strait on 23 May 1941, taking 94 officers and 1,322 men with her. There were just three survivors: Midshipman Dundas, Able Seaman Tilburn, and Signalman Briggs. Vice-Admiral Holland, who flew his flag in the *Hood*, was from this parish. The *Hood* memorials consist of a window to Saint Nicholas, Patron Saint of Sailors; oak benches in the porch with the crest of HMS *Hood*; a painting of the *Hood* by Montagu Dawson; a small model of the *Hood*; a pew runner with the crest of the *Hood*; and a book of remembrance to all those who died on the great ship. (See *Portland*; *Portsmouth*.)

One of the outer doors of the porch is in memory of an only son, Thomas Mostyn Field, aged just 16, lost on board HMS *Queen Mary* at the Battle of Jutland, 31 May 1916.

There is a memorial to Lieutenant Philip Bromfield, who 'in a few years had serv'd with Honour in Ships of every description from a Sloop to a first rate Man of War.' He died, aged 19, in 1795. In 1988 a small brass plaque was unveiled here in memory of the Reverend Richard Jobson, Curate of Boldre, who, with his new wife, sailed on board the storeship *Golden Grove* with the 'First Fleet', and held his first service in Australia on 3 February 1788. (See *Bathampton*.)

Bonchurch, Hampshire
196/569779

A memorial in the church is to Admiral of the Fleet Earl Jellicoe, who in 1882 was one of the survivors of the collision between HMS *Camperdown* and *Victoria*. (See *Bulwick*.) He was later severely wounded in China during the suppression of the Boxer Rebellion. Later, when Commander-in-Chief of the Grand Fleet, Churchill described him as 'the only man on either side who could lose the war in an afternoon.' He subsequently became First Sea Lord, and died in 1935. (See *London – St Paul's Cathedral, Trafalgar Square*.)

Bootle, Lancashire
108/364938

On the war memorial in the Garden of Remembrance in Stanley Park there is a small stone plaque, above the front bronze

Memorial door to a midshipman lost at Jutland, Boldre Church.

panel, which reads: 'In memory of the men of the Liverpool Escort Force who gave their lives 1939–1945.'

Boscastle, Cornwall

190/096909

A simple plaque in the church is in loving memory of Gerald Roose Alford, who was 'lost in the sinking of HMS *Glorious* by enemy action in the North Sea 8 June 1940 in the eighteenth year of his age.' (See *Bearsted*.) Another young man remembered here is Sub-Lieutenant James Kirkness, aged 22, lost on HMS *Captain*, 7 September 1870. (See *Anwick*.)

Bosham, Sussex

197/803039

The church in this lovely village on the shore of Chichester Harbour has two notable maritime memorials. A carving on a grave-stone shows a man falling from a bowsprit, underneath the words: 'In memory of Thomas son of Richard and Ann Borrow, Mafter of the Sloop *Two Brothers* who by the breaking of the horse fell into the sea and was drowned October 13th 1759 aged 23 years', the 'horse' being a foot-rope. Another 23-year-old remembered here, by the churchyard gates – the last work designed by her father – is Jenefer Warnum; 'the sea claimed her' in 1950.

On the wall of the north aisle a memorial to Sub-Lieutenant Edward Robert Gifford RN, aged 23, lost on HMS *Eurydice* off Dunmose Head, Isle of Wight, on 24 March 1878. This sailing frigate, used as a training ship, was returning from the West Indies with about 368 persons on board when she foundered. There were only two survivors, who reported to the subsequent Court of Enquiry that Sub-Lieutenant Gifford had been in command of the six men at the wheel as the vessel was overwhelmed. (See *Brading*; *Gosport*; *Newquay*; *Portsmouth*; *Windlesham*.)

Boston, Lincolnshire

131/326442

A fine memorial plaque to George Bass and others from Lincolnshire who played their part in the exploration of Australia is situated on a wall beneath the tower, though on my last visit this was almost obscured by the church shop. (See *Aswarby*.) A wall-plaque to Thomas Wood, killed in action 13 October 1915, includes Lieutenant Charles Sinclair Wood RNR, killed at sea 19 March 1918.

Nearly three miles away at Scotia Creek is the Pilgrim Fathers Memorial, commemorating the spot from which those later known as

Lincolnshire remembers some of its greatest maritime explorers in St Botolph's Church, Boston.

the Pilgrim Fathers had set sail on their first attempt to find religious freedom. They had embarked on a ship bound for Holland, but the captain had handed them over to the authorities, and their leaders were imprisoned. Not until 1620 did the the Pilgrim Fathers sail for North America. A stained glass window in the church shows John Cotton bidding farewell to more of his parishioners as they leave for America in 1630. He joined them three years later, his son, born on the voyage, being appropriately christened Seaborn. (See *Plymouth*; *Southampton*.)

Bothenhampstead, Dorset

193/470919

In the church a plaque recalls that John C.T. Glossop, a churchwarden here, commanded the cruiser HMAS *Sydney* when she surprised and sank the German commerce raider *Emden* at Cocos Keeling Island, 9 November 1914. At the very eastern end of the village is a redundant church, just inside the gate to which are two maritime gravestones. One is to a Captain Robert Angel, died January 1868; below is a reference to his son Alfred, 'drowned by the foundering of the *Queen of the East* off the Cape of Good Hope in the 30th year of his age.' The other refers to Thomas Jarvis, drowned by the stranding of the *Desert Flower* of Liverpool on the Long Bank off Wexford, 4 March 1864.

Bournemouth, Hampshire
195/071955

A tomb in the churchyard at Kinson is a reminder that this was formerly a lonely stretch of coastline where smugglers plied their trade. One, Robert Trotman, was killed in 1765, his tombstone reading: 'Robert Trotman, late of Road in the county of Wilts, who was barbarously murdered on the shore near Poole the 24th March 1765.

Bradford, Yorkshire
104/168332

A plaque in the Cathedral reads that 'Bradford salutes the memory of Leading Seaman James Joseph Magennis who for his singular bravery in the action by midget submarine *XE-3* against the cruiser *Takao* in the Johore Straits July 31st 1945 was awarded the Victoria Cross.' Lieutenant Ian Fraser had managed to position his craft beneath the cruiser *Takao* so that Magennis could fix six limpet mines to her bottom, but when two side-carriers of amatol explosive were released one became jammed, and the citation for Magennis' Victoria Cross records that 'despite his exhaustion, his oxygen leak and the fact that there was every probability of his being sighted, Magennis at once volunteered to leave the craft and free the carrier rather than allow a less experienced diver to undertake the job. After ten minutes of nerve racking work he succeeded in releasing the carrier. Magennis displayed very great courage and devotion to duty and complete disregard for his own safety.' He was the only Ulster Victoria Cross winner of the Second World War. In 1952, having fallen on hard times, he sold his medal for £75; it was subsequently returned by a well-wisher. Later he moved to Bradford, where he died in February 1986, his medals being sold at Sotheby's a few months later for £31,900.

Brading, Hampshire
196/606873

A memorial exists in the church to three of those lost on HMS *Eurydice*. (See *Bosham*.)

Bradpole, Dorset
193/480943

In the church is a plaque to Arthur Way RN, Captain of Transport *B26*, formerly the SS *Hypernia*, torpedoed in the Mediterranean 28 July 1918. This 3,908-ton ship was sunk some 84 miles NW by N of Port Said with the loss of seven lives, including the master.

Bramley, Hampshire
175/645590

The church has a memorial to Vice-Admiral Noel Stephen Fox Digby (1839–1920), who served in the Crimean War 1854–5, the Baltic 1855–6, and in the Ashanti War of 1872. The Second World War memorial inside the church includes H.J. Miller, who was serving on the submarine HMS *Unity* when she was accidentally rammed off Blyth, Northumberland, in thick fog on the evening of 29 April 1940 by the Norwegian freighter *Atle Jarl*. Four men were lost of whom two, Lieutenant John Low and Able Seaman Miller, went down with their vessel. They had returned below to ensure the rest of the crew had gone up on deck, and that the engines and motors had all been switched off. Both were posthumously awarded the Empire Gallantry Medal, later exchanged for the George Cross.

Bramshaw, Hampshire
184/265167

There are two particularly interesting memorials in the church. One is to seven young men of the parish aged from 17 to 32, lost in the *Titanic* on 15 April 1912. Three by the name Hickman were from the same family. (See *Southampton*.) A white marble memorial is to another youngster, Cadet Peter Vidler, aged 19, 'suddenly recalled' on 3 May 1932 whilst serving on the SS *Nardanna*.

Braunton, Devon
180/489370

A church plaque tells of John Webber, who was lost while in command of the cutter *Sea Flower* in the West Indies in 1793.

Bredon, Worcestershire
150/922360

Lieutenant Hugh Bennett RNR is remembered in the church, one of over 1,400 casualties on one of the darkest days in our naval history. On the morning of 22 September 1914 the armoured cruiser *Aboukir* was patrolling in the Broad Fourteens when she was struck by a torpedo, sinking within 25 minutes. Her sister ships *Cressy* and *Hogue*, stopping to render assistance, were promptly torpedoed in turn. (See *Brook*; *Caister-on-Sea*.)

Bridgwater, Somerset
182/299369

A statue of Robert Blake (1598–1657), a General at Sea, stands in the centre of the town for which he served as a Member of Parliament. During the Civil War he fought for the Parliamentarians, being appointed an admiral in 1649. His naval victories against the Dutch, the Barbary Coast pirates, and Spain, brought him much renown before he died near Plymouth as he returned from a decisive engagement off the Canary Islands. (See *London – Westminster St Margaret's*.)

Bridlington, Yorkshire
101/183682

A memorial in the cemetery is to those lost in the 'great gale' of 1871. Also here is Robert Redhead, who was lost when the lifeboat capsized whilst on service, 19 August 1952.

Bridport, Dorset
193/465926

The plaque in the church to members of the Carpenter family includes a reference to Henry Robert their eldest son 'aged about 14 years, a Midshipman on board HMS *Scout* sloop of war which foundered at sea in November 1802 on the Banks of Newfoundland in her voyage to Halifax in Nova Scotia when all hands perished.'

Brighstone, Hampshire
196/429827

A plaque in the church is in memory of Able-Seaman Henry Hollis, aged 21, who was killed on 23 April 1918 while serving on HMS *Iris II*, one of the two Mersey ferry-boats which accompanied HMS *Vindictive* up to the mole at Zeebrugge and suffered appalling damage and casualties as she withdrew. (See *Dover*; *Wallasey*; *Cardiff*.)

As the result of an appeal from his pulpit following the wreck of three ships in 1860, the Reverend Edward McCall raised enough funds for the purchase of a lifeboat. This and the one at nearby Brook were the first to be established in the Isle of Wight. A plaque records the lifeboat services, including attendance at the wreck of the *Sirenia* in 1888 when the lifeboat capsized and Coxswain Munt and crewman Thomas Cotton were lost.

Brightlingsea, Essex
168/087168

All Saints Church contains a series of remarkable maritime memorials, the like of which I am not aware occurring anywhere else. Oh that others might have emulated this fine example. Some 212 tiles commemorate Brightlingsea people who have died at sea between 9 December 1872 – when David Day and his son, aged 15, were lost in the schooner *William* off Hartlepool – and 30 November 1980, when Jamie Scott was killed

Just some of the marvellous memorial plaques in Brightlingsea Church to those lost at sea.

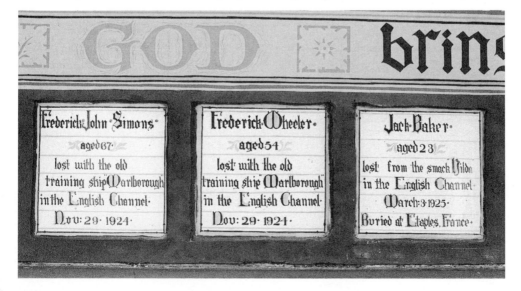

in an accident on board the fishing vessel *Seabien* at Penrhyn. The Reverend John Pertwee was so shocked in 1883 when 19 Brightlingsea fishermen were drowned in a storm on the Terschelling oyster-grounds, leaving 32 orphans, that he decided to record all those from the parish lost since his arrival in 1872. This fine tradition has been continued, though thankfully additions are now of an infrequent nature.

Most of those recorded, particularly in the early years, were fishermen. However, there are some from distant waters, like William Webb on board the emigrant ship *Kapunda* bound for Australia which was in collision off Maceio, Brazil, with the loss of 303 lives. William Everett drowned off Edithburg, South Australia; Alick Burke died off Peru; Sidney Siebert perished on the *Titanic*; and Thomas Farrington was lost with all the crew of the *Miramar* off the Savanah Light, United States. Two of the older casualties, Frederick Simons, 67, and Frederick Wheeler, 54, were lost with the veteran training ship *Marlborough* in the English Channel, 29 November 1924. A youngster commemorated is Melvin Bowles, aged 16, fatally injured on the yacht *Thursa* at Southampton in 1928.

Second World War casualties include Walter Pittick, aged 62, lost on HMY *Campeador V*, 22 June 1940. The gallant little *Campeador*, a steam yacht commissioned for patrol service with its elderly crew, spent 84 days at sea out of the first 95 days of war. *The Times*, when referring to their loss, said: 'As they would have wished, they died together in the service of their country, but their example will long remain an inspiration to the younger generation, and the little *Campeador* will be remembered and talked about long after the war is over by those who served in the same waters.'

Other wartime casualties include Lieutenant Ronald Frost of the submarine *P-33*, lost off Tripoli in August 1941, and Leslie Jeffries, aged 19, washed overboard from the paddle-steamer HMS *Royal Eagle* (serving as an anti-aircraft vessel). Alfred Stone, also 19, was serving in *MTB 218* when she hit a mine and her crew of four were killed during a night attack on a German convoy in the Dunkirk channel on 18 August 1942. Merchant marine war casualties recorded here include George Scott on the tanker *Sourabaya* in the North Atlantic on 26 October 1942, and Leslie Frost, Second Officer of the *Wayfarer*, sunk to the east of Mozambique on 19 August 1944.

Brighton, Sussex

198/322036

An anchor, with a plaque, is a reminder of how in January 1980 25 persons, including

several children, were brought ashore after three separate rescues by the Shoreham lifeboat *Dorothy and Philip Constant*. She had set out in heavy weather to the 3,500-ton *Athina B*, which, with engine problems and a fuel shortage, was being driven ashore in gale force winds. The first rescue took place early in the morning, the second in mid-morning, and the last at about 9.15 pm, by which time the freighter was aground.

Bristol, Gloucestershire

172/584726

In a Missions to Seamen chapel in the Cathedral is a memorial to Richard Hakluyt, who from 1586–1616 was prebendary here. He is best remembered for his massive collection of accounts of voyages, first published in 1588. *The Principall Navigations, Voiages and Discoveries of the English Nation* has appeared in numerous editions throughout the succeeding centuries. Hakluyt died in 1616 and is buried in Westminster Abbey but has a marvellous living memorial, the Hakluyt Society, founded in 1846 and still promoting the history of geographical exploration. The lower light of a window on the south side of the nave is in memory of four members of the RNVR (Bristol Division) who were taken prisoner and died during the First World War. A memorial in the north transept mentions Lieutenant Gilbert Brydone RN, lost at sea in 1851 aged 22.

Across the green from the Cathedral is a statue of John Cabot, standing in front of the City Hall, while on Brandon Hill is the Cabot Tower. Cabot sailed from Bristol on board the *Mathew*, with a crew of 18, on about 20 May 1497 and made landfall at the northern tip of Newfoundland before returning to Bristol in August. Supported by Henry VII, he set out again with five ships the following year; one ship quickly returned, while the others vanished. It was left to his second son, Sebastian, described by one authority as a 'genial and cheerful liar, devoted (insofar as it helped him) to the cause of oceanic discovery' to maintain the family name.

Across the Avon, St Mary Redcliffe Church contains tombs of some of the early Bristol merchants and shipowners, and a superb wall-memorial to Sir William Penn. The text says that he was 'addicted from his youth to maritime affairs' and 'was chosen Great Captain Commander under his Royal Highness in ye signal and evidently successful fight against the Dutch fleet.' He died in 1670, aged 49. There is a painted wooden statue of Queen Elizabeth which is possibly a ship's figurehead, and also a whalebone said to have been brought back by John Cabot as a thanks-offering. The Broughton family are remembered by a floor tablet, one of their number, Francis John, being lost on the *Earl Talbot* East Indiaman in the China Seas in 1801, aged 15.

Brook, Hampshire
196/395844

On the churchyard grave of Henry Gore Browne, who was awarded the Victoria Cross for bravery at the siege of the Lucknow Residency during the Indian Mutiny, is a reference to Geoffrey Gore Browne, lost in HMS *Aboukir* on 22 September 1914. (See *Bredon*.)

Brooksby, Leicestershire
129/671160

The village church stands in the grounds of Brooksby Hall, once the home of Admiral of the Fleet, Earl Beatty of Brooksby and the North Sea. This contains, in addition to his bust and the Union Flag flown on HMS *Queen Elizabeth*, a superb wall-memorial: 'In memory of our friends, Officers and Men who died gloriously for their King and Country in the Battle of Jutland on 31 May 1916.' On either side are listed some of the fallen officers:

— Rear-Admiral Sir Robert Keith Arbuthnot, who commanded the 1st Cruiser Squadron, described as 'gallant and determined as ever lived.' Arbuthnot's ships were surprised by the German battle-cruiser *Lutzow* and four battleships and was 'hit by two heavy salvoes in quick succession and the Admiral and his flagship (*Defence*) disappeared in a roar of flame.' There were no survivors from her complement of 903, which included Captain Stanley Venn Ellis.

— Rear-Admiral The Hon Sir Horace Lambert Alexander Hood, who from *Invincible* commanded the 3rd Battle Cruiser Squadron. His last words were those to his gunnery officer: 'Your firing is very good. Keep at it as quickly as you can. Every shot is telling.' Moments later 'there came the awful spectacle of a fiery burst, followed by a huge column of dark smoke with blackened debris, swelled up hundreds of feet in the air, and the mother of all battle cruisers had gone . . . So in the highest exultation of battle – doing all a man could for victory – the intrepid Admiral met his end, gilding in his death with new lustre the immortal name of Hood.' Captain Lindsay Cay is here, for he was not among the six who miraculously survived.

— Captain Charles Fitzgerald Sowerby was lost with all but two of his crew when *Indefatigable* was hit by shells from the *Von der Tann*. Captain C.I. Prowse in HMS *Queen Mary* suffered a similar fate at the hands of the German battle-cruisers *Derflinger* and *Seydlitz,* disappearing in a 'dazzling flash of red flame . . . and explosion' followed by a 'dark pillar of smoke rising stemlike till it spread several hundred feet high in the likeness of a vast palm tree.' Just seven survived, while 1,268 perished in the holocaust.

— Captain Thomas Parry Bonham, *Black Prince,* found himself shortly after midnight alone in the midst of the German battlefleet and 'in a moment was in a glare of searchlights. A tornado of shell at point-blank rent her from stem to stern, and in two minutes she was a mass of flames. For a while she was seen as a floating furnace, and then, with an appalling explosion, sank with all hands.'

— and finally Captain Charles John Wintour, the gallant commander of one of the smaller vessels, the destroyer HMS *Tipperary*. (See *Clayton West*.)

Brookwood, Surrey
186/960565

Amidst the acres of graves and memorials are a number of maritime interest, like that at Plot 55/57 which includes Wing-Commander Frank Brock, the eldest son of the Brocks fireworks family, who served in naval intelligence. Among his pyrotechnic inventions was an incendiary bullet which brought down several Zeppelins, and the smokescreens, flares, and light-buoys used at Zeebrugge, where 'the value of his contribution was simply incalculable.' Alas, having landed on the Mole during the assault of 23 April 1918 he was never seen again. (See *Dover*.)

There is also the lighthouse-shaped memorial to Captain Frienbergs of the *Katavaldis*, who died in the North Sea in November 1941. Other graves include those of Jane Furley, who served as a nurse for 14 years in the family of Admiral Young, and James Ormiston, senior naval surgeon on the ill-fated Niger expedition of 1840 (see *Wales – Tenby*). The widow of Captain Smith of the *Titanic* (see *Hanbury*; *Lichfield*), who was knocked down by a taxi in Southampton, and Walter Parker, one of the great captains whose career spanned the change from sail to steam, are also buried here, as is Lieutenant Andrew Wood, drowned carrying dispatches in an open boat to the fleet of Lord Cornwallis in 1787. In the same mausoleum as the last is Rear-Admiral Wood, whose service included capture and imprisonment by the French. Finally one must mention the intriguing Yamazaki of Japan, 'a naval officer in the service of Prince Chosiu', who died in 1866.

Bude, Cornwall
190/210061

A memorial stone in the churchyard is to the *Bencoolen* and reads: 'Here lie deposited the remains of the Chief Mate and thirteen seamen, a portion of the crew of the *Bencoolen* which was wrecked at the entrance of this harbour October 21st 1882.'

Budock, Cornwall
204/786324

Lieutenant Charles Norrington, who was at Trafalgar as a midshipman on the *Conqueror*, is buried in the churchyard. He died in 1839 when in command of the *Alert,* one of the fast packet vessels sailing to the West Indies.

Bulwell, Nottinghamshire
129/542450

A window in the parish church, *The Miracle of Dunkerque*, was unveiled on the fiftieth anniversary of the evacuation and shows both a Royal Navy destroyer and a boat (the *Monarch*) used at the time.

Bulwick, Northamptonshire
141/962942

A wall-monument in the church is to Vice-Admiral Sir George Tryon, who is described as a 'man of great energy, zeal and resource who earned a world wide reputation as seaman, strategist and tactician.' His chief claim to fame, however, rests with him at the bottom of the Mediterranean. While flying his flag in HMS *Victoria* he exercised the Mediterranean Fleet in close formation off Lebanon on the afternoon of 22 June 1893, during which the *Camperdown* struck the *Victoria* on the starboard bow, causing her to sink in little more than ten minutes. The Admiral, 22 other officers, and 336 men were lost. (See *Crondall*.)

A plaque records how the Tryon family gave five sons in the Great War, including two sets of brothers. Only one served in the Royal Navy, Lieutenant John Tryon, lost in the Kattegat about 14 January 1918 from unknown causes when in command of submarine *G-8*.

Bunbury, Cheshire
117/569581

In the church there is a representation of a ship on the tomb of Sir George Beeston, who died in 1601. His exact age has been the subject of much conjecture, was he, as some have claimed 102? Whatever the truth, he served four Tudor monarchs in times of war, on both land and at sea, culminating with his

Memorial at Bulwick Church commemorating Vice-Admiral Sir George Tryon, lost on HMS Victoria.

command of the *Dreadnought* during the Armada campaign of 1588.

Burlesdon, Hampshire
196/488097

Another riverside village famous for its shipbuilders, the church memorials to Philemon Ewer and George Parsons, two of the greatest, both include ships.

Burnham Norton, Norfolk
132/835427

The war memorial plaque inside the church records Victor Francis, leading stoker on HMS *Hood*. (See *Boldre*.)

Burnham Overy, Norfolk
132/843429

A father and son loss is recorded on the war memorial within the church. Austin Edward Barnes, a stoker on HMS *Volunteer*, died on 19 April 1941, aged 42, while his son

Anthony Frederick, aged 20, was killed on 21 June 1942 while serving on the submarine *P-514*. She was based in Newfoundland as a training vessel, where she was rammed by the convoy escort *Georgian*. The memorial includes Surgeon Lieutenant William Phillips, killed when HMS *Niger*, a Halcyon class minesweeper, was mined off Iceland on 6 July 1942.

Burnham Overy Staithe, Norfolk

132/845443

A stone tablet on a house at the lower corner of West Harbour Road reads: 'Richard Woodget, Master of the *Cutty Sark* lived here'. He had been born in Burnham Market and retired here to farm shortly after the *Cutty Sark* was sold to the Portuguese in 1895, having been her master for the previous ten years. He died in 1926, two years after he again took the wheel as the *Cutty Sark* made a coastal voyage to Fowey. He is buried at Burnham Norton.

Burnham Thorpe, Norfolk

132/856405

This is Nelson's birthplace, though the house in which he was born – the Rectory – was pulled down two years before his death at Trafalgar. A finger-post points to a plaque on a roadside wall as you approach the village from the south-east. During a period on half-pay (1787–93) he lived at the Rectory and created a pond, the size and shape of a man-of-war, which, though dry and much overgrown, still remains.

The church contains various memorials to the Admiral and his family; his father was Rector here from 1755 to 1802. There is a white marble bust of Nelson surmounted with a wreath of laurel. The lectern and rood-screen are made from oak removed from HMS *Victory*. One of the flags hanging in honour of Nelson was that flown by HMS *Indomitable* at the Battle of Jutland; the other was once flown by the mighty battleship HMS *Nelson*. The flag which flies from the tower on Saints' days and anniversaries is a replica of that flown by Nelson's flagship, the *Vanguard*, at the Battle of the Nile, 1798. (See index under *Nelson*.)

Burnley, Lancashire

103/846325

A plaque in the Sion Baptist Church is 'to the memory of my son and crew of the *Derbyshire*'. The fate of this giant vessel, a bulk carrier of 91,654 gross tons, lost without trace in the South China Sea in September 1980, has been the cause of much speculation. She had left the Sept-Iles in July with a cargo of iron ore concentrates for Japan, where she was expected to arrive on 14 September. On the final stage of the voyage severe weather was encountered, and the last message received was on the morning of 9 September, when she reported being hove to in a violent storm with Force 11 winds and 30-foot waves. On being reported missing an extensive search was undertaken, with an oil slick being sighted in the area of her last known position.

Had she been overwhelmed in the storm,

Plaque marking the site of Nelson's birthplace at Burnham Thorpe.

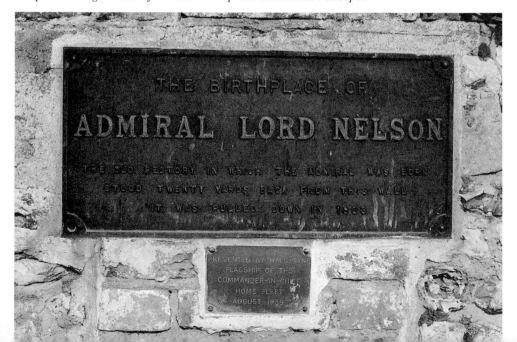

or had there been a catastrophic structural failure? A trade-union financed expedition in 1994 managed to locate the broken-up wreck by video camera at a depth of over two miles. A memorial plaque was subsequently placed on the deck of the forward part of the ship. This reads: 'M.V. *Derbyshire* in our thoughts, in our hearts, in our affections constantly. At the going down of the sun and in the morning we will remember. The whole *Derbyshire* Family.' (See *Liverpool*; *Redcar*; *Salford*; *South Shields*.)

Burntwick Island, Kent
178/869723

A lonely grave, which will surely disappear completely before long, is of Sidney Bernard RN, a surgeon who joined HMS *Eclair* at Madeira as she returned from anti-slavery duty off West Africa in 1845. By the time she arrived to anchor at the quarantine station off Burgh Island 74 officers and men out of 146 had succumbed to illness. Sidney Bernard himself fell ill and died on 9 October, and was buried on the nearby shore. The bronze plaque was subsequently removed to Chatham as the sea encroached, and now only the railings are visible at low tide, a lonely reminder of a brave man 'who departed this life . . . whilst performing quarantine at Stangate Creek aged 27.'

Burton Bradstock, Dorset
193/488895

In the church is a plaque to Commander William Hansford RN, who died 1 June 1799 aged 82, and a marble wall-monument to the wife of Rear-Admiral Ingram which includes a short inscription to the Admiral himself, who died aged 71 in 1826.

Burton in Wirral, Cheshire
117/317743

A plaque in the church is in memory of 'Andrew Boyd Baird of Paisley who died at sea May 22nd 1874 aged 31 years. Erected by the owners of the barque *Maravilla* of Liverpool of which he had command previous to his death.'

Bury St Edmunds, Suffolk
155/855640

A plaque in St Mary's Church is in memory of the men of the Suffolk Regiment lost on the troopship *Birkenhead* when she foundered on the coast of South Africa in February 1852. (See *Beckingham*.)

In the Abbey gardens is a stone from the Dunkirk Mole, now a memorial to 'the men of all services and of all nations' who were evacuated from or left behind during the evacuation from Dunkirk in June 1940. (See *Bulwell*.)

Butleigh, Somerset
183/496337

On the wooded ridge is a tower built in memory of Sir Samuel Hood, 'an officer of the highest distinction amongst the illustrious men who rendered their own age the brightest period in the naval history of their country.' He had gone to sea in 1776, aged 14, on board the *Courageux*, commanded by his uncle, and subsequently saw much service in the North Atlantic, the West Indies, and the Mediterranean, where he commanded the *Zealous* at the Battle of the Nile. In 1802 he was appointed Commander-in-Chief on the Barbados and Leeward Islands station and here, in 1804, captured Diamond Rock, from where he blockaded the French in Martinique. Later, off Rochfort, his arm was smashed by a musket-ball and had to be amputated. The King wept on hearing the news, saying: 'Would to God the French had their frigates again and poor Hood his arm.' In 1811 he took the East India Command, dying at Madras in 1814 'after three days of illness caused by that obstinacy of his, for he would have his palanquin open in the rain.' (See *Netherbury*; *South Perrot*.)

Other Hoods are remembered at Butleigh church, where there is also a window 'in Thanksgiving to Almighty God for the merciful protection of Ralph Neville RN, Phillip Neville RN and Geoffrey Neville RHA during the Great War 1914–18. This window is erected by their parents.'

Cadgwith, Cornwall
204/721152

A plaque in the church is in memory of Admiral E.L.S. King CB, MVO, DL, who was Churchwarden from 1948 to 1971.

Caister-on-Sea, Norfolk
134/520123

A fine memorial in the cemetery, in the form of a broken ship's mast entwined with rope and with an anchor and lifebelt, is to the nine crewmen of the lifeboat *Beauchamp*, which capsized on 14 November 1901. Their names are recorded on the surrounding plaques, and also in the lifeboat house. These include two sons and a grandson of James Haylett, himself a lifeboatman for 59 years, who at the subsequent inquiry uttered the immortal words 'Caister men never turn back.' On this occasion their sacrifice was in vain. The fishing smack they had set out to provide assistance for reached safety, not knowing of the

Memorial at Caister to those lost in the lifeboat disaster of 1901.

the Mediterranean in 1942, and Peter Scandrett died off Freetown the same year. The remaining two casualties were brothers, commemorated in a delightful stained-glass window. Percy Powell was on HMS *Hermes* when she sank following an attack by some 70 carrier-based Japanese aircraft off Ceylon on 9 April 1942. Four months earlier his brother William had been one of 469 casualties when the light cruiser HMS *Galatea* was sunk by *U-557* as she approached Alexandria. Fifty years later the 'In Memoriam' section of the *Daily Telegraph* remembered all who died that day, 'especially "Uncle Sam", leading stoker G. Hutton, Veteran of the

Two brothers lost at sea are remembered by this window at Canon Pyon Church.

attempted rescue. A memorial window is situated in the nearby church, where others lost at sea are also remembered, like Edward Gleadell, chaplain on HMS *Aboukir* (see *Bredon*), and Charles Brown, lost when HM Trawler *Thomas Stratten* was sunk in 1917 by a mine off the Butt of Lewis.

Cambridge, Cambridgeshire
154/451585

A memorial to Captain Cook and his family is in St Andrew the Great's Church. (See *Great Ayton*.)

Canford Magna, Dorset
195/032988

A memorial in the church is to Admiral Macnamara.

Canon Pyon, Herefordshire
149/450492

One would hardly expect such a strong naval connection as this in the heart of Herefordshire, but the 1939–45 roll of honour in the church reveals that four village sons gave their lives in the Royal Navy. Geoffrey Bulmer was lost on a submarine in

Dardanelles Campaign. Never Forgotten. Ralph.' How poignant that, long after, such memories are recorded in this way.

Canterbury, Kent

179/151579

In the Cathedral nave there is a superb marble tablet to the eight killed on board HMS *Kent* at the Battle of the Falklands, 8 December 1914. The *Kent*, which had been the first to clear harbour at Port Stanley when the German ships approached, had chased the *Nurnberg,* though it was only when the latter's boilers burst that she obtained the upperhand and sank her gallant adversary.

In the Warrior's Chapel there is a memorial to Sir George Rooke, who, with Sir Cloudesley Shovel, had captured Gibraltar in 1704. The bell of HMS *Canterbury* which hangs in the Cathedral is struck at six bells in remembrance of all those who face the perils of water in discharge of their duties. There is a model of HMS *Canterbury*, built 1744, and presented in memory of Post Captain Graham Edwards RN, who died on 28 October 1928.

Catherington, Hampshire

197/696145

A stone cross is 'in loving memory of Rear-Admiral Sir Christopher Craddock killed in action off Coronel, All Saints Day 1914, his body rests in the Pacific Ocean.' He had sailed north along the coast of Chile to intercept the German squadron commanded by Vice-Admiral von Spee. Neither knew of the other's close proximity until they met off Coronel that fateful afternoon. Instead of falling back south Craddock pressed on, but the advantages of speed, range, sea conditions, and visibility were all with the Germans. By nightfall both the *Good Hope*, flying Craddock's flag, and the *Monmouth* had been sunk. There were no survivors. (See *Gilling West*; *York*.) When I visited Catherington some years ago I discovered a large tomb of Admiral Sir Charles Napier hidden in undergrowth at the north-east corner of the churchyard, and with most of the inscription illegible. Has this now been lost forever? Such a distinguished commander deserves better. (See *Portsmouth*.)

Chalfont St Giles, Buckinghamshire

176/991835

A memorial in the church is to Admiral Palliser, who may well be best-remembered for his bitter feud with Admiral Keppel, as the result of an unsuccessful attempt to engage the French in the English Channel in July 1778. He died in 1796, still suffering from the wounds received on board the

Monument to Captain James Cook on the hill north-east of Chalfont St Giles.

Sutherland in 1748 when the arms chest exploded.

Admiral Palliser was a strong supporter of Captain James Cook and after Cook's death had a monument tower erected near his house on the hill north-east of the town. This includes a detailed description of Cook and his virtues, concluding: 'If public fervices merit public acknowledgements, if the man who adorned and raifed the fame of his country is deferving of honours, then Captain Cook deferves to have a monument raifed to his memory by a generous and grateful nation.' (See *Great Ayton*.)

Chatham, Kent

178/763680

On the high ground known as the Great Lines stands an impressive memorial 'in honour of the Navy and to the abiding memory of those ranks and ratings of this port who laid down their lives in the defence of the Empire and have no other grave than the sea.' Bronze panels list the major engagements including the great single-ship actions, while 8,515 names are commemorated for 1914–18 and 10,112 for 1939–45. These are by year and rank, though unfortunately the ships on which they served are not included.

St George's Church in the former naval barracks – HMS *Pembroke* – is now the St George's Centre but retains many naval memorials, among them a window to 135 sailors who were killed in the Drill Shed during an air raid in 1917. Another window is to those lost when the submarine *L-12* rammed *H-47* off Pembrokeshire in 1929. A famous action recalled with a plaque is that of the *Jervis Bay*, which took on the *Admiral Scheer* in November 1940 and saved most of her convoy. There is also a window to the Women's Royal Naval Service. Outside, on the south side of the Centre, is a memorial marking the spot where French prisoners-of-war from Napoleonic times are buried. The memorial books have been transferred to the Brompton Garrison Church at 187/761685, which also contains a memorial to Wrens who gave their lives in the two world wars.

One other memorial at St George's should not be overlooked. It is that to 24 boys of the Royal Marine Cadet Corps, who, while marching in Dock Road on 4 December 1951, were hit by a bus and killed.

There are two interesting memorials in the

Part of the Royal Naval Memorial at the Great Lines, Chatham.

Statue of Thomas Waghorn in Viaduct Road, Chatham, with the HMS Barfleur *memorial in the background.*

gardens beside the Chatham New Road viaduct. One, an unmarked obelisk, is to sailors from HMS *Barfleur* killed during the Boxer Rebellion in China in 1900. The other, a fine statue, is to Lieutenant Thomas Waghorn RN, 'pioneer and founder of the overland route' to India, who died in 1850. (See *Snodland*.)

Cheltenham, Gloucestershire
163/945219

Many towns and villages 'adopted' warships during the Second World War, Cheltenham choosing the destroyer HMS *Legion*, which went alongside *Ark Royal* as she slowly sank just 25 miles east of Gibraltar on 14 November 1941, and brought off over 1,000 survivors. On 11 December, in company with the destroyers *Sikh*, *Maori*, and the Dutch *Isaac Sweers*, she sank the Italian six-inch cruisers *Alberto di Giussano* and *Alberico da*

IN·PROUD·MEMORY·OF·VICE-ADMIRAL
WION·DE·MALPAS·EGERTON
D. S. O., R. N. [RETIRED]
WHO·GAVE·HIS·LIFE·FOR·HIS·COUNTRY
IN·THE·BATTLE·OF·THE·ATLANTIC·WHILE
SERVING·AS·COMMODORE·OF·CONVOYS
BORN·16·APRIL·1879·DIED·1·JAN·1943

A plaque in Chester Cathedral to a commodore of convoys in the Battle of the Atlantic.

Barbiano in what the *Official History* described as a 'brilliant action'. Barely three months later *Legion* was bombed at Malta and took no further part in the war. A plaque in the Town Hall commemorates the ship and those who served on her.

Chester, Cheshire
117/405665

A display case in the Cathedral nave contains a number of mementoes of Jack Cornwell VC (see *Greater London – Manor Park, Richmond*) and a roll of those lost on HMS *Chester* during her action at Jutland on 31 May 1916, 35 names in all, including five other boy seamen. A window is in memory of Lieutenant-Commander F. Lewis Copplestone of submarine *D-2*, which vanished in the North Sea in late November 1914, and his brother-in-law Commander A.F. Copplestone-Bougley, killed at the Battle of Jutland on board HMS *Defence*. (See *Brooksby*.) There is also a memorial to Vice-Admiral Wion de Malpas Egerton DSO RN Rtd, who died in the Battle of the Atlantic while a Commander of Convoys, 1 January 1943. The battle ensign of HMS *Broadsword*, flown in the Falklands 1982–3, hangs nearby. A brass is in memory of Arthur Payne, first lieutenant of HMS *Tauranga*, drowned during a gale off the coast of New Zealand 'while in the execution of his duty' October 1904.

Chichester, Sussex
197/859047

The Shipwrecked Fishermen & Mariners' Royal Benevolent Society was founded in 1839 by John Rye of Bath, and C.G. Jones, a former Bristol Channel pilot, who were concerned at the loss of life on the north Devon coast and wondered whether a fund might be established to help the families of drowned seamen. Its patron is Her Majesty The Queen, and the Society office is in Chichester, where the Chapel of St Michael in the Cathedral is dedicated as the Sailor's Chapel. Five memorial plaques have been gathered here including one sacred to the memory of Lieutenant George Pigot Alms RN, killed on board the *Superbe* in action with the French in the East Indies 12 April 1782, aged 16. He was the eldest son of James Alms, who commanded the *Monmouth* in the same engagement. A tablet in the floor of the chapel is to those men of Sussex who gave their lives at sea 1939–45 and who have no known grave. Also to be seen are the Royal Yacht Squadron burgee carried by Sir Francis Chichester on his solo navigation of the world 1966–7; the bell of HMS *Sussex*, the London class cruiser built in 1929 and broken up in 1950; and the ships' crests of the *Sussex*, *Chichester*, and *Peregrine*, the last being the naval air station at nearby Ford.

Two significant flags hang in the chapel: a White Ensign which was worn at the masthead of HMS *Fearless* at the surrender of the German High Seas Fleet in the Firth of Forth, 1918, and the flag of Vice-Admiral H.T. Ballie Grohman, the first British admiral to fly his flag on German soil, May 1945.

Chiddingfold, Surrey
186/959354

A tablet in the church is to Captain Henry George Halahan RN, killed in action at the Zeebrugge Mole on St George's Day 1918. In January, Halahan had written to Admiral Keyes: 'May I say that if the operation for which you said you might want some of my men is eventually undertaken I should very much like to take part in it. I would willingly accept the same condition, viz: that I should not expect to come back. I have lived for three years inside field gun range and I can say (quite impersonally) that I do not suffer from physical fear.' Halahan was shot down on HMS *Vindictive* as she closed up to the Mole. Admiral Tyrwhitt, writing to Keyes immediately after the raid, said of him: 'I did not know him but he must have been a man.' (See *Dover*.)

Chideock, Dorset
193/421929

A gravestone close to the eastern end of the church is to William Brett, who died 9 May 1878, aged 54. It is said that as a boy he was captured by a press gang in Ireland, later fought in the Crimea, and served on one of the Franklin search expeditions. Queen Victoria, on presenting him with his sixth medal, said 'I am proud of you.'

Chislehurst, Kent
177/444699

A plaque is to Sub-Lieutenant Herbert Murray, youngest son of the rector, lost on board HMS *Captain* (see *Anwick*). Another is to the Campbell family, which emigrated to New Zealand, where the Reverend Campbell had been appointed headmaster of Dunedin High School. On the day after their arrival in July 1863 they were crossing from Port Chalmers when 'their small steamer the *Pride of Yarra*, was run down in the darkness of a hazy evening by a large vessel, the *Favourite*. Eleven lives were lost, and nine of these were the family of Mr Campbell', which consisted of the parents and five children, including a five-week-old baby, and two servants.

Church Cove, Cornwall
203/711127

Three Merchant Navy graves in the churchyard – one of Radio Officer R.F. Hampshire, aged 18, the others of unknown sailors – hold a story as epic, and as tragic, as any from the Second World War. These seamen were from the freighter *Gairsoppa*, which, through a shortage of fuel on a voyage from Freetown, became separated from Convoy SL 64. When some 300 miles south-west of Galway on 17 February 1941, she was sunk by *U-101*, one lifeboat getting away with nine Europeans and 25 lascars. They sailed through stormy seas for 13 days, by which time only Second Mate R.H. Ayres and three others were still alive, the further tragedy being that within a few yards of safety they were thrown into the sea. Only Ayres managed to scramble ashore, encouraged by the shouts of four schoolgirl evacuees, who then covered him with their jackets to keep him warm until help arrived.

Clayton West, Yorkshire
110/259110

In the church is a superb carved wooden memorial to Captain Charles John Wintour 'who commanded the Fourth Destroyer Flotilla at the Battle of Jutland and was killed on the bridge of His Majesty's ship *Tipperary* while gallantly leading a night attack on the enemies' ships.' (See *Brooksby*; *Wales – Bosherston*.)

Cliffs End, Kent
179/353643

A replica of the Viking ship *Hugin* commemorates the landing on 28 July 449 of the Danes under Hengist and Horsa; a plaque records this as 'the beginning of English history.' Nearby a beacon is a reminder of a failed invasion, that of the Spanish Armada in 1588.

The Armada beacon at Cliffs End, erected to commemorate the 400th anniversary of the defeat of the Spanish Armada.

Colchester, Essex
168/994252

The passengers and officers of the steamship *Cadiz* contributed to the plaque in the parish church in memory of Third Officer Herbert Wire 'who was drowned in a gale of wind in the China Sea on 27 July 1860 in the gallant discharge of his duty.'

Colne, Lancashire
103/897401

The body of Wallace Hartley, bandmaster on the *Titanic*, was returned to his home town for burial on 18 May 1912. Subsequently a monument was erected in the town park. (See *Southampton*.)

Colwich, Staffordshire
128/016210

Admiral Lord Anson (1697–1762), whose home, Shugborough Park, lies a short distance to the west, is buried in the church. His great voyage of circumnavigation, during which he captured the Acapulco treasure galleon of Spain, commenced with seven ships and 1,939 men in 1740, but only the flagship *Centurion* (60 guns) made the whole journey to return in 1744. His journal, edited by Richard Walter, chaplain during the voyage, and published in 1748, is one of the classics of maritime literature, describing, as it says in the opening line, 'a very singular naval achievement.'

Compton, Surrey
186/954470

A gravestone close to the east wall of the church is in memory of William Julian Shrine, who died in the wreck of HMS *Avenger* on 20 December 1847, aged 14. The steam frigate was wrecked off Galita Island in the Mediterranean with the loss of 247, just four officers and five men surviving. (See *Langham*.)

Constantine, Cornwall
204/731290

Gravestones in the churchyard recall two of the most widely known shipping disasters. James Veal was lost on the *Titanic* (see *Southampton*), while William Bishop died on the *Lusitania* (see *Barnston*).

Cookham, Buckinghamshire
175/896855

A plaque in the church is to Commander Charles Aswell Boteler Pocock RN, clerk in holy orders, who died February 1899. His son

Captain Roger Ashwell Pocock, who died November 1941, was an author and explorer, and in 1904 founded the Legion of Frontiersmen. There are also several memorials to the Young family, including Sir George Young, Admiral of the White, who died aged 78 in June 1810, and his grandsons Captain Sir George Young, who died in 1848, and Admiral Horatio Young, who died in 1879.

Corby Glen, Lincolnshire
130/001250

A plaque in the north aisle of the church records that William Willerton was lost when in command of the *Chazeepore* in the North Sea, October 1882, leaving a widow and three children.

Cornhill on Tweed, Northumberland
74/858393

A memorial in the church records that Thomas Collingwood was lost at sea, 9 May 1859, aged 28.

Corsham, Wiltshire
173/874705

A marble wall-tablet in the church remembers the Edridge family, including Captain John Edridge RN of Pockeridge, who died in January 1856.

Coventry, Warwickshire
140/337790

The Cathedral recalls with a small exhibit the bravery of Petty Officer Alfred Sephton VC, which contains a replica Victoria Cross (the one awarded posthumously having tragically been stolen when thieves broke into the case in September 1990). (See *Wolverhampton*.) The Cathedral's Navy Room contains memorials to those from HMS *Coventry* who died during the battle for Tobruk, and the 19 who died when her successor, a Type 42 destroyer, was sunk by Argentinian aircraft on 25 May 1982 during the Falklands operations.

Cranleigh, Surrey
187/060392

A plaque in the Baynard's Chapel of St Nicholas' Church is to the undying memory of Lieutenant-Commander Waller of the Howe Battalion, Royal Naval Division, who fell at Gallipoli on 9 May 1915.

Crediton, Devon
191/837003

Alexander Spearman, commanding officer of the Collingwood Battalion, Royal Naval

Division, who fell at Gallipoli 4 June 1915, is remembered in the church. As he led his battalion forward he was wounded in the leg 'but nothing daunted, he rose and, taking off his cap, waved it and his revolver, shouting loudly "Come on Collingwoods, don't leave me now".' (See *Pimperne*.)

Cricket St Thomas, Somerset
193/373086

Several of the Hood family are recalled here in the tiny church, including Alexander Hood, Lord Bridport, who died aged 87 in 1814: 'For his Bravery, for his Abilities, for his Achievements in his Profession, for his Attachment to his King and Country, consult the Annals of the British Navy, where they are written in indelible Characters.' A decorated marble plaque is to Horatio Nelson Sandys Hood, who died at Shanghai when in command of HMS *Pegasus* 3 February 1881. (See *Butleigh*.)

There is also a large brass to 'Three Gallant Gentlemen': Lieutenant-Commander Alexander Hugh Gye who, while in command of HMS *Negro*, was lost in the collision with the *Hoste* in the North Sea, 21 December 1916; Lieutenant Henry Nelson Hood of the Hood Battalion, Royal Naval Division, killed on that fateful day at Gallipoli when so many men fell in the battles before Krithia, 4 June 1915; and Lord Edward Seymour, who died of wounds in France 5 December 1917 while serving with the Strathcona Horse.

Cromer, Norfolk
133/220423

In a warriors' corner of the fine church and below a RNLI flag is a small memorial plaque to Henry Blogg GC, BEM, one of Great Britain's finest lifeboat coxswains, some say the finest of all. A splendid bronze bust not far from the cliff-top at the eastern edge of the town gives the bare details of his career as coxswain, spanning the period 1909–47, during which he was awarded the RNLI Gold Medal for conspicuous gallantry three times and its Silver Medal four times. During a total of 53 years' service with the lifeboat he helped save 873 lives. He died on 13 June 1954. Anyone wishing to learn more about 'one of the bravest men who ever lived' should read the book *Henry Blogg of Cromer* by Cyril Jolly.

A plaque in the church records the loss in January 1918 of Lieutenant-Commander Athleston Lennox Fenner, one of our most experienced submarine commanders. On the night of 31 January 1918 he sailed on a combined exercise with no fewer than eight other K-class submarines, together with

Cliff-top memorial at Cromer to Henry Blogg GC, coxswain of the lifeboat.

battleships, battle-cruisers, and escorts, all travelling at high speed out of the Firth of Forth. As this great armada approached the Isle of May the first collisions occurred. *K-22* collided with *K-14*, and then was struck herself by HMS *Inflexible*. Shortly afterwards HMS *Fearless* struck *K-17*, which sank. In trying to avoid these vessels, *K-4* was rammed by *K-6* and almost sliced in two, sinking rapidly with no survivors. The battleships ploughed unknowingly right through the survivors from *K-17*, of which but nine were rescued.

Crondall, Surrey
186/795485

A weathered inscription on one of the gravestones reads: 'Vice-Admiral Gordon Campbell VC DSO 1886–1958'. Campbell was one of the 'mystery VCs' awarded to those who served on the 'Q-ships', the vessels charged with the task of acting as decoys to enemy submarines. He sank his first U-boat (*U-68*) on 22 March 1916, his second (*U-83*) nearly a year later. In the *Pargust* he sank *UC-29*, but was less fortunate in the *Dunraven* for, despite efforts to lure *UC-71* into range, it was the decoy ship that eventually sank. (See *Greater London – Dulwich*.)

Inside the church is a plaque 'in loving remembrance of a Crondall boy's devotion to duty and in the hope that it will be taken as the pattern by other boys in Crondall.' The boy, Midshipman Fraser Sumner Stooks, aged 16, was lost on HMS *Victoria* in June 1893. (See *Bulwick*.) Also a plaque to Lieutenant Patrick Egerton, killed on board the destroyer HMS *Mosquito* during the Gallipoli landings 25 April 1915.

Crosby, Lancashire
108/322988

A plaque in St Faith's Church is to Joseph Bell, chief engineer of the *Titanic*, 'who was lost with all his engineering staff in the foundering of that vessel after collision with an iceberg in the Atlantic Ocean April 15th 1912.' (See *Southampton*.)

Cullercoats, Northumberland
88/365707

A fountain on the sea front is a memorial to Lieutenant-Commander Bryan Adamson, lost with his officers and crew, 73 in all, on board the gunboat *Wasp*, which vanished without trace on a voyage between Singapore and Shanghai in the autumn of 1887.

Culver Down, Hampshire
196/633856

The tall obelisk on Culver Down was erected in 1849 in memory of the first Earl of Yarborough, founder of the Royal Yacht Squadron, who had died on board his yacht *Kestrel* off Vigo, Spain, three years previously.

Dartmouth, Devon
202/886504

The war memorial in the church at the harbour entrance records five men lost on HMS *Monmouth* at the Battle of Coronel, November 1915 (see *Catherington*), and one on HMS *Defence* at Jutland, 31 May 1916 (see *Brooksby*). H.A. Widdicome of HMS *Oppossum* died of exposure on 23 November 1918, while J.C. Atchurst of HMS *Consort* died on the Yangtze. Samuel Codner, a Newfoundland merchant who in 1823 founded what subsequently became the Colonial and Continental Church Society, is remembered here, while James Douglas (1826–98), late engineer-in-chief to the Honourable Corporation of Trinity House, is buried in the churchyard. (See *Plymouth*.) A small plaque at the entrance to Bayards Cove records that Paul Goddard was lost at sea from *Exuberant* in March 1983. The Royal Naval College has, alas, not been visited, but is known to be rich in further memorials.

Dawley, Shropshire
127/687074

Captain Matthew Webb, who in 1875 was the first man to swim the English Channel, and later drowned in the Niagara rapids, was born here and is commemorated by a fountain. (See *Dover*.)

Dawlish, Devon
192/960767

St Gregory's Church contains a memorial to a former curate, Guy Browning, killed at the Battle of Jutland on HMS *Indefatigable*. (See *Brooksby*.) Another is to Mary Fortescue who was lost with 13 other nurses when the hospital ship *Llandovery Castle* was sunk by *U-86* on 27 June 1918, some 114 miles west of the Fastnet Rock. The submarine subsequently shelled the lifeboats and only 24 survived of the 258 on board. (See *Sidmouth*.)

Deal, Kent
179/375530

The war memorial at the gates of St George's includes a major inscription to Arthur Tisdall VC, who, while serving with the Royal Naval Division, landed at Gallipoli, 25 April 1915. The heroism he displayed that day was not reported until correspondence appeared in *The Times* the following December. Killed in action on the afternoon of 6 May 1915, he was posthumously awarded the Victoria Cross the following March.

Also in the churchyard is the tomb of Captain Edward Thornborough Parker, 'a gallant and distinguished commander', who, wounded in action off Boulogne, died on 27 September 1801, aged 23. Elsewhere are recorded the deaths of two sailors ten years later, both on HMS *Niad,* 'in defeating the French fleet off Boulogne in the prefecture of Buonaparte.'

Standing on high ground, the tower of St Leonard's Church was formerly an important landmark for shipping. One of the galleries was built by the Deal pilots and a picture

War memorial at St George's Church, Deal, which includes an inscription to Sub-Lieutenant Arthur Tisdall VC.

commemorates the great storm of 1703 when 13 ships of the Royal Navy were wrecked on the Goodwin Sands with the loss of 1,200

Memorial in St Leonard's Church, Deal, to four sons of Thomas and Sarah Hight, of which three died at sea.

lives. A plaque records that four sons of Thomas and Sarah Hight died overseas, three of them at sea. There are memorials to the Admirals Harvey, Sir Edward and Sir John, who, we are told 'assisted on three different occasions when commanding a ship of the line in the destruction of the squadrons of France and Spain.'

Among the tombstones outside the Museum of Maritime History is one to John Ellbeck, shot by smugglers as he tried to help Customs officers.

Deerhurst, Gloucestershire

150/870290

A plaque in the Saxon chapel has the four verses of *A Little Sanctuary* by Admiral Ronald Hopwood, inspired by a visit here in 1917. His earlier works included *The Secret of Ships*, *The Old Way*, and *The Laws of the Navy*, which commences thus:

> *Now these are the laws of the Navy.*
> *Unwritten and varied they be;*
> *And he that is wise will observe them,*
> *Going down in his ship to the sea;*
> *As naught may outrun the destroyer,*
> *Even so with the law and its grip,*
> *For the strength of the ship is the Service,*
> *And the strength of the Service, the ship.*

Devonport, Devon

201/451553

The Church of St Nicholas, the patron saint of seafarers, in the heart of the great dockyard, contains many memorials and mementoes. A particularly striking one is a tribute to those who died during the actions of HMS *Tiger* at the Dogger Bank, Jutland, and Zeebrugge.

The silver replica of Drake's Drum was presented to HMS *Devonshire* in 1904, but when moved to the new *Devonshire,* a cruiser, in 1929, the ship experienced a run of ill-fortune which the crew associated with the drum and Drake's spirit. During a fleet regatta the *Devonshire* won the first race, but once the drum was beaten in celebration, won no more. In 1936, following the death of a telegraphist by falling from the mast, the drum was brought ashore to the church. Good fortune then followed, for the *Devonshire* survived the 1939–45 war, to be broken up in 1954.

An illuminated scroll and the christening font, which depicts the conditions of Arctic warfare, are 'in memory of those who gave their lives in the Arctic Campaign of the Second World War', and were provided by the Arctic Campaign Memorial Trust. (See *Liverpool*; *Portsmouth*.)

Overlooking the exit to Plymouth Sound is

a fine statue, perhaps the most dramatic of all the memorials to Captain Scott, who died with his four companions – Edward Wilson, Henry Bowers, Lawrence Oates and Edgar Evans – on the return from the South Pole in March 1912. (See *Binton, Portsmouth; Scotland – Greenock.*)

Set on a low granite pedestal in Devonport Park is a gun captured from the Boers, a memorial to men from the cruiser HMS *Doris* who fell during the Boer War as they stemmed the Boer advance, first at Stormberg and later at Graspan, where the casualties occurred.

Donnington, Lincolnshire

131/208359

Matthew Flinders is well remembered here in the church of his native parish. He entered the Royal Navy as a lieutenant's servant on HMS *Alert* in 1789. At the Glorious First of June he was on the *Bellerophon.* Later he surveyed the coast of New South Wales, and between 1801 and 1803, now in command, he circumnavigated Australia on board HMS *Investigator.* While returning home he was detained at Mauritius for six and a half years by the French, who considered him a spy. A decorated wall-plaque refers to his 'restoration to his native land', where he died in 1814. A stained-glass window with his chart of *Terra Australis*, made in 1802, shows him together with Joseph Banks and George Bass. A small display includes paintings of his ship, and of Flinders himself, together with information about his life.

Dover, Kent

179/316417

In a quiet corner of the cemetery are the

An ornamental wall-plaque in Donnington Church to the memory of Matthew Flinders.

graves of 66 sailors lost at Zeebrugge on St George's Day 1918, and their doughty leader, Admiral of the Fleet Sir Roger Keyes, 1st Baron of Zeebrugge and Dover, who died 26 December 1945 after 60 years of outstanding service. He was Chief of Staff during the Dardanelles operations, where he 'rose to the occasion with all the fire and enthusiasm for which he was famous.'

War graves in Dover cemetery of those lost on the Zeebrugge Raid, with the grave of Admiral Sir Roger Keyes in the background.

Summoned before the newly-appointed First Sea Lord, Admiral of the Fleet Wester Wemyss (see *West Wemyss*), in December 1917, Keyes was told: 'Well, Roger, you have talked a hell of a lot about what ought to be done in the Dover area, and now you must go and do it.' He did just that, and the raid on Zeebrugge and Ostend was the culmination of his career. At the unveiling in 1950 of a memorial in St Paul's Cathedral to the Admiral and to his son, Geoffrey Keyes VC, Winston Churchill said: 'In many ways his spirit and example seemed to revive in our stern and tragic age the vivid personality and unconquerable and dauntless soul of Nelson himself.' (See *Brighstone*; *Scotland – Aberchirder*; *Wales – Cardiff*.)

Among the graves elsewhere in the cemetery are others with maritime connections, including a reference on one stone to the loss of Leading Seaman Walter Saunders, killed when a bomb hit HMS *Warspite* during operations in the Mediterranean on 2 August 1943.

In St Mary's Church there is a memorial window to those lost in the *Herald of Free Enterprise* disaster of 1987 (see *St Margaret's at Cliffe*), also a roll of honour to the Cinque Ports pilots who lost their lives during the Second World War, and a window to all the pilots who served from 1526 to 1988. Another fine window, in memory of Captain Payne, shows the ferry *Invicta*, while among the flags is a Red Ensign which flew during the evacuation from Dunkirk. The Air-Sea Rescue service of the Royal Air Force is also remembered here, a window showing a launch going to the rescue of an airman adrift in a tiny dinghy off the white cliffs of Dover. On the East Cliff there is a memorial to Captain Webb. (See *Dawley*.)

Dovercourt, Essex

169/238311

A grave in the churchyard is the final resting place of Captain Charles Fryatt, master of the Great Eastern Railway Company steamer *Brussels* plying between Harwich and then-neutral Holland. On 28 March 1915 he tried to ram a U-boat, an act widely reported at the time. Over a year later two destroyers stopped the *Brussels* and took her captain prisoner. He was subsequently tried and executed by the Germans, his body being returned to this country in 1919. (See *London – Liverpool Street Station*.)

Down Ampney, Gloucestershire

163/099965

Admiral Charles Talbot gave a window to the church as a thanksgiving for the preservation of himself and his ship's company from ship-

wreck off Sebastopol during a gale on 14 November 1854.

Durham, County Durham

88/274426

The fine statue of Neptune which graces the Market Place was 'given to the City by George Bowes MP of Gibside and Streatham as a symbol of the scheme to link Durham to the sea by improved navigation of the River Wear.'

Dursley, Gloucestershire

162/756981

Hanging in the church is the bell of the submarine *Trident*, bequeathed by her commander Captain G.M. Sladen, DSO, DSC and Bar, and erected to his memory. The submarine had a distinguished service in the Arctic, North Atlantic, Mediterranean, and Far East. She badly damaged the German cruiser *Prinz Eugen* at the entrance to the Leads off Trondheim in the early morning of 23 February 1942.

Dyrham, Gloucestershire

172/742758

The church contains the splendid tomb of George Wynter and his wife, surrounded by four sons and five daughters. One of the sons, John, went with Francis Drake on his circumnavigation of the world, but did not complete the voyage. As master of the *Elizabeth*, the Queen's own ship, he became separated and returned home. His failure resulted in a long spell in prison, though he did serve as a lieutenant on the *Britannia* at the time of the Spanish Armada.

Eastbourne, Sussex

199/601973

A plaque on No 14 Milnthorpe Road records that Polar adventurer and explorer Sir Ernest Shackleton and his family once lived there. (See *Greater London – Dulwich*.)

East Clandon, Surrey

187/060518

A plaque in the church is to Petty Officer Peter Joseph Day of HMS *Nelson*, who died at sea February 1930.

East Coker, Somerset

194/538122

William Dampier was born nearby at Hymerford House and is remembered as 'Buccaneer, Explorer, Hydrographer' by two plaques in the church: 'Thrice he circumnavi-

To the memory of the following Islanders
who were shot by the Press Gang,
during its unlawful raid on the Royal Manor of Portland
in what was known as the Easton Massacre,
on April 2nd. 1803,
Alexander Andrews, Quarryman,
Richard Flann, Quarryman,
William Lano, Blacksmith,
and Mary Way who died later of
wounds received in the same raid.
This plaque was unveiled by
Rear Admiral G.I. Pritchard on April 23rd. 1978

Masons {B.H. Otter
        C.A. Durston}

Victims of the press gang remembered at Easton.

gated the Globe and, first of all Englishmen, explored and described the coast of Australia . . . Born East Coker 1651 he died in London 1715 and lies buried in an unknown grave.'

East Farleigh, Kent
188/734533

Donald Maxwell, who during the First World War was Official Artist to the Admiralty and later accompanied the Prince of Wales on his world tour on HMS *Renown,* is buried here. He died in 1936.

The four sons of John Skynner remembered at Easton-on-the-Hill include Lancelott, who perished on the La Lutine.

Eastham, Cheshire
108/360800

A plaque in the church is to Frederick Archer, a captain in the Allan Line, who died in June 1888 and is buried in mid-Atlantic.

Easton, Dorset
194/686720

A dreadful incident involving a press gang is recalled on a plaque in St George's Church, recording the names of two quarrymen, a blacksmith, and a woman, Mary Way, who were shot in what became known as the Easton Massacre of April 1803.

Easton-on-the Hill, Northamptonshire
141/011047

On a memorial to the Reverend John Skynner is a reference to a son, Lancelott, a post captain in the Royal Navy who 'at the age of 33 years perished by shipwreck off the coast of Holland in *La Lutine* frigate, October 9th, 1799.' She was carrying a large quantity of coins and bullion, and her bell, recovered during the subsequent salvage operations, was taken to Lloyds, where it is still rung whenever a ship is lost, or an overdue ship reported safe.

East Pennard, Somerset
183/597375

Names on the war memorial in the church include Royal Marine Reginald Little of HMS *Hampshire.* (See *Scotland – Marwick*

Head.) A plaque recalls Admiral Bernard John Napier who died in 1901, while a gravestone close to the east end of the church records that Sub-Lieutenant Edward Goldney RN 'departed this life 27 December 1869 aged 21 and is buried at 16 N Long 45 25' W'. This is in mid-Atlantic between the Cape Verde Islands and the West Indies.

East Rudham, Norfolk
132/828283

Sir Aylmer de Mordaunt, a Crusader saved from shipwreck on his return from the Holy Land about 1290, donated a fine window to the church in thanksgiving.

Eastry, Kent
179/311547

A splendid marble relief of the Glorious First of June is to Captain John Harvey of the *Brunswick*, whose starboard anchor became hooked in the forechains of the French ship *Vengeur*. When it was proposed she be cut free Harvey said 'No, as we've got her we'll keep her', and so they remained throughout the battle. He was severely wounded and died on 30 June 1794. (See *London – Westminster Abbey*.) His son Edward also served on the *Brunswick*. (See *Deal*.)

Ebony, Kent
189/922306

In this lonely Romney Marsh church is a hymn board to the memory of Vice-Admiral John Armstrong, who died in 1949.

Edenfield, Lancashire
109/799191

A drinking fountain to Alexander Barlow, who died suddenly on board the *St Tudno* at Llandudno in July 1897.

Edensor, Derbyshire
119/250699

In the church lies George Alexander Barker, who as a lieutenant served on board HMS *Swiftsure* at the Battle of Trafalgar. He died the following year, aged 31. (See *London – Westminster Abbey*.)

Egerton, Lancashire
109/711143

On a churchyard stone, below the crest of HMS *Glamorgan*, John Stroud is remembered by his wife and son. He was killed off the Falkland Islands on 12 June 1982. (See *Portland*; *Portsmouth*; *Wales – Merthyr Tydfil*.)

Eglingham, Northumberland
81/106195

The curtain rail below the tower of the church is in memory of Captain Edward Ormsby RCN, buried at sea in 1973.

Elvedon, Suffolk
144/823700

In the church a plaque tells how Augustus Keppel, 'who having discharged his duty in a series of faithful services to his country as a naval commander, a statesman and a citizen ended his days in the village', where he died in 1786. He had joined the *Oxford* in 1735 aged just 10, and five years later sailed round the world with Anson (see *Colwich*) on board the *Centurion*. Subsequently he served in many actions, including Quiberon Bay in 1759, and the capture of Havana in 1762. In 1778, off Ushant, the French were again encountered but not brought to full action, an incident which resulted in a violent quarrel with Palliser (see *Chalfont St Giles*). A courtmartial acquitted him, a verdict received with much popular acclaim. (See *Wentworth Woodhouse*.)

Endon Bank, Staffordshire
118/928538

On his parents' grave is a reference to Gordon Harding, one of 69 who perished when the submarine *M-1* was accidentally rammed by the Swedish steamship *Vidar* on the morning of 12 November 1923 off Start Point, Devon.

Epsom, Surrey
176/210606

A small plaque in the parish church is in memory of William Maunsell Reeves, lost on 21 February 1907 when the *Berlin* ran aground off the Hook of Holland. (See *Wales – Henfynyw*.)

Erith, Kent
177/497779

In 1857 the Shipwrecked Mariners' Society provided funds which enabled a home to be opened at nearby Belvedere for 'aged, disabled and worn-out mariners'. Later, when Prince Alfred, Duke of Edinburgh, became patron, the institution became what is now known as The Royal Alfred Seafarers' Society, with several homes and funds to assist seafarers. In the cemetery are two memorials commemorating residents from the original home.

Etal, Northumberland

75/929395

The war memorial in the church includes the Reverend William Hall, chaplain and naval instructor. The cannon outside the castle is from the *Royal George*. (See *Portsmouth*.)

Exbury, Hampshire

196/427003

Captain Henry Mitford, lost with all his crew on 'His Majesty's ship *York* while cruising in the North Sea supposed Christmas Day 1803', is remembered by a plaque in the church.

Exeter, Devon

192/921925

The Cathedral has a rich collection of maritime memorials including one to Arthur Corfe Angel, an officer on the *London*, which foundered in the Bay of Biscay on 11 January 1866. Only one boat got away, carrying the chief engineer, three passengers, and 15 crew; some 244 persons were lost, including six stowaways.

A bronze memorial is to the battling Sandford brothers 'who in a dark hour of peril on St George's Day 1918 together maintained the highest traditions of the Navy.' Hugh Sandford, who had served at the Dardanelles and on the Dover Patrol, and lost an eye whilst minelaying in the Gulf of Smryna, devised the scheme by which two submarines packed with explosives would ram the Mole viaduct at Zeebrugge, thus cutting off its defenders. In the event only *C-3* reached its destination, blowing open a 100-foot breach. She was commanded by his younger brother Douglas, who was awarded the Victoria Cross. (See *Dover*.)

Several Admirals are remembered, including Sir Edward Thornborough, who died in 1834. He went to sea aged seven, as a servant to his father on board the *Arrogant,* and after nearly 60 years of service had 'very few rivals and certainly no superior; and this knowledge of a seaman's duty extended to managing the fleet better than any man I ever served with.'

There are two flags of interest. One was flown by Captain Scott's last expedition, while the other, a battle-scarred signal flag from HMS *Exeter*, was flown during her engagement (together with the *Achilles* and *Ajax*) against the German pocket battleship *Graf Spee* off the mouth of the River Plate on the morning of 13 December 1939. (See *London – St Paul's*.)

Exton, Rutland

130/920112

A plaque in the church to Commander

Montague Wrothesley Noel RN records that he was twice decorated with the Royal Humane Society's Bronze Medal for saving life at sea before giving his own life while on convoy duty 6 April 1941.

Fairford, Gloucestershire

163/150012

Lieutenant Frederick Wade, Royal Engineers, returning home after serving in the Cameroon Expeditionary Force, was one of 77 lost from the *Apapa* and is remembered on a plaque in St Mary's Church.

Falmouth, Cornwall

204/808329

A memorial at the harbour has been erected 'to the memory of their comrades' by the St Nazaire Society. Together they had taken part in Operation Chariot in March 1942, when a raiding force from Falmouth sailed to St Nazaire. Their objective was the destruction of the great *Normandie* lock, the only place on the west coast of France where the *Tirpitz*, should she venture into the Atlantic, could be repaired. The raiding parties suffered some 169 men killed, with many others wounded or captured. The latter included Lieutenant-Commander S. Beattie, who had commanded the *Campbeltown*, and Lieutenant-Colonel A.C. Newman of the Commandos. Both were subsequently awarded the Victoria Cross, as were Commander R.E.D. Ryder, naval force commander, and, posthumously, Able Seaman Bill Savage, who manned the forward pom-pom of *MGB 314*, and Sergeant T.F. Durrant of the Commandos. In addition four DSOs, 17 DSCs, 11 MCs, four CGMs, five DCMs, 24 DSMs, 15 MMs and 51 mentions in despatches, were awarded to participants.

On Fish Strand Quay a plaque tells of the arrival on 4 November 1805 of Lieutenant John Lapenotiere of the *Pickle* bringing the despatches from Trafalgar. He left at noon 'by post-chaise for London where he reported to the Admiralty some 38 hours later. Normal stage coach services took a week for the journey.' (See *Penzance*; *Whitchurch*.)

Near the public library is an obelisk to the memory of the 'gallant officers and men of HM Packet Service sailing from Falmouth 1688–1852'.

Fareham, Hampshire

196/575061

St Peter & Paul Church contains several memorials, including one to Captain John Everett, killed by a cannon-ball on board HMS *Ruby* off Hispaniola in June 1779. Another is to the crew of HMS *Hero*,

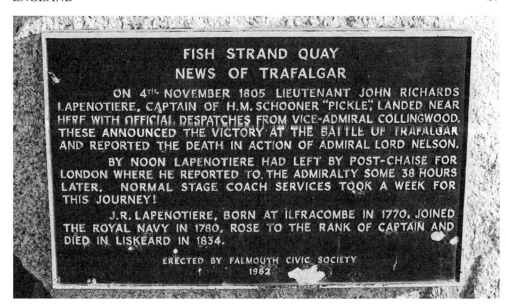

Plaque at Fish Strand Quay, Falmouth. (Tony Grimmer)

wrecked off Holland in December 1811. (See *Somerton*.) Two Admiral Chads are remembered, Henry being on board HMS *Java* when she fought the USS *Constitution*, and later serving in the First Burma War. At Holy Trinity a memorial lists the many services of Vice-Admiral Charles Thompson, who died in command of the Channel Fleet, 1799.

Farncombe, Surrey
186/976450

A plaque in the church is 'in memory of John George Phillips aged 26 years formerly a chorister of this Church, Chief Marconi Officer on RSM *Titanic* which sank at sea April 15th 1912. Faithful to his duty to the last.' (See *Godalming*; *Southampton*.)

Farnham, Surrey
186/838467

A tablet tells that the porch and door were restored in 1948 in memory of Charles Tanner and his son, also Charles, George Medal, RNVR, who was killed in action 1943.

Faversham, Kent
178/011617

Michael Greenwood, who died in 1812 aged 80, is buried in the churchyard. The headstone includes the inscription: 'In Lichfield I was wrecked upon a barren shore; For 14 months in slavery I toiled with many more.' The 50-gun *Lichfield* was a fourth rate battleship which ran ashore in Morocco in 1758.

On being released the survivors received the longest leave granted to any returning prisoners, some six weeks.

Felton, Northumberland
81/179001

In the church there is a memorial to Alexander Davison, victualler to the Admiralty in Nelson's time. (See *Swarland*.)

Filey, Yorkshire
101/117811

A stone in St Oswald's churchyard tells of 'a fearful shipwreck' when the Italian barque *Unico* was wrecked on Filey Brigg in January 1871. Twelve of the crew and the pilot perished.

Fittleton, Wiltshire
184/145496

In September 1976 the minesweeper HMS *Fittleton* closed up to the frigate HMS *Mermaid* for a mail transfer during a NATO exercise in the North Sea. The ships collided, and within a minute *Fittleton* had capsized with the loss of 12 crewmen. A plaque in the church lists their names. Later she was raised, and her crest, White Ensign, and name plaque are all here.

Fleetwood, Lancashire
102/339486

The memorial on the seafront includes the

'The real price of fish is the lives of men', and here at Fleetwood the names of their vessels are listed.

words: 'The real price of fish is the lives of men'. Then follows: 'The Fleetwood-based trawlers listed here came to grief on fishing operations at the cost of life. Many other Fleetwood fishermen have been killed or injured in ships great and small during peace and war from Morecambe Bay to beyond the Arctic Circle.'

A tall obelisk just opposite is to James Abram and George Greenall 'who lost their lives in the storm of November 1890 whilst heroically endeavouring to save others.' A barnacle-encrusted boulder close by is 'in memory of all those who lost their lives at sea.'

Flushing, Cornwall
204/807340

A plaque in the church is to Lieutenant Commander Dermot Vallancey Garde RN, who was killed on 22 March 1942 while serving as squadron torpedo officer to Rear-Admiral Phillip Vian on board HMS *Cleopatra* during the Second Battle of Sirte. This engagement with units of the Italian fleet was described as 'one of the most bril-

liant actions of the war, if not the most brilliant.' Below a handsome portrait of Commander Adoniah Schuyler RN, Post Office packet captain 1786–1807, who died in 1814, we are told that 'after a conversion experience in a great storm at sea he left a legacy for this church to be built.'

Folkestone, Kent
189/234361

Standing above the harbour is St Peter's Church – the mariners' church. Here hang the Red Ensigns of the last conventional ferries to sail from Folkestone, the *Hengist* and *Horsa*. There is but a single memorial to a seaman, to 'James Fagg, fisherman, ten years Churchwarden of this Parish. He died on St Peter's Day 1881'.

Forest Row, Sussex
187/424351

A memorial in the church is to one of those lost when the *Roumania* was wrecked in heavy weather on the coast of Portugal, 1892, with the loss of 113. There were just nine survivors.

Framlingham, Suffolk
156/282639

Among the memorials in the church at Framlingham College is a framed replica Victoria Cross to Captain Augustus Willington Shelton Agar VC, DSO, a former pupil here. In June 1919 he dashed into Kronstadt harbour in a fast motor boat and sank the Russian cruiser *Oleg*. The citation for his Victoria Cross, deliberately vague in view of the fact we were not technically at war with Russia, records 'his conspicuous gallantry, coolness and skill under extremely difficult conditions in action.' Two months later he took part in the famous 'Scooter Raid' at Kronstadt, when eight coastal motor boats sank two battleships and a depot ship.

Freshwater, Hampshire
196/326853

Alfred Tennyson lived at Farringford, near the Down which bears his name. Here once stood a wooden beacon known as Nodes Beacon, but in 1897 a huge granite Celtic Cross was unveiled in memory of the poet, as 'a beacon to sailors.'

Frimley, Surrey
186/879581

A plaque in the church is to Harold Gambier, a midshipman on HMS *Victoria* when she sank after collision with the *Camperdown* 22

June 1893. (See *Bulwick*.) In the churchyard lies Admiral Doveton Sturdee, who, as Commander-in-Chief South Atlantic, had destroyed Admiral von Spee's squadron at the Battle of the Falklands in December 1914. On retirement he was closely involved with the early preservation of Nelson's *Victory* at Portsmouth.

Frome, Somerset
183/777478

The submarine *Thunderbolt* was adopted by the town during 'warship week' in February 1942, and a ship's crest hangs in the Royal British Legion Club, together with a small exhibit. *Thunderbolt* was formerly the *Thetis*, which sank in Liverpool Bay. (See *Wales – Holyhead*.) Subsequently raised and repaired, she re-entered the service but was lost on her fifteenth patrol, 14 March 1943.

Fulmer, Buckinghamshire
176/999857

In the church is a memorial to George Nembhand, late of HM steamship *Vesuvius*, who died off Gibraltar 19 June 1844, aged 33.

Gedney, Lincolnshire
131/403243

'More glass than wall', said John Betjemen of St Mary Magdalene, one of the most beautiful of the fenland churches. Here the cross on the screen was given in honour of Penry

Osmond Bertie, Royal Navy cadet, who passed away 22 March 1917, aged 15.

Georgeham, Devon
180/464399

On 10 February 1799 the revenue brig *Weazel*, sailing for Falmouth, was wrecked near Baggy Point. William Kidman, one of the 107 who died, is buried against the church wall. The *Weazel* had spent the previous day at Appledore, where a farewell party had taken place on board; no doubt confiscated liquor had been liberally handed out. A plaque inside the church is to Henry Tinker, drowned when trying to save a life at Croyde Bay in 1916.

Gilling West, Yorkshire
100/616769

A plaque to the brave and dashing Rear-Admiral Sir Christopher Craddock, killed off Coronel, Chile, on 1 November 1914. He wrote *Whispers from the Fleet,* a book for aspiring officers. (See *Catherington*.)

Gillingham, Kent
178/789680

Buried in the cemetery is Lieutenant-Commander Eugene Esmonde VC, DSO, RN, who led his Swordfish squadron against the battle-cruisers *Gneisenau* and *Scharnhorst,* and the heavy cruiser *Prinz Eugen*, during the daring dash through the English Channel on 12 February 1942. Admiral Ciliax, who flew

A memorial to a 15-year-old naval cadet at Gedney Church.

The Phillips' Memorial cloister at Godalming.

his flag in the *Scharnhorst,* wrote admiringly of this 'mothball attack by a handful of ancient planes, piloted by men whose bravery surpassed any other action by either side that day.' A fine portrait of Esmonde hangs prominently in the Town Hall.

The clock-tower fountain beside the A2 is a memorial to William Adam, born here in 1564, who in 1598 joined a Dutch fleet sailing to Japan. He found much favour in the Royal household, and remained until his death there in 1620. A street in Yedo was named after him, and a festival held each year in his honour for he found 'such favour with two Emperors of Japan as never was any Christian in these parts of the world.'

Godalming, Surrey
186/968440

A superb cloister in the public gardens is to the memory of John Phillips, Chief Wireless Telegraphist on the *Titanic* who 'died at his post' on 15 April 1912. 'May no man or woman who seeks rest in the cloister leave without an inspiration towards that high courage which is in truth the liberator of souls.' (See *Farncombe*.)

Godstone, Surrey
187/357515

A wall-tablet in the church is to Lieutenant Evelyn Greenwell RNVR, who died at

Portland in 1919. Another is to Rear-Admiral John Saumarez Dumaresq, who died in 1922 during a cruise to Manilla when in command of the Australian fleet.

Goole, Yorkshire
105/744241

The town church has fine series of maritime memorials including one to the officers and men of the Mercantile Marine who died during the First World War. Plaques tell of the SS *Colne*, lost in the North Sea 12 March 1906; the SS *Calder*, which disappeared in the North Sea when homeward bound from Hamburg in April 1931; and the *Broomfleet*, 'which sailed from this port on Dec 13th 1933 and foundered in the North Sea off the Norfolk coast.'

George William Cawthorn, who perished in the SS *Merville* while crossing with coal from Goole to Ghent in 1923, is remembered here, while the belfrey clock was installed in memory of George William Proudfoot, Master Mariner, who died aged 46 in 1926, and Sub-Lieutenant Harry Proudfoot RNR, 'for many years a chorister of this church who died on active service aged 33 years when HMS *Princess Victoria* was lost 19 May 1940.'

Gorleston, Norfolk
134/524044

The church tower was restored as a memorial

Plaque in Godstone Church. (Rachel Woodfield)

to all Gorleston lifeboatmen, there being a memorial in the cemetery to four lost on service in November 1888.

Gosforth, Cumberland
89/072036

The village church contains a wooden plaque to Lieutenant-Commander Austin Noel Rees Keene RN, who was lost on HMS *Glorious* on 8 June 1940. (See *Bearsted.*) A marble plaque is to the memory of Captain Charles Alan Parker RM, who in 1854 'nobly fell leading the attack on Petropaulovskoi, Kamtschatka'. Another Parker commemorated here is Charles, who served in the Royal Navy from 1799, and spent seven years as a prisoner of war in France. Yet another memorial records how Sir Humphrey Le Fleming Senhouse of Seascale 'who having faithfully served his country for more than forty years lost his life in consequence of great mental and bodily exertions.' These were occasioned in 1840 after the taking of the heights of Canton, where he was senior naval officer. Next to the memorial is a Chinese bell, and two large cannon-balls brought back from the Dardanelles.

Gosport, Hampshire
196/620991

At the Joint Services Marina is the Coastal Forces Memorial listing 15 of the bases used by those in small, high-speed craft who 'cut into the enemy's coastal lifelines and shipping reserves, harrying the E-boats and preventing them attacking our convoys, enabling our Commandos to make vital raids'. (See *Wickersley.*)

In the gardens at the harbour ferry point is a fine bust of Admiral of the Fleet The Lord Fieldhouse of Gosport GCB, GBE (1928–92). Close by is a fountain erected in 1870 by Rear-Admiral R.F. Gambier and 'EMS'. I wonder who EMS was? In the churchyard of Holy Trinity there is a memorial stone which includes a reference to Lieutenant George Sprent RN, who went to sea aged 12 in 1803, but shortly after receiving his lieutenant's commission was invalided home from the West Indies to die aged 25.

The huge cemetery contains almost countless maritime memorials and graves and is worth exploring at length. One of the largest is a boulder draped with chains, commemorating those lost on HMS *Eurydice* on 24 March 1878. (See *Bosham.*) Four A-class submarines are remembered on a single memorial: *A-1*, the first submarine to be lost by the Royal Navy, was rammed by the liner *Berwick Castle* off the Isle of Wight in March 1904; *A-3* was rammed by the submarine tender HMS *Hazard* in December 1912, also off the Isle of Wight; and in 1905 *A-5* and *A-8* both suffered internal explosions, the latter just outside the Plymouth breakwater.

Coastal Forces' memorial at Gosport, which lists the bases from which the small craft operated during the Second World War.

Another prominent memorial, though you may have to move a cemetery seat to read the whole inscription, is to the 42 officers and men of *L-55*. She was sunk by the Russians near Kronstadt in the Baltic on 9 June 1919, and subsequently raised in 1928 when the bodies were returned for burial.

One more Gosport memorial must be mentioned, though, alas, public viewing can only be by appointment, for it is inside HMS *Centurion* in Grange Road. This is to a dog, a Great Dane named Just Nuisance, well-known to many naval personnel at Simonstown, South Africa, during the Second World War. His home was the Union Jack Club, but he travelled back and forth on the trains between Simonstown and Cape Town, boarded countless ships, had his own bunk, and his own seat on the last bus.

Grange over Sands, Lancashire
96/406776

A plaque in the church has been erected by Margaret Leigh to her husband Evan of Yewbarrow Hall, who lost his life in the sinking of the *Lusitania*. (See *Barnston*.)

Grasmere, Westmorland
90/337074

Near the churchyard gate is the gravestone, now almost illegible, of Sir John Richardson. He had joined the Royal Navy in 1807 as surgeon on the frigate *Nymphe* and, subsequently, on other ships until he retired in 1815. During the first Franklin expedition to the Canadian Arctic in 1819 he shot an Iroquois *voyageur* in self-defence after

Midshipman Hood had been killed. He went north with Franklin on his second expedition, and later (in 1848–9) led one of the first search parties to look for his old leader, though without success. He died in 1865. The Arctic skua was formerly known as Richardson's skua.

Gravesend, Kent
177/649744

St Andrew's Waterside Church, now a community centre with the Thames lapping against its walls, was a traditional departure point for ships. The daughter of Rear-Admiral Francis Beaufort helped provide the funds for the church, which was dedicated in memory of her father, hydrographer to the Royal Navy. (See *London – Hackney*.) A plaque recalls the *Loch Ard*, one of the many emigrant ships which left here, wrecked at the approaches to Melbourne with just two survivors from a complement of 54.

Three windows, and a plaque listing the petty officers and seamen, were donated by Lady Franklin in memory of her husband and all those who sailed from here on board *Erebus* and *Terror*, 19 May 1845. The ships, trapped by ice in Victoria Strait, were eventually abandoned off Victory Point in April 1848, leaving some 105 officers and men to try to make their way south. Illness and exhaustion beset them, and the last of the party probably succumbed in the vicinity of Starvation Cove on the desolate north shore of the Adelaide peninsula. (See *London – Waterloo Place*; *Spilsby*; *Northern Ireland – Banbridge*.)

Just to the east of the former church is the

The statue of Pocahontas, wife of Captain John Rolfe, in the town churchyard at Gravesend.

pier-head, where a large mural in a shelter depicts scenes from the maritime history of Gravesend, including the famous Watermen's Riot. Nearby in the town churchyard you may be surprised to find a statue of an American Indian princess, Pocahontas, wife of Captain John Rolfe. (See *London – Ludgate Hill*.)

Grays, Essex
177/615775

To demonstrate the past links with coastal trading there is a steel sculpture of a Thames barge mounted on a plinth bearing the words of T.S. Elliot: 'The barges drift with the turn-ing tide, Red sails wide, To leeward swing on heavy spar.' Nearby a pavement plaque remembers the accidental burning on the night of 22 December 1875 of the *Goliath,* a wooden battleship moored offshore as a training vessel for pauper boys. Nineteen boys and one officer died in the fire.

Great Ayton, Yorkshire
93/590101

On the summit of Easby Moor stands an obelisk in memory of Captain James Cook, who came to live in Great Ayton as a boy. The site of his cottage is marked by a rock brought from Point Hicks, the first land he sighted in Australia. After service on merchantmen he entered the Royal Navy in 1755, and in *Endeavour* began his first voyage of exploration in 1768. During his second voyage he penetrated the Antarctic regions as well as visiting Tahiti and other Pacific islands. His third voyage ended with his death at Karakakoa Bay in Hawaii in 1779. (See *Cambridge*; *Chalfont St Giles*; *London – Admiralty Arch*; *Marton-in-Cleveland*; *Stowe*; *Whitby*.)

Great Mongeham, Kent
179/345515

A plaque on the outside of the church tower is to Captain Robert Maynard who died in 1750, a 'faithful and experienced commander in the Royal Navy who . . . distinguished himself by many brave and gallant actions'.

Great Torrington, Devon
180/495191

Among several maritime memorials in the church is one to Arthur Rudd, who gave his life 'for King and Country on 11 May 1917 whilst minesweeping in the North Sea'. The White Ensign here flew at the Normandy landings, while a memorial window and plaques to the Colby family include Midshipman Henry Colby, who died in 1809.

Great Yarmouth, Norfolk
134/530055

Rising above the south end of the town is Nelson's Monument, a fine fluted column rising to 144 ft, completed in 1819 as Norfolk's memorial to its great son. A climb of 217 steps takes one to the viewing plat-form. On the four sides of the capital are the names of the ships on which he gained his principle victories – *Vanguard*, *Captain*, *Elephant*, and *Victory* – while at the top of the pedestal are the names of the victories – Aboukir, St Vincent, Copenhagen, and Trafalgar. (See *Burnham Thorpe*.)

Greater London

Crystal Palace Park *177/346708*

On 6 June 1931 HRH The Prince of Wales unveiled a memorial to mark the service of the Royal Naval Volunteer Reserve in the First World War, including no fewer than 125,000 who had been trained here since the first intake in 1914. Many of those who passed through HMS *Victory*, as it was called, were destined for the Royal Naval Division. (See *Blandford.*) The memorial, often referred to as the Royal Naval Volunteer Reserve Trophy, is in the form of a replica bell suported by two bronze dolphins, mounted on a massive teak table and situated within a stout shelter surrounded by low railings.

Deptford *177/375777*

Before it was damaged by enemy bombing, the church of St Nicholas 'contained a wealth of naval and maritime monuments and records which few churches if any in the kingdom can rival.' Nowadays it suffers insidious vandalism. High in the outside north wall is set a stone to John Addey, 'one of the King's Master Shipwrights', who died in 1606, Deptford having been formerly a Royal Dockyard.

A table-tomb in the churchyard, though it is now impossible to say which as the inscriptions are illegible, is where Captain George Shelvocke rests. He was a wonderful seaman of 'wild and truculent independence', who, while sailing round the world between 1719 and 1722, was wrecked on Juan Fernandez off Chile. It was during this voyage that an albatross was shot, an event which formed the basis of Coleridge's poem *The Rhyme of the Ancient Mariner*. (See *Ottery St Mary*.)

One of the wall-memorials which remains is unusual in commemorating two unrelated people, the upper panel remembering the Earl of Cork's eldest son, Roger Boyle, who died at school at Deptford aged 12, while the lower one relates to Edward Fenton, 'adventurer and navigator of outstanding truculence and daring'. He went with Frobisher on his second attempt to discover the North-West Passage in 1577, and commanded the *Mary Rose* during the Armada campaign of 1588.

Look for the remains of two shipbuilders' memorials, those of Peter Pett who died in 1652, inventor of the frigate (one formerly featured on the ornamental surround), and Jonas Shish, described by John Evelyn as 'a plaine honest carpenter, master builder of this dock, but one who can give very little account of his art by discourse, and is hardly capable of reading'.

There is a marble wall-plaque, formerly part of a larger memorial, to Sir Richard

M.S
LIEUT: PETER BUTT R.N. Ætt17.
Eldest Son of PETER BUTT Esq.
who died 7th July 1780, of wounds
received on board H.M.S. Conqueror
R. Adm! Rowley, on the 19th of May
preceding, in the Fleet under
the Command of V. Adm¹ Sir
George Rodney, in Action with
the French Fleet in the West
Indies .
Also of
LIEUT: JOHN BUTT ,
Second Son of PETER BUTT Esq.
who was drowned while in Command of an Armed Ship in the
North Sea, 24th Sept. 1799. Æt 26.
Mʳˢ GRACE BUTT, Mother of the
above PETER and JOHN BUTT,
died 24th Dec. 1824 .

Two sons of Peter Butt who died at sea, remembered in St Nicholas's Church, Deptford.

Hughes, 'one of the principal officers and commissioners of his Majesties Navy', who died in 1779. The Butt family are remembered here, including two sons of Peter Butt, clerk of survey in the Deptford Yard: Lieutenant Peter Butt, aged just 17 when, in July 1780, he died on board HMS *Conqueror* of wounds received in action against the French in the West Indies, and Lieutenant John Butt, drowned while in command of an armed ship in the North Sea, 24 September 1799.

In St Peter's Church is a fine decorated memorial to James Sawyer, Vice-Admiral of the White, who died in 1776. In the war of 1739 he received the 'thanks of the Assembly of Barbados for his distinguished conduct in the protection of their Trade.'

Dulwich *177/334730*

In the north cloister of Dulwich College is the *James Caird*, the open boat in which Shackleton and five companions sailed the 800 miles from Elephant Island to South Georgia in 1916 to seek help for the stranded crew of his ship, *Endurance*. He had attended classes here from 1887 to 1890. (See *Eastbourne*.) Elsewhere in the college is a

The James Caird, *Shackleton's boat, at Dulwich College.*

Binnacle from the Q-ship HMS Loderer *at Dulwich College, one of the ships of a distinguished old boy, Gordon Campbell VC.*

superb painting, the *Epic of the Sea* by Norman Wilkinson, which shows the *James Caird* during her voyage.

In the Hall are paintings of Old Boys who were awarded the Victoria Cross, among them Gordon Campbell, while close by is the binnacle, minus compass, of HMS *Loderer*, later *Farnborough* and *Q-5*, on board which he won his Victoria Cross. (See *Crondall*.)

East Greenwich *177/398782*
The wall-plaque close to the entrance of the Pleasaunce records that about 3,000 men, formerly pensioners of the Royal Hospital, are buried here: 'They served their country in the wars which established the Naval Supremacy of England, and died the honoured recipients of her gratitude.' The tombstones include those of such individuals as Captain Parker, a midshipman on the *Belleisle* at Trafalgar; Captain Mark Sweny, who served on the *Colossus* in the same action; and James Sherard RN, a Crimean veteran who for 18 years was 'with her late Majesty Queen Victoria as Boatswain's Mate on the Royal Yacht *Victoria and Albert*.' There are a number of graves of instructors at the Royal Naval College, and also two curators of the Royal Naval Museum.

Eltham *177/432762*
The fine tower known as Severndroog Castle was built to commemorate the achievements of Sir William James in the East Indies, and

The grave of Captain Mark Sweny in the East Greenwich Pleasaunce.

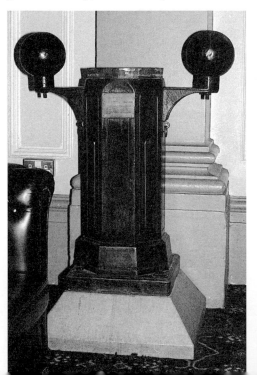

MARK HALPEN SWENY,
CAPTAIN ROYAL NAVY,
SERVED IN H.M.S "COLOSSUS"
AT TRAFALGAR,
DIED 25TH NOVR 1865,
AGED 82 YEARS.

Severndroog Castle, standing on the highest point in south London, above Eltham, was erected to commemorate the achievements of Sir William James.

in particular his conquest of the castle of Severndroog on the coast of Malabar in 1755.

Forest Gate *177/417854*

The Drewry family are remembered in All Saints Church, in particular George Drewry, who as a midshipman was one of those valiant souls who helped effect the landings from the *River Clyde* at 'V' Beach, Gallipoli, on 25 April 1915. (See *Deal; Wales – Chepstow.*) For this he was awarded the first Victoria Cross of the war to a member of the RNR/Merchant Navy. Later he served in the North Sea, and while loading the armed trawler *William Jackson* at Scapa Flow on 2 August 1918 was struck by a balancing block from a derrick, dying later that day from his injuries. His brother officers on the Northern Patrol erected the window here in his memory. (See *Greater London – Manor Park.*)

Greenwich *177/383779*

Facing the Thames on the western end of the Royal Naval College building, busts of some of our greatest naval commanders, from Sir Francis Drake to Earl St Vincent, are set high in the wall. Elsewhere in the College there is a memorial to the men of the Royal Naval Division which formerly stood outside the Admiralty. (See *Blandford.*)

In a small chapel behind the altar of the main chapel is a marble memorial to Sir John Franklin and his men, together with the remains of Lieutenant Henry Le Vesconte of the *Erebus*. The skeleton discovered by Captain Hall was brought back to England and identified, then placed in an oak coffin and buried at Greenwich. The plaque simply reads: 'Beneath lie the remains of one of

The wall-plaques of some of our greatest naval heroes at the Royal Naval College, Greenwich.

Franklin's companions who perished in the Arctic regions 1848.' (See *Gravesend*.)

On the riverside walk is a tall obelisk with just a single name – Bellot. This French Navy lieutenant joined Captain William Kennedy's expedition to search for Franklin in the *Prince Albert* in 1851 and was lost in the Arctic in 1853 when he set off across the ice to deliver dispatches to Sir Edward Belcher, trapped in the Wellington Channel. 'The last that was seen of Lieutenant Bellot was on his going round a hummock, out of sight of his companions; the rest is mere conjucture, for he never returned.'

The first permanent memorial in London to all of those lost on the *Titanic*, a garden, at the National Maritime Museum, was opened in April 1995 in the presence of the oldest living survivor. Mrs Haisman, now aged 98, was a 15-year-old girl when she and her mother were among those saved, her father being lost in the tragedy. (See *Southampton*.)

Lower Edmonton *177/345937*
In the church a fine memorial to Robert William Eastwick tells that he died in December 1865 'aged 93 years 6 months and 6 days'. He had many adventures: he was one of just seven men who escaped from the wreck of a ship in August 1793 at Cape Negrais on the coast of Burma; he was captain of the *Endeavour* when she was taken in Belasore Roads by the *La Forte* and then recaptured by the *La Sybille* in the celebrated action of 28 February 1799; and in 1810 he escaped from the wreck of the *Elizabeth* at Dunkirk when 360 persons perished, only to be taken prisoner by the French. Following his release he was imprisoned again after a severe action against the American privateer *Anaconda*. His final command seems to have been the *Asia*, wrecked on the coast of Holland in 1825.

Manor Park *177/421863*
George Drewry VC is buried in the City of London Cemetery. (See *Greater London – Forest Gate*.) In Manor Park Cemetery lies another holder of the Victoria Cross, Jack Cornwell: in nearby Jack Cornwell Street is the Victoria Cross public house, and in Grantham Road a block of flats is known as Jack Cornwell VC House. (See *Chester*.)

Putney Vale *176/223726*
Here lies 'one of England's best loved Sons, Charles William De la Poer Beresford, Sailor and Patriot.' He had entered the Royal Navy in 1859 and had sailed round the world on HMS *Galatea*. Later he was prominent in the action at Alexandria in 1882 and in the Nile Campaign. His bitter feud with Admiral Fisher over naval reforms and policy domi-

nated his later career. (See *London – St Paul's Cathedral*.)

Richmond *176/184737*
A ward at the Star and Garter Home is named after Jack Cornwell VC. (See *Chester*.)

Upper Norwood *177/332697*
Admiral FitzRoy, who committed suicide in 1865, is buried in the churchyard. He commanded the *Beagle* during the famous cruise with Charles Darwin on board which commenced in 1831. Later he was Governor of New Zealand, and then became interested in meteorology, inventing the rather splendid FitzRoy barometer.

Greystead, Northumberland
80/771858

The church here, together with those at Humshaugh, Thorneyburn, and Wark, were built after the Battle of Trafalgar to accommodate redundant fleet chaplains. They are often referred to as the 'Admiralty churches'.

Grimsby, Lincolnshire
113/264079

As you come into the town on the A16 you will pass a statue of Grim the Viking, a fictional character who is said to have settled here as a fish merchant. A memorial plaque to the Royal Naval Patrol Service now in the National Fishing Heritage Centre was formerly in the Dock Tower. There is a Fishermen's Chapel in the Methodist Hall, Duncombe Street, with a fine memorial providing details of the ships lost during peace and war. Windows recall three separate tragedies, those of the *Epine*, *St Oswald*, and *Sheldon*. Since the chapel was opened in 1966 almost 250 further names of Grimsby seafarers have been added to the memorials here, bringing the total to almost 3,000.

Guildford, Surrey
186/987500

Although there is no special link between Guildford and the sea a large wooden cross made from timbers from the old training ship HMS *Ganges* was erected in 1933 at the site for the Cathedral. It remains to this day, just to the east of the building. There is a painting of the *Ganges* in the Cathedral, while the chapel of the Queen's Royal Surrey Regiment has reminders of the maritime traditions of the Regiment, for its men served afloat in several notable engagements. Two small stained glass windows should be noted. One was given by the Royal Naval Association, the other, which marks the Diamond Jubilee of the Women's Royal Naval Service, having

The 'Ganges' cross at Guildford Cathedral.

been dedicated on 8 July 1979 in the presence of Earl Mountbatten of Burma, his last public engagement before his murder.

The church of St Nicholas contains a memorial to Admiral Sir Charles Knowles, born in Jamaica in 1754 when his father, also an Admiral, was Governor. The inscription refers to him being a 'brave officer' who had 'fought and bled in defence of his country in several parts of the globe.'

Guiseley, Yorkshire

104/194422

The parish church contains a White Ensign given in thanksgiving by Commander J.M. Howeson RN, for 'rescue from drowning in a naval action during the Great War'. The first Guiseley man to lose his life in that war was Royal Marine Fred Greep, at Antwerp, while in the Second World War the first was George White on HMS *Courageous*. The town adopted HMS *Bramble*, and there is a memorial to her company of 121 lost on 31 December 1942 as she helped escort Convoy JW.51B to North Russia. A plaque records the name 'Richard Emly Choir Boy 1953–1964 killed in action HMS *Sheffield* 1982.' A sub-lieutenant, he died when the *Sheffield* was sunk on 4 May 1982. (See *Stubbington*.)

Gunwalloe, Cornwall

203/660205

The church is situated at Church Cove some two miles south of the village itself, past Hazelphron Cove and the cliffs where ship-wrecked mariners were formerly buried. The rood screen is made from timbers taken from the wreck of *The St Anthony of Lisbon* (or *Padua*) wrecked here on 19 January 1527. The four winches at Fishing Cove come from the wreck in 1890 of the *Brankelow*.

Gwithian, Cornwall

203/586413

The war memorial in the church consists of a small framed water-colour of a soldier, sailor and Union Jack. The names recorded include Thomas Bate, H. Sydney Hearn, and James Mehennet, who went down with their ship at Coronel. (See *Catherington*.)

Hamble, Hampshire

196/481067

Outside the church gate is a bronze listing 46 names from TS *Mercury* who died in the First World War. Inside are memorials to the Bradby sons, both captains, who died of yellow fever at Martinique. A tablet, Red Ensign, American flag, and a painting all recall US Army Tanker *Y17* and her crew of 18 lost through enemy action on 9 April 1945.

Hambledon, Hampshire

196/646152

A stone tablet tells of Erasmus Gower, Admiral of the White, the eldest of 19 children. In 1764 he sailed round the world on HMS *Dolphin* then went straight away to the *Swallow* and a further circumnavigation, which did not conclude until 1769. When in command of the *Medea* he captured a large French storeship and an even more valuable prize, the *Vryheid*. Later he took command of

HMS *Lion* on a momentous voyage to China, bringing home cargo valued at £5 million. On board the *Triumph*, in action against the French on 17 June 1795, it was reported that 'the cool and firm conduct of his ship was such that it appeared to me that the Enemy's ships dared not come near to her.' He died in 1814 aged 72. (See *Wales – Cilgerran.*)

The base of the war memorial is made from wood taken from HMS *Britannia*, training ship at Dartmouth 1869–1905. A rather beautiful wall-plaque is to John Goldsmith, a Royal Marine Light Infantry captain who gave his life in France 11 May 1917. Then there is a plaque to Stoker Arthur Parvin, who, together with 737 others, was lost when the battleship HMS *Bulwark* exploded while taking ammunition aboard at Sheerness, 15 November 1914. (See *Blakeney*; *Little Marlow.*)

Hamworthy, Dorset

195/017920

The lych-gate of St Michael's Church contains plaques to those lost on landing craft during the Normandy operations of June, and the Walcheren operations of November 1944. 'Those who fell that week most worthily upheld the traditions of the great corps to which they belonged, and which had already visited that battlefield. For the Royal Marines were no strangers to Walcheren, and in 1809 had earned the commendation of Admiral Sir Richard Strachan, the naval commander . . . He praised them for their excellent manage-

Memorial at Hamworthy to those from 3 Commando Brigade who gave their lives in the Falklands, 1982. (Royal Marines)

The 'Cockleshell Heroes' memorial at Hamworthy. (Royal Marines)

ment and discipline . . . That same excellent management and discipline enabled the officers and men . . . to avenge the ghosts of their ancestors, who from the shadows must surely have watched their prowess and rejoiced.'

In the Royal Marines base there is a memorial to the officers and men of 3 Commando Brigade, HMS *Fearless*, and 846 Naval Air Squadron lost in operations in the Falklands in 1982, 32 names in all. Six were on board the landing craft *Foxtrot Four*, operating from *Fearless*, when it was attacked by Argentinean aircraft between Goose Green and Fitzroy. Corporal M.D. Love DSM, an aircrewman, was killed when his Sea King helicopter crashed, while others were killed during the actions ashore.

Within the main camp is a fine memorial to the 'Cockleshell Heroes' who participated in Operation Frankton, the canoe-borne raid on shipping at Bordeaux in December 1942. Only Major H.G. Hasler and Marine Sparks returned. The inscription is provided by the words of Earl Mountbatten of Burma: 'Of the many brave and dashing raids carried out by the men of Combined Operations Command none was more courageous or imaginative than Operation Frankton'.

Hanley, Staffordshire

118/883473

The former town hall of Hanley, now the Registry Office, contains a large framed photograph of Captain John Smith of the *Titanic* above a plaque which informs the visitor that he was 'born in Hanley 27 January 1850, died at sea 15 April 1912. Be British.' For that was his last message to his crew as the great ship settled. (See *Lichfield*; *Southampton*.)

Happisburgh, Norfolk

133/379312

A fishermen's corner inside the church includes a cross made of ships' timbers as a memorial to the nine 'fishermen and lads of this village lost at sea since the Great War'. The bells restored at Easter 1924 are in memory of the officers and men of the Royal Navy and Merchant Navy 'who made the supreme sacrifice in the North Sea 1914–1919'. One of these same bells was a gift 'in memory of Nelson's men wrecked off Haisboro in 1801.' These 119 sailors from HMS *Invincible* were on their way to join the Admiral off Copenhagen but now rest in the large mound on the north side of the church. In December 1770 HMS *Peggy* was wrecked here and 32 of her crew buried in the churchyard. In 1804 the crew of the revenue cutter HMS *Hunter*, also wrecked here, joined them.

Memorial at Happisburgh to those lost in the wreck of the Young England *1876.*

Harpley, Norfolk

132/788260

Jermyn, third son of Rector Pratt, who fell from the rigging aged 16 while serving as a midshipman on the *Maidstone*, bound for Calcutta in 1856, is remembered by a wall-plaque.

Hartlepool, County Durham

93/532338

On 16 December 1914 a German squadron bombarded several east coast towns. Winston Churchill describes, in *World Crisis*, how he heard the news: 'At about half-past eight I was in my bath, when the door opened and an officer came hurrying in from the War Room with a naval signal which I grasped with dripping hand "German battle-cruisers bombarding Hartlepool." I jumped out of the bath with exclamations. Sympathy for Hartlepool was mingled with what Mr George Wyndham once called "the anodyne of contemplated retaliation." Pulling on clothes over a damp body, I ran downstairs to the War Room.' A plaque on the seafront records the place where the first shell struck, and that the bombardment resulted in the first death of a soldier on British soil by enemy action during the First World War.

Haslemere, Sussex
186/903335

St Christopher's Church contains a large painted crucifix and a memorial plaque to a former curate, Christopher Tanner, who was awarded the Albert Medal (now the George Cross). In December 1939 he volunteered for the Royal Navy, a service which had already claimed the lives of two of his three brothers. Posted to the cruiser *Fiji* he was lost when the ship was sunk in an air attack south-west of Crete on 22 May 1941. One of the survivors described how, as the *Fiji* began to settle, Padre Tanner ensured all the wounded were brought from the sick bay, and was one of the last to leave the ship. In the water he was 'indefatigable in helping fellows to floats or wood; and swam about tirelessly that when they ultimately got him aboard, he collapsed and died.'

Hawkeshead, Lancashire
97/352980

A grave in the churchyard records an examiner of ships' masters at Liverpool, Captain Charles Louis Albert Lecoustre, who died 16 May 1933.

Heacham, Norfolk
132/682379

In the churchyard is a gravestone to a victim of pneumonia, Petty Officer James Mallett, who died in Scotland 7 November 1918, aged 27.

Hebburn, County Durham
88/308638

In the town cemetery are buried 27 crew members of HMS *Kelly*, killed in action against E-boats in the North Sea when the ship almost sank. Less than a year later, on 23 May 1941, she was sunk off Crete during a fierce aerial onslaught with the loss of 128, who are also remembered here. At the Swan Hunter shipyard where she was built a plaque also records these events.

Heighington, County Durham
93/248224

Captain Cumby RN was born in a cottage overlooking the green, while his fine house of later years, appropriately known as Trafalgar House, stands at the eastern edge of the village. Following the death of her captain in that battle he took command of the

Bellerophon 'which was then opposed in the hottest of the action . . . being in close contact with the French ship *L'Aigle*, closely engaged with the Spanish ship *El Monarca* and exposed to the fire of several other ships'. Two fine chairs are said to be made from timber taken from the *Bellerophon* (See *Wales – Pembroke Dock*.)

Helston, Cornwall
203/659275

In the town centre is a cannon from HMS *Anson*, raised by divers from HMS *Seahawk*, the nearby naval air station. The mounting and carriage are replicas of the original, and were presented by descendants of Henry Trengrouse of Helston, who has a large memorial stone directly opposite the church door. This records that he 'rendered most signal service to humanity by devoting the greater portion of his life and means to the invention of the "Rocket Apparatus" for

Close to the door of Helston Church is the memorial to Henry Trengrouse, inventor of the rocket apparatus.

A cannon from HMS Anson *in the centre of Helston.*

communicating between stranded ships and the shore, whereby many thousands of lives have been saved.' (See *Loe Bar*.)

Hereford, Herefordshire
149/513396

A fine pillar on a knoll in the park is in memory of Nelson. The plaque refers to him having 'terminated a career of unexampled glory off Cape Trafalgar . . . in a battle which nearly annihilated the marine of France and Spain and confirmed in the eyes of Europe and the World the naval superiority of Great Britain'. (See *Burnham Thorpe*.)

Heswall, Cheshire
108/265812

A small plaque in the church remembers Arthur Watkinson, lost on HMS *Thetis* in June 1939. (See *Wales – Holyhead*.)

Highfield, Hampshire
196/425147

A massive model of a sixteenth century ship hangs in the church in memory of Captain John Creaghe, who died in 1931, so that all who see it 'may remember and pray for our sailors.'

Highworth, Wiltshire
174/201924

The Warneford family chapel contains a plaque 'placed here by members of the Warneford family throughout the world' in memory of Reginald Warneford, who, after service in the Merchant Navy, joined the Royal Fusiliers before transferring to the infant Royal Naval Air Service in February 1915. He had qualified as a pilot within 15 days, his boyhood daredevil attitude causing one squadron commander to write that 'he hoped Warneford would become a Hun killer, but he was a darned nuisance at Eastchurch.' On 7 June he destroyed a Zeppelin near Bruges, but 10 days later he was thrown out of a biplane and killed. King George V wrote to Warneford's mother: 'It is a matter of sincere regret that the death of Flight Sub-Lieutenant Reginald Alexander John Warneford deprived me of the pride of personally conferring upon him the Victoria Cross, the greatest of all Naval Distinctions.' (See *London – Brompton Cemetery*.)

Hinderwell, Yorkshire
94/791171

In the cemetery is the grave of Robert Patton, 30 years a lifeboatman, who was dragged

overboard and crushed between the lifeboat
and the salvage steamer *Dispenser* during a
rescue in February 1934. Before he died he
said: 'I could not let the poor man go, as he
might have drowned.' He was posthumously
awarded the RNLI Gold Medal.

Holbrook, Suffolk
169/165353

The Royal Hospital School was founded in
Greenwich in 1712 but moved here in 1933.
It is primarily for the children and grandchildren of seafarers.

Holy Island, Northumberland
75/125418

A husband lost on the minesweeper HMS
Holdene when she was sunk by a mine off
Orfordness in February 1917 is remembered
in the church, along with a post captain who
died aged 70 in 1825. The churchyard
contains gravestones to a number of lifeboatmen, and opposite the Heritage Centre are
some information panels recording the
history of the Holy Island lifeboats and their
services.

Hornchurch, Essex
177/540865

At the Battle of Jutland, the cruiser HMS
Chester was in action against the German
cruisers *Frankfurt, Wiesbaden, Pillau,* and
Elbing 'and in a minute or two the *Chester*
was smothered in bursting shell. Within five
minutes she had three of her guns disabled'.
Admiral Beatty's dispatch says. 'Boy 1st
Class John Travers Cornwell of *Chester* was
mortally wounded early in the action. He
nevertheless remained standing alone at a
most exposed post, quietly awaiting orders
till the end of the action, with the gun's crew
dead and wounded all round him. His age
was under 16 years. I regret that he has since
died, but I recommend his case for special
recognition in justice to his memory, and as
an acknowledgement of the high example set
by him.'
    The special recognition was a posthumous
Victoria Cross for Jack Cornwell, the
youngest naval winner of the award. A public
appeal raised sufficient funds for the building
of three commemorative semi-detached
houses, laid out in the form of the Victoria
Cross. These are administered by The John
Cornwell VC National Memorial, whose
object is to provide homes for disabled and
infirm sailors. Other memorials include a
ward at the Royal Star and Garter Home,
Richmond; a hospital bed in Grimsby; a Sea
Cadet Unit, the J.T. Cornwell VC (TS
Chester) in Newham; and the Cornwell Scout

Badge. (See *Chester*; *Greater London –
Manor Park*.)

Hove, Sussex
198/286047

A plaque in St Andrew's Church records that
Admiral Sir George Westphal who died in
1875 was 'the last surviving officer of the
glorious battle of Trafalgar', where he was
wounded on board the *Victory*.

Hoylake, Cheshire
108/214889

In the parish church are two memorials to
lifeboatmen. One is 'in pleasant memory' of
John Roberts, who, while serving on the
night of 15 November 1906, was washed
overboard and drowned. The other is to
Thomas Dodd, 40 years a member of the
Hoylake and Hilbre Island lifeboats, for 22 of
which he was coxswain.

Hull, Yorkshire
107/081277

On the Hessle Road is a memorial to three
fishermen killed by naval gunfire, not in

*A trawlerman on a plinth in Hessle Road,
Hull, commemorates the three killed during
the Dogger Bank incident of 1904, when their
vessels were fired upon by the Russian fleet.*

wartime, but as a result of being shelled by the Russian fleet in the North Sea on the night of 22 October 1904. Mistaking the lights and flares of trawlers for Japanese torpedo-boats (!), the Russians opened fire and several trawlers suffered casualties. The incident nearly caused a war: the Channel Squadron was readied for action, and British cruisers shadowed the Russian fleet on its voyage to almost total annihilation by the Japanese at the Battle of Tsushima on 27 May 1905.

A memorial at the entrance to the old fish docks is dedicated to all those who passed through the St Andrew's Lock Gates 1883–1975 and 'fished the Arctic grounds of Murmansk, Greenland and Iceland. In 1914 and 1939 men and trawlers went to war. This tablet commemorates the many who did not return.'

Towards the eastern end of the Spring Bank Cemetery is the tomb of Captain Gravill, the last of the Hull whalers, who had died when his ship *Diana* was trapped in the Davis Strait in the winter of 1866–7. (See *Scotland – Lerwick.*)

A superb bronze plaque in Queen's Gardens shows Robinson Crusoe complete with musket and parasol, and the words: 'Robinson Crusoe most famous character in fiction sailed from here September 1651. Sole survivor from shipwreck he was cast up on a desert island where he spent 28 years, 2 months and 19 days. An example of resolution, fortitude and self reliance.' This is followed by the words: 'Had I the sense to return to Hull I had been happy.'

A plaque overlooking the former Humber Dock Basin commemorates the departure of the *Forfarshire* from here on 5 September 1838. (See *Bamburgh*.) A number of sculptures in public places link with the maritime past, as does a mural at the Edinburgh Street Community Centre, depicting the fishing industry. A recent initiative has been the creation of a Seven Seas Fish Pavement, a trail throughout the city in which a series of 35 plaques, carvings, and sculptures depicts different types of fish ranging from the anchovy to the zander.

Hunstanton, Norfolk
132/673401

An epitaph on a stone in the churchyard is in memory of William Webb, late of the 15th Light Dragoons, who was shot from his horse by smugglers, 26 September 1784.

Hythe, Kent
189/161349

Lionel Lukin in 1785 produced a pamphlet *The Invention, Principles of Construction*

and Uses of Unimmergible Boats, and his tombstone in the churchyard to the northwest of the tower records that he 'was the first who built a lifeboat and was the original inventor of that principle of safety by which many lives and much property have been preserved from shipwreck.' Herein lies a controversy, for Henry Greathead and William Wouldhave are also claimed to have designed and built the first lifeboat. (See *South Shields.*)

Ilderton, Northumberland
75/017218

A small mausoleum contains members of the Roddam family including Admiral Robert Roddam, who, when in command of the sloop *Viper* in 1746, showed particular skill at Cadeiro Bay on the north-west coast of Spain where he destroyed the guns of a battery, burnt 25 merchant ships, and captured several others. A subsequent command included the guardship *Lennox* at Portsmouth, where the future Admiral Collingwood served under him. (See *Tynemouth.*)

Immingham, Lincolnshire
113/175150

The church has an impressive array of memorials to the little ships of the Royal Navy that sailed from the port, and of men lost on them, during the First World War. These include the *Margate*, sunk off Spurn Head, Yorkshire, on 24 April 1917 after a gallant fight with an enemy submarine; and the *Epworth*, lost as a result of collision a month later. HMS *Cotsmuir*, another ship remembered here, disappeared without trace in February 1917.

Inner Farne, Northumberland
75/218358

A plaque in St Cuthbert's Chapel is inscribed: 'To the memory of Grace Horsley Darling a native of Bamburgh and an inhabitant of these islands who died October 20 1842 aged 26 years.' (See *Bamburgh.*)

Irton, Cumberland
89/091004

The church contains a memorial tablet to Skeffington Lutwidge, who had sailed in 1773 as second-in-command of the bomb-vessel *Carcass* on the Arctic expedition (during which a very young Nelson had his famous encounter with a Polar bear). Members of the Brocklebank family are remembered, including Daniel Brocklebank who commenced shipbuilding in Whitehaven in 1782.

The Roddam mausoleum at Ilderton. (Phil Rowett)

Iver, Buckinghamshire

176/040812

Admiral James Gambier, who died in 1833, is buried here and also remembered by a plaque in the church. In the *Defence* he had been the first to break the line at the Glorious First of June. However, his sea service was short – a mere five and a half years – and he 'seems indeed, to had a very distinct preference for life on shore'.

Another tablet records S. Snook, senior captain in the Indian Navy, who died in 1844, aged 74. He had assisted in bringing Christianity to the Pelew Islands in the Pacific. James Whitshed, an 18-year-old midshipman on the *Berwick* who fell in action against French vessels in the Mediterranean in 1813, is also commemorated. His father was much more fortunate in a naval career which spanned 71 years, becoming Admiral of the Fleet in 1844 aged 82.

Jarrow, County Durham

88/325654

Just outside the hospital is a stout monolith erected by the Palmer Shipbuilding Company to all 1,543 men of their works who joined the forces in the First World War. It lists those that fell, and the department in which they worked. A fine statue of Sir Charles Palmer, who died in 1907, stands overlooking the river. A brief inscription outlines his achievements, and reliefs show some of ships built in his yards, including the first, the paddle-tug *Northumberland* (1851).

Kettering, Northamptonshire

141/867784

The names of seven local men are recalled on a memorial to all those lost when the troopship *Transylvania* was sunk by a submarine in the Gulf of Genoa, 4 May 1917. Of some 3,000 on board that morning 411 passengers and crew, including the captain, were casualties. (See *St Albans*.)

Kilverstone, Norfolk

144/894840

In the churchyard, close to his beloved Hall, lie the ashes of one of Britain's most dynamic Admirals – Admiral of the Fleet and 1st Baron Fisher of Kilverstone. Born in 1841, John Arbuthnot Fisher entered the Royal Navy in 1854 on board Nelson's *Victory*. During the Crimean War he was with the Baltic Fleet, and later served in the Far East, at Canton in 1858 and the disastrous attack on the Taku Forts in 1859. His experiences there caused him to write: 'When by-and-by the Chinese know their power they have only to walk slowly westwards and, like the locusts in Egypt, no Pharohs in Europe with all their mighty boats will stop them.' Such eloquence was matched in countless letters, minutes and memorandum and two books, *Memories* and *Records*. Though he retired as First Sea Lord in 1910 (to grow roses, which, as a friend said, 'will dammed well have to grow'), he was brought back in October 1914. At first he and the new First Sea Lord, Winston Churchill, worked in harmony, but strains soon became apparent on a number of issues, in particular regarding the deployment of ships at the Dardanelles.

Admiral Fisher died on 10 July 1920, the state funeral in Westminster Abbey being described as an unforgettable sight. His ashes were buried at Kilverstone alongside his wife. On the tombstone is his motto: 'Fear God and Dread Nought'.

Kineton, Warwickshire
151/335510

'A brave man to be remembered' is the inscription on the gravestone of Admiral Sir Walter Cowan, who died in 1956, while in the north aisle of the church hangs his rear-admiral's flag, flown in HMS *Caledon* of the First Light Cruiser Squadron at the surrender of the German Fleet on 21 November 1918. His career commenced in 1884 and concluded in 1945, his last action, just two years earlier, being in a commando operation on the coast of Dalmatia, for which, aged 73 and 'beginning to fill the strain', he was awarded a bar to his DSO.

King's Lynn, Norfolk
132/617198

A town steeped in maritime history has many reminders of the wealth the sea brought here, including a Customs House, a Pilot Street, and the Greenland Fishery. In Nelson Street there was a pre-Tudor inn, now a private house, which for part of its existence was known as the Valiant Sailor, after Jack Mowbray. (See *Sunderland*.)

St Margaret's Church has an ornate wall-memorial to Sir William Hoste RN, born 1780, which provides the bare details of an epic career which commenced at the Battle of the Nile. His most gallant action was the famous victory off the Isle of Lissa on 15 March 1811, when, in command of just three frigates and a brig, he defeated the entire Franco-Venetian squadron. As he manoeuvred before battle commenced, Hoste made the signal: 'Remember Nelson'. (See *London – St Paul's Cathedral*.) His two sons also entered the Royal Navy and are remembered here. The eldest, William, rose to the rank of rear-admiral, but Theodore died on board the *Volage* in the Mediterranean, aged just 16, on 3 April 1835, 'cut off like a flower.'

This ornate memorial in the parish church of King's Lynn is to Sir William Hoste and his two sons, who all served in the Royal Navy.

Another famous son of King's Lynn, born in New Conduit Street, was George Vancouver, the youngest of six children. A plinth now marks the spot where the house stood, while the shopping precinct is named the Vancouver Centre and there is Vancouver Avenue on the south side of the town. (See *Petersham*.)

Kington, Herefordshire
148/291567

A plaque in the church tells of James Parker who was lost with 78 others on the *British Admiral* in the Bass Strait on 23 May 1874. Chartered to the White Star Line, she ran aground on rocks near King Island, Tasmania. There were just nine survivors.

Kirkby Stephen, Westmorland
91/775086

At the centre of the town, cloisters to provide

shelter for churchgoers and market-people were 'built by direction of the Will of John Waller Esq. a Purser in His Majesty's Navy and a native of this town, 1810.'

Kirkwhelpton, Northumberland
81/996845

Sir Charles Parsons, who developed the high speed turbine in 1884 and the first turbine-driven steamship, the *Turbina*, in 1897, and took out over 300 patents on his work, is buried here. It is said that 'of all his many inventions and experiments, an attempt to make diamonds was the only one in which he failed to achieve his aim.'

Knotty Ash, Lancashire
108/404916

The tall obelisk in memory of Nelson is now much defaced, while the original plaques were removed long ago. The memorial was offered to the Liverpool City Corporation by a local shipping merchant, but turned down because it was too small. Instead he erected it in a prominent position on his estate, now a park. (See *Burnham Thorpe*.)

Knowlton, Kent
179/282533

Fine tombs in the church contain the bowels of Sir John Narborough, who in 1688 died at sea of fever in the West Indies, and tell of his two sons, who died with their stepfather, Sir Cloudesley Shovel, in the terrible wreck of his fleet in the Isles of Scilly in 1707. (See *Oxford*; *Rochester*.)

Lancaster, Lancashire
97/473619

The graveyard of St Mary's Priory Church contains a number of memorials of maritime interest, including one to Thomas Walmsley, who served on the *Majestic* at Camperdown, and his brothers, Joseph, lost as the *Harriett* left Liverpool in 1808, and William, who died on passage to Barbados, 'a victim of the climate.'

Lancing, Sussex
198/196066

A window in the war memorial cloister at Lancing College is to HMS *King Alfred*, based here 1940–45, the White Ensign of which hangs in the chapel.

Langham, Norfolk
133/007413

Near the church tower lies Captain Frederick

Marryat. A plaque tells little of his life, but he was a naval officer with as adventurous a career as any, and was able to use many of his experiences in his numerous novels and children's books, which included *Masterman Ready* and *Mr Midshipman Easy*. He was elected a Fellow of the Royal Society after devising a signalling code for merchant ships. The loss in 1847 of his son Frederick, also remembered here, a lieutenant on HMS *Avenger* (see *Compton*), hastened his own death the following year.

Langton Matravers, Dorset
195/998789

There is a plaque in the church to Admiral of the Fleet 1st Baron Tovey, who was on the *Amphion,* the first British warship in action in 1914, when she sank the German minelayer *Konigin Luise*, only herself to be sunk by a mine the following day. At Jutland he commanded the destroyer *Onslow* and was promoted 'for the persistent and determined manner in which he attacked enemy ships.' In the Second World War, when flying his flag in *King George V*, his forces sank the *Bismarck* in May 1941. As Commander-in-Chief The Nore he made, in the words of the

Plaque in Langton Matravers Church to Admiral of the Fleet John Tovey.

Admiralty, 'an outstanding contribution' to the success of the Normandy invasion.

Lea, Lincolnshire
121/831867

The church contains an unusual plaque to Francis Foljambe Anderson, who died in South Africa in September 1881 but was buried at sea in October, the plaque thoughtfully including a map indicating the precise spot, 230 miles NNW of Ascension Island. A rector of Lea and his wife, who 'died by the foundering of the *Liberia* with all hands on their voyage to Madeira April 13th 1874', are also remembered.

Leatherhead, Surrey
187/166562

The parish church contains a memorial to Admiral Sir James Wishart, died 1723, whose commands included the *Oxford*, which, at Barfluer in 1692, put an end to James II's hopes of regaining his crown. He was also with Rooke at the breaking of the boom at Vigo, and the capture of Gibraltar in 1704.

Statue of Captain John Smith of the Titanic *in the park at Lichfield.*

Leckhampton, Gloucestershire
163/944194

A plaque in the church is to the memory of Captain John Campbell, Royal Marines, who died in London in August 1848.

Leconfield, Yorkshire
107/021435

Royal Engineers lost in the sinking of the *Lancastria*, 17 June 1940, are remembered in the Garrison Church by a plaque dedicated in 1991 in the presence of three survivors. (See *London – Leadenhall Street*.)

Lee-on-Solent, Hampshire
196/558010

The large roadside memorial to officers and men of the Fleet Air Arm who have no grave but the sea. The names are listed by year and rank, so it is not easy to learn their story.

Leeds, Yorkshire
104/299334

James Watt (1736–1819), whose statue is in the City Square, was a Scottish engineer and inventor whose works included the improvement of harbours, while his son, also James, in 1817 fitted the engine to the first steamer to leave port, the *Caledonia*.

Leicester, Leicestershire
140/600012

Denzil Jarvis, who was lost on the *Titanic*, is remembered in the churchyard of St Mary Magdalene, Knighton. (See *Southampton*.)

Lichfield, Staffordshire
128/116097

In the central park is a fine statue of Captain John Smith of the *Titanic* by Lady Scott, wife of Captain Scott of the Antarctic. It includes the words: 'Commander Edward John Smith RD RNR. Born January 27 1850, died April 15 1912. Bequeathing to his countrymen the memory and example of a great heart, a brave life and a heroic death. Be British.' (See *Hanley*; *Southampton*.)

As you walk back towards the main road past the former Free Library and Museum, note the figure of an armed sailor from HMS *Powerful*, which had contributed sailors and marines to man field-guns at the siege of Ladysmith in 1900.

Lincoln, Lincolnshire
121/978718

The Cathedral contains a memorial window

to Matthew Flinders, one of Lincolnshire's sailor sons. (See *Donnington*.)

Lindale, Lancashire
96/414804

Out of 16 names on the war memorial plaque inside the church just one is naval, Robert G. Hutchinson of HMS *Good Hope*. (See *Catherington*.)

Little Berkhamstead, Hertfordshire
166/295081

Stratton's Folly, a tall circular tower, was built by John Stratton in the hope that he might see his ships anchored on the Thames some 20 miles away.

Little Dunham, Norfolk
132/887125

An obelisk to the peace of 1814 includes a plaque to 'Nelson of the Nile and Trafalgar.' (See *Burnham Thorpe*.)

Littleham, Devon
192/029812

Admiral Nelson's wife Frances, a widow he had married in 1787 while serving in the West Indies, is remembered in the church by a fine memorial which also recalls her son Josiah Nisbet, who rose to be a captain in the Royal Navy. Her tomb in the churchyard is surrounded by stout railings.

Little Marlow, Buckinghamshire
175/874878

A memorial window in the church is to Edward Finch who was lost on HMS *Bulwark*. (See *Blakeney*.) A wall-plaque to Admiral of the Fleet Sir Charles Edmund Nugent, who died 1844 aged 86, tells us that 'he entered the service very early in life, and served in Europe and America above 70 years, most honorably and with great credit, having distinguished himself, both on sea and land, on various occasions'.

Liverpool, Lancashire
108/337903

This city must vie with London and Portsmouth for the honour of having the greatest number of maritime memorials. Start at Pier Head, where a tall pillar, often thought to commemorate the Merchant Navy, is, in fact, to those officers and men of the Merchant Navy who died while serving with the Royal Navy 1939–45, and have no grave but the sea.

The engineer-heroes memorial was origi-

Memorial window in Little Marlow Church to Edward Finch, lost on HMS Bulwark.

nally designed to commemorate the engineers and firemen lost on the *Titanic*, but was over-taken by the First World War and is now for 'all heroes of the marine engine-room'. Nearby is a plaque to 831 Belgian merchant seamen who lost their lives in the Second World War, and another to the 'Norwegian sailors and airmen who participated in the Battle of the Atlantic'.

Opposite the entrance to the Cunard Building is the company memorial to those lost in the two world wars. It follows the design of the columns erected by the Romans to commemorate their naval victories during the Punic Wars. Inside the Royal Liver build-ing is a memorial to the staff of the Canadian Pacific Company lost in the world wars. In the foyer of the Port of Liverpool building are war memorial plaques to the staff, includ-ing those lost in the pilot boat disasters. (See *Birkenhead*.)

In the grounds of the parish church a mast from HMS *Royal Arthur* is a memorial for all those who lost their lives during the Arctic

Arctic Campaign memorial at Liverpool parish church. (George Donnison)

Campaign, 1941–5. Some 119 vessels were lost, together with 2,773 men and women, many aircraft and their crews. (See *Devonport*.) Elsewhere in the grounds, which are a memorial to James Harrison (see *Wallasey*), is the bell of the Blue Funnel ship *Sarpedon*, though sadly the details have been removed. On a low plinth is a plaque to the 12 men who lost their lives when the *Atlantic Conveyor* was sunk by Argentinean aircraft in June 1982. (See *Blackpool*.)

Inside the church the maritime chapel was dedicated in 1993 as part of the fiftieth anniversary of the Battle of the Atlantic. A fine kneeler depicting a ship passing a lighthouse is just one of several references to those lost. A book of remembrance contains the names of many lost at sea, while a roll of honour presented by the Liverpool Steam Ship Owners Association is maintained in a

case made of wood from the RMS *Aquitania* (1914–50). The bell of the Cunard Line tender *Skirmisher*, which served at the port 1884–1945, hangs here, as do four marble war memorial plaques originally in the Cunard building, two of which list the seagoing officers and shore staff who lost their lives in the Second World War.

Not far away, in the centre of Exchange Flats, is a remarkable, huge, and very ornamental memorial, standing 25 feet high, to the memory of Nelson. The four lower figures represent the victories at St Vincent, the Nile, Copenhagen, and Trafalgar, with reliefs showing some of the naval actions. Nelson himself is shown together with figures of Victory and Death.

In the Bibby Line offices there is a memorial plaque listing those lost on the *Derbyshire* in 1980. (See *Burnley*.) Hidden away in a passage behind the stage of the Philharmonic Hall is a plaque to the eight musicians lost on the *Titanic*. This has an interesting history, as the Hall was burnt down in July 1933 and the plaque was rescued shortly before much of the debris collapsed. (See *Colne*; *Southampton*.)

Don't neglect a visit to the Cathedral, with its bell of HMS *Liverpool* in memory of those lost during the Battle of the Atlantic, and plaques to the two Admirals, architects of the victory, Sir Percy Noble, Commander-in-Chief Western Approaches 1941–2, and Sir Max Horton, who served here 1942–5: 'May there never be wanting in this Realm men of Spirit and Imagination, Discipline and Valour, humble and unafraid to serve England in her hour of need.'

A small cenotaph with a book of remembrance was placed here in 1994 to record the Battle of the Atlantic in honour of all members of the armed forces and civilians who took part. The metal frame of the book is inscribed to one of the great captains of our

Admiral Sir Max Horton, Commander-in-Chief Western Approaches 1942–5, is remembered in Liverpool Cathedral.

escort forces, Vice-Admiral Sir Peter Gretton.

The Liverpool cemeteries contain many maritime memorials and deserve further urgent study. One in particular, however, must be mentioned: the grave of Joe Rodgers in the Roman Catholic Cemetery at Ford, on the northern edge of the city. Rodgers was one of just 39 survivors from the wreck of the *Royal Charter*. (See *Wales – Moelfre*.)

The Western Approaches Project, which uses the underground combined operations centre constructed for the Battle of the Atlantic, is a living memorial to the 120,000 servicemen and women who died fighting this, the longest campaign of the Second World War.

Loe Bar, Cornwall

203/646237

A white cross here is 'sacred to the memory of about 100 officers and men of HMS *Anson* who were drowned when the ship was wrecked on Loe Bar 29th December 1802 and who are buried hereabout.' (See *Helston*.)

London

Admiralty Arch
Immediately west of the Arch on the north side of the Mall is a fine bronze of a Royal Marine which commemorates the Corps' service in the South African War. On the south side is a statue to Captain James Cook. (See *Great Ayton*.)

Aldersgate
In St Botolph's churchyard is a unique wall

The memorial cross above Loe Bar, commemorating those lost when HMS Anson *sank offshore, was erected in 1949.*

with plaques to heroes, now sadly neglected. Several are of maritime interest, such as those of Joseph Onslow, a lighterman, who

Plaques to several heroes at Aldersgate.

tried to save a boy from drowning in 1885, and David Selves, aged just 12 in 1886, when he drowned off Woolwich with his playfellow in his arms. Mary Rogers, stewardess on the *Stella* in 1899, is also here. (See *Southampton*.)

Aldwych
The church of St Mary le Strand is the Wrens' church, a memorial to all those who served in the Wrens and particularly those who lost their lives. The kneelers have been given in their memory. A tall Paschal candlestick is to those Wrens who were lost when the *Kedhive Ismail* was sunk off the Maldives by a submarine in February 1944, a terrible disaster in which just 136 survived from a complement of 1,407.

Brompton Cemetery
A memorial paid for by donations from readers of the *Daily Express* inscribed with the words 'Courage, Initiative, Intrepidity', is to Flight Sub-Lieutenant Reginald Warneford VC. (See *Highworth*.)

Buckingham Gate
The office of John Swire & Sons contains two plaques, one listing by ship the China Navigation Company officers, the other the Chinese shore and floating staff, who lost their lives during the Second World War. Their deep-water vessels included the *Hoihow*, sunk off Mauritius by a German submarine, and the *Szechuen*, lost off Port Said, possibly by sabotage. A number of river steamers were captured or lost in action against the Japanese, including the *Woosung*, mined on the Yangtze. The captured *Wulin* was torpedoed by HMS *Shakespeare* off the Andaman Islands.

Bunhill Fields, City Road
A pillar of Italian marble recalls Daniel Defoe, born at Stoke Newington in 1660. Though he had an adventurous life he never served at sea. He wrote some 250 books and pamphlets, the best known being *Robinson Crusoe* in 1720. (See *Hull*.)

Camden Town
In St Martin's Gardens is a tall Celtic cross memorial to Charles Dibdin, who died in 1814, and is claimed by many to have been our greatest song-writer. Certainly his output was prodigious, and the outbreak of war with France inspired him to write numerous patriotic songs, many of a naval character. He became so well-known that, when elements of the Fleet mutinied, he was despatched by the Admiralty to sing to the sailors, in the hope that by restoring their pride he might bring them to their senses.

Cheapside
A statue of Captain John Smith stands in the churchyard at St Mary's. (See *Ludgate Hill*.) The bust of Admiral Arthur Philip was originally in St Mildred's, Broad Street, and was salvaged from the ruins after an air-raid in 1941. (See *Bath*.)

Chelsea
The *Tyndareus* memorial stone at the National Army Museum commemorates the occasion in 1917 when the troopship struck a mine off Cape Agulhas and men of the Middlesex Regiment, the 'Die-Hards', mustered on deck *Birkenhead*-fashion. A colonnade in the nearby Hospital recalls this shipwreck and the epic bravery of the troops on board. (See *Beckingham*.)

Covent Garden
In St Paul's Church (the Actors' Church) is a plaque to the Royal Naval Division: 'The Survivors held their Annual Memorial Service in this Church from 1920 onwards.' (See *Blandford*.)

Embankment
This part of London is a rich hunting-ground for memorials. The bust of Samuel Plimsoll (1824–98) was erected by 'members of the National Union of Seamen in grateful recognition of his services to the men of the sea of all nations.' The 'Plimsoll mark' painted on the hulls of ships, down to which a vessel might be loaded with safety, is his living memorial.

Near Blackfriars Bridge is a wall-plaque to the men of the London Division RNVR who were killed in action. HMS *Wellington* of the Honourable Company of Master Mariners is an unofficial memorial. She is the last escort vessel to have taken part in the Battle of the Atlantic still afloat in Britain.

Beyond her is a superb bronze to 'the memory of the officers and men of the British Navy who lost their lives serving in submarines 1914–1918 & 1939–1945.' This gives the names of all the submarines lost, starting with *AE-1*, which disappeared in St George's Strait between New Britain and New Ireland in September 1914, and concluding with *XE-11* lost as the result of a collision in Loch Striven, 6 March 1945.

Fulham Road
The Oswald Stoll Gate to what was formerly an ex-serviceman's housing estate forms a handsome war memorial, listing several notable naval engagements such as the Heligoland Bight, Dogger Bank, and Jutland.

Hackney
In the churchyard lies Admiral Beaufort (1774–1857), whose name will be immor-

talised long after his tomb has vanished. Despite a career of high adventure, service and achievement – he was Hydrographer to the Navy for 26 years – and despite his books and scientific papers, few would know of him if it was not for the wind-scale which he devised and which is still used on both land and sea. As his biographer observed, 'it is a neat, handy and efficient piece of systematization and, like many other useful things, is so simple and obvious that its chief wonder is why no one ever thought of it before.' (See *Gravesend*.)

Hammersmith
St Paul's Church contains a memorial to Edmund Lord Sheffield, confirmed as a Knight of the Garter for 'his valiant service in '88 against the Spaniards he being a captain of the ship called the *Beare* and commander of a squadron of ships.'

Hill Street
In the doorway of the Naval Club is a plaque to the officers of the RNVR who 'gave their lives for the good of mankind, and for the security of such as pass on the seas upon their lawful occasions.' Ask to see the painting in the hall by Peter Scott, of Lieutenant-Commander Robert Hichens DSO and bar, DSC and two bars, greatest leader of those who fought in small boats in what his friend Scott called the Battle of the Narrow Seas. (See *Penrhyn*.)

Holborn Viaduct
Described as a 'rather hot-tempered, downright sailor-like man, of unmistakable honesty and sterling goodness of heart', Captain Thomas Coram established the Foundling Hospital in Bloomsbury for abandoned children. He died in 1751 aged 85. His tomb is in the church of St Andrew, the pulpit, font and organ having been brought there from the Hospital chapel, where Handel gave recitals in support of his work.

Horseguards
Standing between Downing Street and King Charles Street is a statue of Earl Mountbatten of Burma, First Sea Lord 1959–65. (See *Romsey*.)

Hyde Park
Not far from the boat-house is a memorial stone erected by the Norwegian Navy and the Norwegian Merchant Fleet, to 'thank the British people for friendship and hospitality during the Second World War, you gave us a safe haven in our common struggle for freedom and peace.'

Lambeth, Tradescant Museum
Admiral William Bligh spent his last years

A fine portrait of Lieutenant-Commander Robert Hichens graces the Naval Club, Hill Street.

further east along the Lambeth Road, and is buried in the churchyard here, the inscription informing the reader that he was a 'celebrated navigator who first transplanted the bread

Captain William Bligh's tomb in the tiny churchyard at the west end of Lambeth Road.

fruit tree from Otaheite to the West Indies, bravely fought the battles of his country and died beloved, respected and lamented on the 7th day of December 1817 aged 64.' No mention of the mutiny on the *Bounty*!

Nearby in the headquarters of the Sea Cadet Corps is a plaque to the Bounty Boys, those Sea Cadets who joined the Royal Navy during the war as wireless operators and signallers, originally training on the *Bounty* but later on other vessels.

In the entrance hall of Lambeth North underground station a plaque records that the Maudslay works, 'famous for marine and general engineering', stood here from 1810 until 1910.

Leadenhall Street
Below a memorial window in St Katharine Cree is a simple wooden memorial to more than 4,000 who died when the troopship *Lancastria* was sunk on 17 June 1940, and in honour of all who took part in the rescue, with 19 ships listed. It is difficult to know just how many were lost in this terrible tragedy when the liner was attacked in the Loire by German aircraft. Each July survivors and friends, all linked by the common bond of the Lancastria Association, pay tribute here to their shipmates and friends lost that day, and who have died since.

Liverpool Street Station
A bronze relief bust of Captain Charles Fryatt

A wooden plaque in St Katherine Cree, Leadenhall Street, remembers all those lost from the Lancastria, *and the names of the vessels involved in the rescue operation.*

was erected by 'neutral admirers of his brave conduct and heroic death. (See *Dovercourt*.)

Lombard Street
Formerly there was a memorial in St Mary Woolnoth to 'Sir William Phips, Knight, who in the year 1687, by his great industry discovered among the rocks near the Banks of Bahama, on the north side of Hispaniola a Spanish plate-ship, which had been under water fourty-four years.' Now there is a simple framed statement to his memory.

Ludgate Hill
Captain John Smith (1580–1631) is buried in the Church of the Holy Sepulchre. He was first and foremost a soldier of fortune whose early adventures, or rather misadventures, included being captured by the Turks. This may have been a not unpleasant experience since he named what is now Cape Anne on the coast of New England 'Cape Tragabizanda', after a beautiful Turkish princess. Later, during his exploration of Virginia, he was captured by Indians, but was saved from execution by the intervention of Pocahontas, daughter of Chief Powhatan. She was later to marry Captain John Rolfe, and died of smallpox in 1617. (See *Gravesend*; *London – Cheapside*.)

Mansion House
In the entrance to St Michael Paternoster Royal is a wooden plaque: 'In 1835 Reverend John Ashley saw a fleet of vessels in Penarth Roads and heard a call to undertake missions to crews on board.' So was founded the Missions to Seamen.

Mark Lane
The Institute of Marine Engineers is situated in The Memorial Building, dedicated to all marine engineers who gave their lives in the two world wars. The first page of the 1939–45 roll of honour commences with John Esmond Ackery of the submarine *Narwhal*, who died 1 August 1940.

A plaque is dedicated to the memory of the engine room staff of the *Titanic*: Joseph Bell, chief engineer, is followed by 34 other names. The Institute's Guild of Benevolence is the only charity linked to the *Titanic,* being established to assist the 18 widows, 25 children and other dependents of the ship's engineers, all of whom died at their posts. Now it provides assistance to elderly marine engineers and their dependents, and runs a residential home at Littlehampton. (See *Liverpool*; *Southampton*.)

Piccadilly
In St James' Church there is a memorial to the Van der Veldes, father and son: 'After the year 1673 these eminent Dutch Marine

Ornate memorial to Admiral Earl Howe in St Paul's Cathedral.

Artists lived and worked in this Country as Painters of Seafights'.

Rotherhithe

The church of St Mary the Virgin contains a number of important maritime memorials including one to Joseph Wade, King's Carver in the nearby shipyards where he was 'equalled by few and excelled by none.' Also commemorated is Roger Tweedy, who left money to be distributed 'among 12 Poor seamen or seamen's widows in bread.' A fine chair is made of oak from the 'Fighting *Temeraire*', broken up here in 1838. A plaque inside, and a grave outside, help reveal the story of how the East India Company packet *Antelope* was wrecked on the Pelew Islands in the Pacific. Here the crew were helped by the natives to build a vessel, in which they sailed to China. They took with them the king's second son, Prince Lee Boo, who, some six months after arriving in London, contracted smallpox and died nearby in December 1784, aged 20.

St Paul's Cathedral

As with Westminster Abbey, the numerous maritime memorials and the services they record are to be marvelled at. In the nave lie Richard Burges of the *Ardente* 'who fell in the 48th year of his age while bravely supporting the Honour of the British Flag in a daring and successful attempt to break the enemy's line near Camperdown'; George Westcott, killed 'in the Victory obtained over the French fleet off Aboukir'; and Captain Edmund Lyons, 'so bright an ornament to the Navy,' who was killed in HMS *Miranda* as he engaged the batteries of Sebastapol in 1855.

The memorial plaques to HMS *Captain* list all on board. (See *Anwick*.) There are fine monuments to Nelson, who is buried in the crypt (see *Burnham Thorpe*), Collingwood (see *Tynemouth*), Hoste (see *King's Lynn*), and Howe (see *Melton Mowbray*). As well as the famous and those who fell in epic actions there are memorials to men who died in minor skirmishes, such as Granville Loch of HMS *Winchester*, who 'fell in the service of his country near Donabew on the River Irrawaddy' in 1853.

A descent into the crypt is like entering Valhalla, the home of heroes, and what heroes are remembered here. There is the huge tomb of Nelson, while on nearby walls and on the floor are memorials to others who served nobly at sea, men such as William Earl of Northesk and Admiral of the Red, third-in-command at Trafalgar; Captain George Duff of the *Mars*, killed early in the same battle; Captain John Cooke of the *Bellerophon*, slain in the hour of victory; and Edward

Nelson's tomb is to be found in the crypt of St Paul's Cathedral.

Coddrington (1770–1851), who had been a lieutenant at 'The Glorious First of June', commanded the *Orion* at Trafalgar, and was Commander-in-Chief at Navarino in 1827. There is a huge memorial to Admiral Rodney (1719–92) who had fought, and won, earlier naval victories. (See *Old Alresford*.)

More recent admirals remembered here include a lovely wall-monument to Sir James Scott (1787–1872) which lists his numerous actions, including the cutting out of 300 merchant vessels. Other heroes include Sir John Hawley (1829–85), Frederick Richards (1833–1912), Henry Jackson (1855–1929), and Sir Harry Rawson (1843–1910), who had 'commanded 1,300 Chinese troops at the defence of Ningpo'. There is a plaque to Admiral Beresford (see *Greater London – Putney Vale*), but not to his great rival Admiral Fisher (see *Kilverstone*). Fisher's protégés, Beatty (see *Brooksby*) and Jellicoe (see *Bonchurch*) are here, while there are plaques to Keyes (see *Dover*) and Charles Madden, chief-of-staff to Jellicoe throughout the crucial period of the First World War.

From the 1939–45 war there is Admiral of the Fleet Dudley Pound, who commanded the *Colossus* so skilfully at Jutland, and had risen to become First Sea Lord from 1939 until his death on Trafalgar Day 1943. Of him Winston Churchill said: 'Your vast and precise knowledge of the sea war in all its aspects, your fortitude in times of anxiety and misfortune, your resourcefulness and readiness to run the risks without which victory can never be won, have combined to make your tenure as First Sea Lord memorable in the records of the Royal Navy.'

Pound's successor, Cunningham (see *Bishop's Waltham*), is also here, as is that most dashing of officers Sir Phillip Vian who, in the destroyer *Cossack*, had intercepted the German supply-ship *Altmark* in Norwegian waters and rescued nearly 300 seamen taken by the surface raider *Graf Spee*. (See *Exeter*.)

A recent memorial is to members of the South Atlantic Task Force of 1982; another is to those who served in the Gulf War, while those from an earlier conflict, Gallipoli, 1915, have also recently been remembered. Two others must be noted: that of George Jackson, the Arctic explorer who rescued Nansen; and a plaque to Professor Edward Palmer, Captain William Gill RE, and Lieutenant Harold Charrington of HMS *Eurylasus* who, 'while travelling on public duty into the Sinai desert were cruelly slain in the Wady Sadr August 11 1882 . . . Their

Above *Plaques in the crypt of St Paul's Cathedral commemorating Admirals of the Fleet Sir Roger Keyes and Charles Madden.*

Right *Bust of Samuel Pepys, the diarist and Secretary to the Navy, in the gardens of Seething Lane.*

tragic fate shared by two faithful attendants the Syrian Khalil Atik and the Hebrew Bakhar Hassun whose remains lie with them.'

Seething Lane
In the gardens is a fine bronze bust of diarist Samuel Pepys, Secretary to the Navy in the reigns of Charles II and James II. He is buried just opposite in St Olav's Church. There are also memorials to those from the shipping company of William Cory and Sons who lost their lives in the two world wars. A window is to all those associated with the Corporation of Trinity House who laid down their lives in the same wars.

Shadwell
In the churchyard of St Paul's there is an inscription to Thomas Marwood of Whitby, who died on board the *Dowthorn* in the Gulf of St Lawrence, 1861. Walk through King Edward Memorial Park and close by the river you will find the Mariners' Memorial in

memory of 'Sir Hugh Willoughby, Stephen Borough, William Borough, Sir Martin Frobisher and other navigators who in the latter half of the sixteenth century set sail from this reach of the River Thames near Ratcliff Cross to explore northern seas.'

South Kensington
A statue of Sir Ernest Shackleton stands in a niche high on the wall of the Royal Geographical Society in Exhibition Road. He first went to sea on the *Hoghton Tower* in the guano trade, and then served in a variety of ships before joining the *Discovery* expedition of 1901–4 under Captain Scott. Later he led his own Antarctic expeditions on the *Nimrod* 1907–9 and *Endurance* 1914–16. (See *Eastbourne*; *Greater London – Dulwich*.)

Stepney
A fine memorial in St Dunstan's is to Thomas Spert, a sailing master and later a shipowner, who founded the Trinity House Corporation in about 1511.

Southwark
A large marble floor plaque in the Cathedral is 'in remembrance of all those drowned when the MV *Marchioness* was struck near Southwark Bridge, Sunday 20 August 1989.'

Tower Hill
Facing directly on to the busy road is a cloister 'to the honour of twelve thousand of the Merchant Navy and Fishing Fleets (1914–1919) who have no grave but the sea.'

Here on bronze plaques, vessel by vessel, their names are recorded. Beyond are the memorial gardens with more plaques, recording the ships and those lost with them in 1939–45, down to the smallest fishing boat.

Nearby is Trinity House, the officers of which have striven for several centuries to ensure the highest safety standards for mariners around Britain's coasts. The memorial registers for the Merchant Navy Memorial are here and requests to inspect them can be made at the enquiry desk. This also provides one with an opportunity to examine the maritime paintings hanging there.

Just along the road in All Hallows by the Tower a blue-veined ivory figure of Christ is said to have come from an Armada ship, while the crucifix on which it is mounted is made of wood from the *Cutty Sark*. Among the memorial windows is one to a terrible peace-time tragedy when the Houlder Bros refrigerated vessel *Royston Grange* collided with the oil tanker *Tien Chee* in the River Plate on 11 May 1972. The resultant massive fire completely engulfed the *Royston Grange* and all 75 persons aboard were lost.

In memory of the 1st Baron Sandserson there is a fine model of the *Passat*, built in Hamburg in 1911, which, together with the *Pamir*, in 1947 carried the last cargoes to leave Australia under sail. On one wall is a ship's crest of HMS *Hood* and the words: 'In Memoriam.' (See *Boldre*.) There is a plaque to four Sea Scouts drowned off Gravesend on 25 October 1913, erected by their comrades from the *Daily Mirror* troop. The reredos is

The Merchant Navy Memorial at Tower Hill.

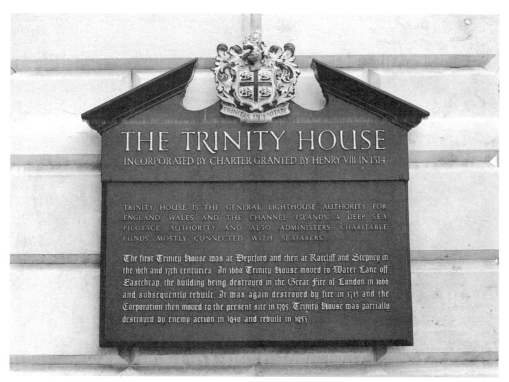

Above *Trinity House wall-plaque at Tower Hill.*

Below left *Another plaque in All Hallows by the Tower remembers those lost on HMS* Hood.

Below right *This window in All Hallows by the Tower commemorates the crew of the* Royston Grange, *lost in 1972.*

in memory of 'Taffrail', the pseudonym of Captain Henry Taprell Dorling DSO, a prolific writer of naval fiction and the author-ative *Ribbons and Medals*, first published in 1916. The book of remembrance is to those lost at sea who have no known graves.

In the crypt is the crow's-nest from the *Quest*, Shackleton's last ship, a former Norwegian whaler of 204 tons in which he had planned to sail around the Southern hemisphere. Alas, the great explorer died at South Georgia on 5 January 1922, surrounded by many of those who had accompanied him on the *Nimrod* and *Endurance*. (See *Eastbourne*; *London – South Kensington*; *Greater London – Dulwich*.) Look also for the two memorials to 'Old Worcesters' killed in the world wars, listing the names of 266 men who, as boys, had trained for the Royal Navy on the *Worcester*.

Trafalgar Square
At the very heart of London stands Nelson's Column, the best-known of all maritime memorials. His 16-ton, 17 ft 4 in statue stands atop a fluted column, the whole structure being 184 ft 11 in tall, almost three feet higher than the mainmast of HMS *Victory*. The foundation stone was laid in 1830 by Charles Davison Scott, whose father John – Nelson's secretary – was also killed at Trafalgar.

On the north side of the square, barely glanced at by visitors, are bronze busts of those who led our navies in later conflicts: Admiral Beatty (see *Brooksby*; *London – St Paul's Cathedral*); his Commander-in-Chief at Jutland, Sir John Jellicoe (see *Bonchurch*; *London – St Paul's Cathedral*); and Admiral Cunningham, who, on 11 September 1943, sent the famous signal: 'Be pleased to inform their Lordships that the Italian Battle fleet now lies at anchor under the guns of the fortress of Malta.' (See *Bishop's Waltham*; *London – St Paul's Cathedral*.)

Nearby, in St Martin's-in-the-Fields, are laid up the flags of the East India Station established in 1744, and the Queen's Colour of the South Atlantic and South American Station.

Waterloo Place
On the west side is a fine statue of Sir John Franklin, below which a plaque depicts a scene from his last and ill-fated expedition. In addition there are plaques listing all the crew, starting with Franklin and ending with the boy seaman David Young, none of whom returned from the attempt to discover the North-West Passage in 1845–7. (See *Gravesend*.)

Across the square is Captain Robert Scott, another ill-fated Polar explorer, the fine statue sculpted by his widow Kathleen. Scott

had commanded the National Antarctic Expedition of 1901–4 on board the *Discovery*. Among those who served were a number who also took part in subsequent Polar expeditions, including Edward Wilson, who was to die with Scott on the return journey from the South Pole in March 1912, as well as Cheetham, Crean, Evans, Joyce, Lashly, Shackleton, and Wild. (See *Binton*.)

Westminster Abbey
In such surroundings the visitor may be excused for missing a modest but poignant memorial in the north-west corner of the nave. This is the memorial book to the 848 sailors and marines of HMS *Barham* lost when the mighty battleship was torpedoed in the Mediterranean on 25 November 1941. A pair of gilt candlesticks on the nave altar also perpetuates their memory.

Nearby is an ornate memorial to Hardy, Nelson's flag-captain to whom he muttered his last words at Trafalgar. (See *Portesham*.) You can hardly miss the huge memorial to James Montagu, killed on board the *Montagu* at the Glorious First of June. A floor plaque near the West Door is to Admiral of the Fleet Earl Mountbatten of Burma, murdered by the IRA while on a family holiday in County Sligo in 1979. (See *Romsey*.)

Just across the way hangs the bell of HMS *Verdun*, the destroyer which brought the body of the Unknown Warrior from Boulogne to Dover on the eve of Armistice Day, 1920. He lies close by, representing the dead of two world wars whose final resting places are unknown.

Further up the central aisle is buried Thomas Cochrane, who died in 1860. He was one of our greatest seamen – some would go so far as to claim that he was greater than Nelson. He served in the Royal Navy, then led Chile's and Peru's fledgling navies against that of Spain, with memorable success, and later served in the Brazilian and, briefly, the Greek navy.

A large marble wall-memorial to Philip de Saumarez tells us that he was 'one of the few whose lives ought rather to be measured by their actions than their days' Another memorial is to John Baker, Vice-Admiral of the White Squadron, who died at Port Mahon 10 November 1716: 'A sincere friend and a true lover of his country'. John Balchen, Admiral of the White Squadron, is also remembered here. After nearly 60 years of continuous naval service he died, aged 75, when HMS *Victory* disappeared off the Channel Islands during a violent storm on the night of 7 October 1744, with the loss of over 1,000 officers and men. Also lost with his ship and remembered here is Richard Kempenfelt of the *Royal George*. (See *Portsmouth*.)

The East India Company erected a monument in 'grateful testimony to the valour of Captain Edward Cooke, Commander of His Majesty's Ship *Sybille* who on 1 March 1799 after a long and well contested engagement captured *La Forte* a French frigate of very superior force in the Bay of Bengal, an event not more splendid in its achievement than its importance in its result to the British Trade in India. He died in consequence of the severe wounds he received in this memorable action on the 23 May 1799 aged 27.'

Another killed in 'the flower of his age' was Richard Le Neve, just 27 years old during 'that sharp engagement with the Hollanders' in August 1673. Even younger was Midshipman William Dalrymple, 'who though heir to ample estates, preferred to a life of indolence and pleasures the toilsome and perilous profession of a seaman when his country was in danger. At the age of 18 he was killed off the coast of Virginia in a desperate encounter in which Captain Salter in the *Santa Margareta* took the *Amazone*, a French ship of superior force almost in sight of the enemy's fleet'.

Aubrey Beauclerk, so his monument tells us, had his legs shot away at Cartagena but still gave the order 'to fight his ship to the last extremity'. Then, after giving directions about his private affairs, he 'resigned his soul with the dignity of a hero and a Christian', and 'dying he bid Britannia's Thunder roar, and Spain still felt him when he breathed no more.'

Among shared memorials is one to Charles Harbard of the *Royal James* and Charles Cottrell, killed at the Battle of Sole Bay, 28 May 1672. A magnificent monument, for which the Treasury paid £4,000 in 1793, is to three of Rodney's captains killed in April 1782. William Bayne was killed by a stray shot in a skirmish with the French three days before the engagement off Dominica on 12 April. During the latter the 64-gun *Anson* was 'warmly engaged' from the beginning and her commander, William Blair, was killed. The third captain remembered is Lord Robert Manners, commander of the *Resolution*, which sailed in the centre of the line at Dominica. Here he was severely wounded, dying of lockjaw several days later.

There is a small memorial to Sir John Franklin (see *Gravesend*), below which is a plaque to Admiral Sir Leopold McClintock (1819–1907). McClintock first went to the Arctic with Sir James Clark Ross during the search for the North-West Passage in 1848–9, and two years later, as first lieutenant of the *Assistance*, sledged 760 miles in 80 days. As commander of the *Intrepid* he accompanied Captain Belcher on a search for Franklin. After the official searches had failed McClintock sailed again, on board the *Fox*, at the request of Lady Franklin, and succeeded in finding traces of the ill-fated expedition.

An addition in late 1994 to those commemorated in 'engineers' corner' was John Smeaton (1724–92), who built the Eddystone lighthouse. Others remembered here include Isambard Kingdom Brunel, James Watt, and George and Robert Stevenson.

In the Abbey cloisters look for the bronze figure 'to the officers and men of the submarine branch.' Nearby is the figure of a Commando, dedicated to 'all ranks of the commandos who fell in the Second World War.' A little further on a wall-plaque commemorates great circumnavigations. It shows the world and three vessels – those of Sir Francis Drake, Captain James Cook, and Sir Francis Chichester.

Westminster, St Margaret's
A memorial window and plaque tells us that

The plaque to Robert Blake, Admiral at Sea, tells of his removal from the nearby Abbey and reburial here.

In memory of
WILLIAM GORDON RUTHERFURD, C.B.
Captain of H.M.S. Swiftsure at the
BATTLE OF TRAFALGAR,
DIED 14. JANY 1818.
Also of
LILIAS RUTHERFURD, HIS WIFE,
DIED 5. NOV. 1831.
Both buried here.

A captain at the Battle of Trafalgar is remembered in St Margaret's, Westminster.

Colonel Robert Blake, Admiral at Sea who died on 7 August 1657, was 'ejected from his grave in the Abbey and buried in St Margaret's Churchyard Sepr. 1661.' (See *Bridgwater*.) Beside this is one to William Rutherfurd, captain of the *Swiftsure* at Trafalgar, who died 14 January 1818. (See *Edensor*.) Just inside the door is a small (when compared to those in the Abbey) but ornate memorial to Sir Peter Parker, whose brilliant but short naval career was brought to an end when he was shot during a skirmish on the Chesapeake River in 1814. The multi-talented Sir Walter Raleigh is also remembered here. He served in naval expeditions against Spain as well as exploring the coasts of North and South America. In 1618 he was beheaded following his last, disastrous, mission to search for gold along the Orinoco.

Look for the memorial to First Lord of the Admiralty William Smith, who, parodied in Gilbert and Sullivan's 'HMS Pinafore' as Sir Joseph Porter, became known as 'Pinafore Smith'. (See *Portsmouth*.) Appropriately the crest of HMS *Speaker*, an escort carrier commissioned in 1943, hangs here.

Longhoughton, Northumberland
81/243151

A gravestone in the churchyard is to David Williams, master of the *Epsilon* of Blyth, who was drowned off Dunstanburgh Castle in January 1857 with all his crew.

Long Melford, Suffolk
155/865467

The church contains memorials to the Hyde Parkers, one being to Commander Sir Hyde

Parker, lost at sea in 1782 on board the *Cato* while proceeding to the East Indies. Another is to his famous second son, knighted for his actions while commanding frigates in the war with America, who was later Commander-in-Chief in the West Indies and at the Battle of Copenhagen, 1801, where he flew his flag in the *London*. His eldest son rose to be Senior Lord of the Admiralty, dying in 1854 less than two months before his own eldest son, captain of the steam frigate HMS *Firebrand*, fell while leading his men at the attack on the Russian fortifications at the Sulina mouth of the Danube.

Long Sutton, Lincolnshire
131/432229

A wall-monument in the church is to Richard Delamere, who for 20 years traded as a merchant ship captain to Jamaica.

Lowestoft, Suffolk
134/550944

Towards the north end of the town, on the hill known as Cart Score, Gallows Score or

The Royal Naval Patrol Service Memorial at Lowestoft.

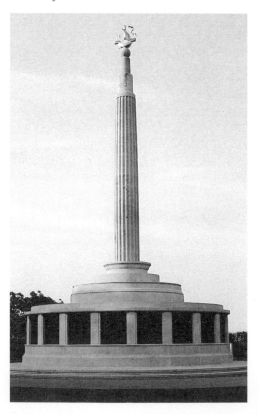

Hangman's Hill, where the town gibbet once stood, and close to the remains of a beacon erected in 1550 to warn of coastal attack, is a fine monument to those who lost their lives in the little vessels – minesweepers, anti-submarine vessels and the like – of the Royal Navy Patrol Service, 1913–45. Known as 'Harry Tate's Navy' after a comedian of the day, the Patrol Service grew to become a force of some 66,000 men and 6,000 ships, with its headquarters at the 'Sparrows' Nest', a requisitioned pleasure ground in Lowestoft, officially HMS *Europa*. Some 13,650 men from the RNPS were lost during the Second World War, of whom 2,385, having no grave but the sea, are especially remembered here. Winston Churchill instituted the unique award of a silver badge to all those in the RNPS who had completed at least six months' sea service.

Make a point of visiting St Margaret's Church with its memorials, especially the wooden panels listing the names and vessels of all those who sailed from here and did not return. The bells of St Margaret's provide a further unique memorial, for they include several of maritime interest. One is known as the 'Trawler Bell', another as 'The Drifter's Bell', while others are dedicated to the Lowestoft Fishermen and in memory of Thomas Crisp VC, skipper of the trawler *Nelson* who was mortally wounded fighting a U-boat on the Jim Howe Bank in the North Sea, August 1917. His son received the DSM for the same action.

Ludlow, Shropshire
137/511747

A wooden grave marker to Leading Seaman Henry Thomas Hill, who died on 29 January 1921, stands in the church porch. Inside is a White Ensign flown by HMS *Ludlow,* formerly the *Stockton,* one of the 50 destroyers provided by the American government to help Great Britain in its hour of greatest need. They were renamed in accordance with an Admiralty decision that they should bear names common to towns in both countries.

Lustleigh, Devon
191/785813

Hidden away in the lanes on the south-east edge of Dartmoor, the church contains a lovely oval plaque to Leopold Amery, born in India in 1873. On his death in 1955 Churchill was to write: 'I mourn the loss of my friend Leo Amery. Statesman and man of letters, he was above all a great patriot.' During a long career as a Member of Parliament he served as First Lord of the Admiralty from 1922 to 1924.

Lychett Minster, Dorset
195/960931

Church memorials to the Lees family include a window to Katherine, aged 19, who was lost at sea on 28 July 1909. In the porch there is a plaque to Captain James Lees, Kings Royal Rifle Corps, Special Boat Service, who died of wounds in Dalmatia, 11 March 1943.

Lydd, Kent
189/043209

A number of maritime references are easily located on gravestones in the churchyard, including that of Edward Greenland, who fell from the rigging of HMS *Barosa* off Yokohama in 1870.

Lyme Regis, Dorset
193/344922

An ensign, bell, and two photographs in the church tell of the town's link with HMS *Lyme Regis*, a Bangor class minesweeper. The ensign, flown during the D-Day landings, was presented by the officers and crew in recognition of the work of the Lyme Regis Brownies in 'supplying the ships company regularly with comforts.' There is a model of the sailing and rowing lifeboat *Thomas Masterman Hardy*, which was on station here 1915–32. The plaque to members of the Hillman family remembers Edward, who died aged 30 on 3 October 1825 while in command of HMS *Pylades* on the West India Station.

Lymington, Hampshire
196/332958

A tall obelisk provides a handsome memorial to Admiral Sir Harry Burrard Neale, who died at Brighton in February 1840. During his long career he distinguished himself in many well fought actions, with 20 enemy warships taken or destroyed. It was in the *San Fiorenzo*, in company with *La Nymphe* – both French prizes – that he captured the French *Resistance* and *Constance* off Brest on 9 March 1797, a classic action subsequently depicted by the marine artist Nicholas Pocock (1741–1821).

In the parish church is a small plaque to Richard Sheepshanks and his brother-in-law Robert Castle, who were lost with HMS *Captain*. (See *Anwick*.) A particularly fine memorial is to Captain Josiah Rodgers of HMS *Quebec*, who 'during the American War, braved every danger and suffered all the severities of Wounds and Imprisonment.' He died at Granada of yellow fever in 1795. The previous year his younger brother and nephew, serving with him as lieutenants, had died 'of the same dreadful disorder.'

Lyonshall, Herefordshire
149/331562

A monument to Marianne, a granddaughter of Captain Charles Colby, recalls that he distinguished himself at the taking of Portobello in 1739.

Lytham St Anne's, Lancashire
102/319285

On the South Promenade is a superb statue to Coxswain William Johnson of the lifeboat *Laura Janet*, lost with her crew of 13 on the night of 9 December 1886 during Great Britain's worst lifeboat disaster. In heavy weather the German barque *Mexico* had come ashore on the Horse Bank on the south side of the Ribble. Somewhere out of the sight of those watching from the land, the *Laura Janet* was overwhelmed, being found on the Ainsdale sands the following morning. Seven of her crew lie in the churchyard of St Cuthbert's, Lytham, where there is another memorial, and five in St Anne's churchyard below a plain Celtic cross. The remaining crew member is buried in Layton cemetery, Blackpool.

The Lytham lifeboat *Charles Biggs*, which had arrived on station just a few days earlier, was launched on the same mission, and after a journey of some seven miles, during which she was thrown on her port beam, she reached the *Mexico* and eventually rescued all her crew. Those on board had no idea that not only had the St Anne's lifeboat been lost but so had that from Southport. (See *Southport*.)

Madron, Cornwall
203/453318

A Nelson banner in a glass case is a reminder that, in early November 1805, this church held the first memorial service for Nelson and a Thanksgiving for the victory at Trafalgar. (See *Burnham Thorpe*.)

Malborough, Devon
202/707398

A plaque tells of Lieutenant John Kelly RN, a 'brave and intelligent officer' and 'a good and amiable man'. He was 'shipwrecked off this coast on 3 September 1802.' Outside there is a memorial stone to James Cook, aged 52, lost off Ushant in the schooner *Swallow* with all his crew in March 1862. Also here lies William Barrow, one of 15 lost when the submarine *B-2* was rammed off Dover by the liner *Amerika*. There was just one survivor, Lieutenant Richard Pulleyne, who was subsequently lost when *E-34* failed to return from a North Sea patrol in July 1918.

Manchester, Lancashire
109/838983

The National Westminster Bank in King Street contains a memorial book listing the staff killed in the two world wars, several of whom served at sea.

Marazion, Cornwall
203/516305

A large block of stone records that the greatest of all battleships, HMS *Warspite*, ran aground near here – at Prussia Cove, a little

Roadside memorial in Marchwood to the men of the Royal Fleet Auxiliary who lost their lives during the Falklands conflict.

to the south-east – as she was being towed to the breakers' yard in 1947. Completed in 1915, she served at Jutland, where a jammed rudder caused her to steam in circles like a giant target for the German battle-cruisers, receiving at least 13 hits. In the Second World War she was at Narvik, and in the Mediterranean, where she was at Matapan before being badly damaged off Crete two months later. After repairs she saw service in the Pacific before returning to Europe, being seriously damaged again off Salerno. Her final actions were the bombardment of targets in France and Holland during the invasion of 1944. She notched up the largest number of battle honours of any ship in the Second World War.

Marchwood, Hampshire
196/385102

At the roadside outside the church are remembered the Royal Fleet Auxilary ships which served in the Falklands conflict – *Sir Bedivere*, *Sir Geraint*, *Sir Galahad*, *Sir Tristram*, *Sir Lancelot*, and *Sir Percivale*. In

addition there are the names of five men lost from *Sir Galahad*, two from *Sir Tristram*, and three from the *Atlantic Conveyor*.

Margate, Kent
179/350707

A memorial on the sea-front to the eight crew, and the superintendent of the Margate Ambulance Corps, lost in the surf lifeboat *Friend of all Nations* when on 2 December 1897 going to the rescue of the sailing ship *Persian Empire*, which had been in collision with a steamer during a tremendous storm. As she passed the Nayland Rock, just offshore of the memorial, she capsized, there being just four survivors, one of whom was trapped beneath as the boat washed ashore. There is another large memorial in Margate cemetery to those who died.

Marlow, Buckinghamshire
175/851862

Close to the bridge is a nude figure of a lady set on a pedestal, formerly a fountain, which the inscription tells us is 'in happy memory

The lifeboat memorial on the sea front at Margate commemorating those lost when the Friend of all Nations *capsized in 1897.*

The Charles Frohman memorial in Marlow-on-Thames.

of Charles Frohman.' There is nothing to connect the statue with the sea, but Charles Frohman was an American impressario lost on the *Lusitania* in May 1915. Pauline Chase, an American actress who had taken the lead in Frohman's production of *Peter Pan*, was instrumental in raising funds for the statue. The 'un-draped figure', described as a nymph, may well be of Pauline Chase herself. A further mystery is the origin of the inscription: 'For it is not right that in a house the muses haunt morning should dwell; such things befit us not.' (See *Barnston*.)

Martindale, Westmorland
90/436192

A window in the church is dedicated to the memory of those lost on HMS *Glorious*, sunk off Norway in June 1940. (See *Bearsted*.)

Marton-in-Cleveland, Yorkshire
93/515163

A memorial marks the site of the cottage in which Captain Cook was born in 1728. (See *Great Ayton*.)

Martyr Worthy, Hampshire
185/515328

A plaque in the church is to Admiral Sir Thomas Palsey, who, after a long and distinguished service, commanded a division of Lord Howe's fleet in the victory over the French on 29 May and 1 June 1794. Flying his flag in the *Bellerophon*, he lost a leg during this great encounter.

Maryport, Cumberland
89/037365

A plaque on Ropery House records that 'in this house lived through his boyhood Thomas Henry Ismay born in Maryport 7 January 1837. Founder of the White Star Line.' (See *Thurstaston*.)

Melksham, Wiltshire
173/904636

A plaque in the church records the loss of a complete family on the *Titanic*: 'Frederick and Augusta Goodwin with their six children . . . The children were all in the Sunday School and the three older boys in the choir of this church.' (See *Southampton*.)

Melton Mowbray, Leicestershire
129/753190

A plaque records that Earl Howe was married in the church in 1757 and was granted the privilege of choosing the subsequent incumbents. He entered the Royal Navy in 1739 and served under Anson in the Pacific, and later played a distinguished part in the Seven Years War. In 1794, while in command of the Channel Fleet, he gained the great victory off Ushant of the Glorious First of June. (See *London – St Paul's Cathedral*.)

Meonstoke, Hampshire
185/611202

A tablet in the church to the daughter of a rector also records the loss of her brother Edward Plantagenet Hume, a sub-lieutenant on HMS *Captain*. (See *Anwick*.)

Micheldever, Hampshire
185/512391

Another memorial to an HMS *Captain* casualty is in the chancel here. Midshipman Arthur Napier Thomas Baring, aged just 16, is said to have won his place on board from his cousin Alexander by the toss of a coin.

Memorial in Micheldever Church to a midshipman lost on HMS Captain.

ARTHUR NAPIER THOMAS BARING,
MIDSHIPMAN R.N.
SECOND SON OF THOMAS GEORGE
AND ELIZABETH HARRIET BARING.
BORN THE 3RD OF JUNE 1854.
LOST AT SEA IN H.M.S. CAPTAIN
OFF CAPE FINISTERRE,
THE 7TH OF SEPTEMBER 1870,
AGED 16.

His friends presented the tower and clock of the village school, just opposite the church gate, in his memory. (See *Anwick*.)

Look for the simple plaque to Vice-Admiral Sir Norman Denning (1904–79), whose 'work in Naval Intelligence was of outstanding value in the war of 1939–1945.' Throughout the whole of the war he spent six days and nights per week in the Admiralty, almost continuously on call, his 'contribu-tion, both in respect of pre-war planning and war-time control of surface ship intelligence, was of no less importance than Winn's great work against the U-boats.'

Minster Abbey, Kent

178/986730

A reference occurs in a floor-memorial to someone who worked in their Majesties' Dockyard at Sheerness in the time of William and Mary.

Minsteracres, Northumberland

87/024556

The little church of St Elizabeth's contains a memorial plaque to Commander Arthur Silvertop, lost on HMS *Defence* at Jutland, 31 May 1916. (See *Brooksby*.)

Minterne Magna, Dorset

194/659044

Among the numerous memorials in the church is one to Sir Henry Digby, who commanded the third-rate HMS *Africa* at Trafalgar.

Mistley, Essex

169/116320

Mistley Towers were retained as a landmark for shipping on the Stour when the church was demolished in 1870.

Morden, Surrey

176/250670

Augustus Schermuly, inventor of the pistol rocket life-saving apparatus is buried in the churchyard of St Lawrence's. After serving at sea he devoted his life to the invention of the rocket line, carrying out his early experi-ments on the nearby common. However, it was not until 1929, the year of his death, that it became law that every British ship exceed-ing 500 tons should carry a line-throwing apparatus. Nearby lies Alexander Maconochie, the prison reformer who had entered the Royal Navy at the age of 15 in 1803 and was captured following the wreck of the *Grasshopper*. In 1837 he accompanied Franklin to Tasmania, and subsequently

became governor of Norfolk Island. Another buried here is Captain William Chaplin, who died in 1974. His commands included the London Missionary Society ship *John Williams*.

Moretonhampstead, Devon

191/755861

A gravestone here is of a French prisoner-of-war, Lieutenant Ambroise Quanti of the 'Artillerie de Marine', who died in 1810 aged 33.

Morpeth, Northumberland

81/198853

Admiral Collingwood's house is in the town. (See *Newcastle*.)

Morwenstow, Cornwall

190/205153

At the most northerly village in Cornwall the figurehead of the *Caledonia* is a reminder of how all but one of the crew were drowned here in 1834. A few days earlier they had gone ashore in Falmouth to attend the funeral of the cook, leaving behind the cabin boy who managed to break the barometer, their only weather forecasting facility; the tragic wreck was the result.

Mousehole, Cornwall

203/469263

On the Ship Inn is a plaque to Charles Greenhaugh, landlord, one of the crew of the lifeboat *Solomon Browne* which was lost with all hands during the unsuccessful attempt to rescue the crew of the *Union Star* in 1981. (See *Paul*; *Penlee*; *Truro*.) A memorial with a difference is Starry Gazy Pie, which is eaten in Mousehole on Tom Bawcock's Eve, 23 December. This is a pilchard pie recalling how the village was saved from starvation by Tom Bawcock's skill as a fisherman.

Mundesley, Norfolk

133/310369

Robert Delpratte, aged 18, a 'youth of the most amiable disposition and of the most promising acquirements', is remembered in the church. He was drowned in 1819, whilst bathing, 'by an unforseen and rapid current on the neighbouring coast.'

Mylor, Cornwall

204/820352

There is a memorial here to those from HMS *Ganges*, launched in 1821, the last sailing ship to be used as a sea-going flag-

A shipwreck memorial in the churchyard at Mylor. (Catherine Saunders)

ship. At the end of her active career she was moored in the nearby Carrick Roads as a training ship for boys, and not broken up until 1929. Elsewhere in the churchyard is a stone to 'the warriors, women and children who on their return to England from the coast of Spain unhappily perished in the wreck of the *Queen* transport on Trefusis Point, January 14 1814.' Inside the church a plaque tells of John Warren of HMS *Ranger*, who caught a fever from negro slaves which he had helped rescue, and died at St Helena in 1862.

Naburn, Yorkshire
105/599454

A memorial in the church tells of William Baines, senior apprentice on the *Port Yarrock* of Glasgow, who died when his ship was wrecked with all hands in Brandon Bay, County Kerry, on 29 January 1894, after having fought through storms right across the Atlantic. They had been at sea for 206 days

and were making for the coast 'through stress of weather, want of provisions and sickness.'

Nacton, Suffolk
169/216397

In the churchyard lies Lieutenant Hugh Montgomery, master's mate on HMS *Niad,* the first ship to sight the enemy fleet at Trafalgar. Nearby Orwell Park was owned by Admiral Vernon (1684–1757), and in the church there is a plaque to the memory of 'Old Grog', a nickname which resulted from his preference for grogram coats. He is best remembered for his order that the naval rum ration should be diluted with water, a mixture thereafter known as 'grog'.

The Broke family lie here, including Rear-Admiral Sir Philip Bowes Vere Broke, whose most famous command was the 38-gun frigate *Shannon*. On 1 June 1813 off Boston, the US *Chesapeake,* also 38 guns, ventured forth and the vessels joined in a short but bloody battle in which Broke was victorious, though badly wounded. He was made a Baronet and would for all time be remembered as 'Broke of the Shannon'. There is a plaque to Admiral Sir George Broke Middleton, who died in 1887 aged 74, having served at the Battle of Navarino in 1827, the taking of St Jean de Acre in 1840, and in command of the *Gladiator* in both the Baltic and the Black Sea during the Crimean War.

Netherbury, Dorset
193/470995

A plaque remembers three Hood brothers. Lieutenant Arthur Hood was drowned in the West Indies from HMS *Pomona* in 1776. Captain Alexander Hood, who had sailed with Cook, died in the hour of victory while commanding HMS *Mars* in her duel with the French ship *Hercule* in 1798. The third brother, Samuel, saw much action as he rose to become an admiral. (See *Butleigh.*)

Nettleham, Lincolnshire
121/007754

A wooden cross standing in the church nave is to Captain A.E. Haward, Merchant Navy, who died 23 May 1943.

New Brighton, Cheshire
108/301943

On the sea-front is a memorial plaque which details the lifeboat launches and rescues from 1863 to 1991, a proud record of 1,055 launches and 1,167 lives saved by 14 lifeboats, together with temporary vessels and inshore craft. A plaque in St James'

Church includes Charles Malan, lost on HMS *Opal* when she was wrecked with her sister ship *Narborough* off Scapa Flow in January 1918. (See *Scotland – Windwick*.)

Newcastle upon Tyne, Northumberland
88/249641

In the Cathedral is a memorial to Admiral Collingwood, while close by at Millburn House, the site of his birthplace, his bust may be seen. Look out too for Collingwood Street. (See *Tynemouth*.) A memorial window to Sir Charles Parsons shows the *Mauretania*, one of his famous vessels, which held the 'Blue Riband of the Atlantic' for nearly a quarter of a century. (See *Kirkwhelpton*.) During the Second World War the city became the home of the Danish merchant fleet, which lost 1,406 seamen. A memorial to them in the Cathedral includes a book of remembrance.

New Ferry, Cheshire
108/338852

There is a plaque to Leading Seaman Maddocks, who died on HMS *Diana*, a second-class cruiser, in October 1916.

Newhaven, Sussex
198/446015

The Dieppe Raid of 19 August 1942, in which painful lessons were learned at the cost of many lives, is remembered in the Memorial Park, at one end of which is the Allied navies memorial, a small plaque and a holm oak. A little distance away is the Canadian Memorial and a maple tree, for the Canadians suffered particularly heavy losses in the operation.

The 'Transport' Memorial is soon to be moved to the Memorial Park, commemorating the crews lost during the First World War while operating ferries to France. There is a plaque close to the Roman Catholic Church recalling the *Maine*, a supply ship lost off Start Point in 1917.

In St Michael's churchyard the 104 crew of HMS *Brazen* are remembered. Their ship sank in 1800 with but a single survivor. Nearby is Brazen Road, and also a Hanson Road in memory of the *Brazen*'s captain, James Hanson, who had accompanied George Vancouver during his explorations on the Pacific coast of North America. (See *King's Lynn*.)

Nearby is a plaque to those of the Newhaven branch of the RNVR who lost their lives in the two world wars, while in the cemetery on the Lewes road is a memorial to the men of the Auxiliary Patrol.

Newport, Hampshire
196/499893

A bust of Earl Mountbatten is in St James' Square. (See *Romsey*.)

Newport, Shropshire
127/745192

When the church at Longford was closed the memorials were removed to St Nicholas's. These included a window in memory of two brothers of the Leake family killed in the First World War. A third brother, who served on board HMS *Warspite* at Jutland, is remembered close by.

Newquay, Cornwall
200/802615

The grave of Captain Jenkins includes a reference to the wreck of the *Eurydice*. (See *Bosham*.)

Norham, Northumberland
75/901472

A number of maritime graves in the churchyard extend back to 1750, including a mother and son drowned on their passage to Australia in 1853. Inside is a model of a salmon fishing coble, with the words: 'God bless the Tweed fisheries.'

Northam, Devon
180/448292

The flagstaff set in a cairn of 60 large pebbles from the shore was erected in the sixtieth year of Queen Victoria's reign. Each pebble bears the name of a famous sailor. Nearby in the churchyard is a memorial to the 21 men of the cargo ship *Thistlemoor*, which foundered in Bideford Bay, December 1909.

Northill, Bedfordshire
153/149466

A gun tompion in the church is from HMS *Iron Duke*, Jellicoe's flagship at the Battle of Jutland, and was presented to commemorate the placing of a plaque on a cottage in nearby Ickwell where Thomas Tompion, 'father of English watchmakers', was born in 1639.

North Shields, Northumberland
88/354687

In the Seamen's Chapel of Christ Church an inscription tells us that 'the Watch Ashore on the North-east coast caused the wall of this chamber to be pierced to make the window that looks towards the sea' as a memorial to those in the Merchant Navy who gave their lives the Second World War. A memorial in the recreation park is one of three erected by Smith's Dock Company in memory of their employees who gave their lives in 1914–18, the others being in South Shields and Middlesbrough. At Preston Towers is a memorial to the men of the 3rd Regiment Maritime Royal Artillery who lost their lives defending Allied merchant shipping 1940–45. (See *Sunderland*; *Scotland* – *Lochwinnoch*.) Look for the 'Wooden Dolly', the figure of a fisherwoman, in Northumberland Square, the fifth such figure to have been erected here. The first three were ships' figureheads, the tradition having begun when a local shipowner erected one in about 1814 as a memorial to his son, killed off Yarmouth in a pirate action.

North Stoneham, Hampshire
185/440173

Admiral Hawke is remembered in the church by a monument which depicts his most famous victory, at Quiberon Bay in November 1759, when he destroyed the French fleet and so prevented an invasion. His prowess elsewhere at sea is elegantly recorded by the inscription: 'wherever he sailed victory attended him.'

North Wootton, Somerset
182/563418

In the village church is the simplest of memorials, a small framed paper memorial to Gerald Arthur Pike AB, killed in action on board the frigate HMS *Affleck* on 26 December 1944, aged 18.

Norton, County Durham
93/442222

Here you will find Robert Gregory, a captain in the Royal Navy, 'who bore with manly fortitude a long and painful illness, the consequence of a broken constitution acquired in the service of his country'. He died in 1774 aged 39. Rear-Admiral Taylor, who spent most of his service in the West Indies, is also here, having died in 1780 at the age of 74.

Norwich, Norfolk
134/236088

A statue of Nelson in the Cathedral Close is hard by the school which he attended. The latter now has, appropriately, a Nelson House. (See *Burnham Thorpe*.)

Nottingham, Nottinghamshire
129/576396

The Union Jack hanging in St Mary's Church was flown by the cruiser HMS *Nottingham* at the Battle of Jutland. The plaque which records the presentation of the flag by Admiral Tennant, then her navigating officer, tells us that two months after Jutland she was sunk by *U-52* with the loss of 22 of her company. (See *Upton-on-Severn*.) Nearby is a memorial to Lieutenant James Still of HMS *Pheasant*, who 'fell a victim to the Yellow Fever' off Sierra Leone in 1821. At St Peter's Church the Launder family memorial includes Philip, killed at the Battle of the Nile in 1799, while the font cover is in memory of Lieutenant Frank Woodward of HMS *Neptune*, mined off Tripoli with considerable loss in December 1941. (See *Wales* – *Llanyre*.)

Old Alresford, Hampshire
185/588336

In the church is a superb marble monument to Jane, first wife of Admiral Rodney, who died in February 1757. Though he subsequently remarried, on his death in 1792 he was buried here near his first wife. He entered the Navy at 13 and quickly made his mark. In 1780 he gained a brilliant victory, at night, in stormy weather and close to a lee shore, over a Spanish force near Cadiz. Two years later his victory over the French at Dominica could, in the opinion of Hood, have been even greater if the enemy had been pursued. He has been described as a 'man quick to see an opportunity, prompt to seize it, and tenacious to an extreme degree of his dignity and authority', and as someone whose 'two passions – the love of women and of play – carried him into many excesses.' (See *London – St Paul's Cathedral*; *Wales – Breidden Hill*.)

Old Bonchurch, Hampshire
196/569779

Buried in the churchyard is Ewan Law RN of HMS *Seringapatam*, who died in 1838 'from the effect of climate' following service in the West Indies, aged 19.

Osmington, Dorset
194/725830

A plaque tells the visitor that Lieutenant-Commander Hardinge Shephard was lost at sea on 13 or 14 January 1915.

Ottery St Mary, Devon
192/098956

One of our best-known poems with a maritime theme, *The Rhyme of the Ancient Mariner* by Samuel Taylor Coleridge, needs no introduction. Nearly 40 years after his death a great-great-nephew, with no formal

Plaque in Osmington Church to Lieutenant-Commander Hardinge Shephard.

training, sculpted the head and shoulders of the poet, and proudly set it in the churchyard wall. Unsurprisingly an albatross is depicted over the poet's head.

The gates are in memory of Captain N.J.W. William-Powlett RN (1896–1963). A plaque inside the church is to Frederick Smith: 'During the great French war he served in the Mediterranean and afterwards on the west coast of Africa where in the year 1822 he helped to rescue from a slave ship a Negro boy now well known as Bishop Crowther of the Niger, but a wound the consequence of a gun explosion soon after compelled his retirement.'

Oundle, Northamptonshire
141/042883

A plaque in the church to Kathleen Coombs includes her son Arthur, a lieutenant on board the cruiser HMS *Hawke* sunk on the morning of 15 October 1914, shortly after picking up mail from the cruiser *Endymion*. There were just 70 survivors. (See *Southam*; *Stow-on-the-Wold*.)

Overstrand, Norfolk
133/241408

Above an arch in the church is a marble tablet to Anna Gurney, who died in June 1857. She lived at nearby Northrepps Hall and, although an invalid, desired to be carried to the clifftop whenever shipwrecks occurred.

Owermoigne, Dorset
194/769853

A plaque to the Ingram family records that one was wounded 'at Aboukir Bay under Nelson.'

Oxford, Oxfordshire
164/515060

An ornate plaque in the Cathedral is to James Narborough, younger son of Admiral Narborough, who was devoted to the College and assisted generously. Aged 22, James 'joined those we mourn along with his step-father Cloudesley Shovell and his brother'. (See *Knowlton*.) There is a memorial window to Richard Hakluyt in the nearby Hall. (See *Bristol*.)

The war memorial at Balliol College includes Hugh O'Beirne of the Diplomatic Service, lost on HMS *Hampshire* in June 1916 (see *Scotland – Marwick Head*), Wallace Moulton de Patourel, a chaplain who fell at Jutland, and Patrick Shaw Stewart, a Gallipoli veteran, killed in France with the Royal Naval Division.

A chair given to the Bodleian Library in 1662 was made from timber taken from Sir Francis Drake's ship the *Golden Hind*, in which he sailed around the world from 1577 to 1580, one of the greatest adventures undertaken by a British sailor. At least three other such chairs are known to exist.

Padstow, Cornwall

200/915754

A lifeboat tragedy remembered on a plaque in the church concerns the four crew who perished in the *Albert Edward* lifeboat while endeavouring to assist the crew of a vessel at the harbour entrance on 6 February 1867.

Painswick, Gloucestershire

162/866097

A fine model, made in about 1885, of Sir Francis Drake's flagship *Bonaventure* hangs in the church, to which it was presented in 1961.

Parham, Sussex

197/058140

Lieutenant Charles Bishopp RN, who died in Jamaica in 1808, is remembered in the church, another victim of the 'baneful effects of the West Indian climate'.

Parkgate, Cheshire

117/280780

Mostyn House School chapel contains a plaque presented by the cadets of HMS *Conway* as a token of thanks for hospitality received during the blitz of 1941, when mines on the Mersey had posed a threat to their ship. (See *Wales – Plas Newydd*.) The Grenfell family have provided headmasters at the school for five generations, one of their relations being Julian Grenfell, 'Grenfell of Labrador', whose escape from an ice-floe off the coast of Newfoundland in 1908 is remembered, together with the names of the dogs whose sacrifices saved his life – Moody, Watch, and Spy. Sir Richard Grenville of the *Revenge*, also a relative, is shown in a fine window. (See *Bideford*.)

Paston, Norfolk

133/323344

Sons of the Mack family given in the service of the Royal Navy in both world wars are remembered in the church. Ralph, a lieutenant-commander, was lost in action with the enemy on board HMS *Tornado* in the North Sea, 23 December 1917. There is a window to his memory, while a plaque from his old shipmates on HMS *Lucifer* and HMS *Phoebe* tells of their 'regret that they were not with him at the end.'

Rear-Admiral John Mack, who commanded the 14th Destroyer Flotilla in the Mediterranean from May 1940 until March 1942, is commemorated by a plaque. He was killed 'flying on active service 29th April 1943.'

Paul, Cornwall

203/464271

In the church is an imaginative memorial to those lost on the Penlee lifeboat *Solomon Browne*, consisting of a glass 'ship's lantern' atop a granite boulder brought from Lamorna Cove. (See *Mousehole*; *Penlee*.) High on the wall is recorded another disaster which befell young men of the parish, this time from want and exposure, in South America, where they were taking the Gospel to the inhabitants of Terra-del-Fuego in 1850. A window provides a fine memorial to Lieutenant Torquill MacLeod of HMS *Serpent,* a cruiser wrecked on the Punta Buey Reef near Cape Vilano, north-west Spain, in 1890 with the loss of all but three of her 176 crew. His cousin, Midshipman Torquil MacLeod, and five seamen from the parish were lost when the battleship *Goliath* was sunk at the Dardanelles in the early hours of 13 May 1915. An ornate marble is to Captain Andrew Elton, commander of the galley *Godfrey*, 'killed in an engagement with a French privateer off the Lands End of England' on 4 September 1710.

Pear Tree Green, Hampshire

196/439115

Lying on the ground in the churchyard, the gravestone of Richard Parker, aged 17 refers to his death at sea in 1884 after 'nineteen days suffering in an open boat in the tropics having been shipwrecked in the yacht *Migonette*'. This had left Southampton for Sydney on 19 May, having an uneventful voyage until early July when, 1,900 miles north by west of the Cape of Good Hope, she foundered in heavy seas, leaving her crew of four adrift in a 13-foot open boat. In dire straits after 19 days, they killed Richard Parker, drank his blood, and ate parts of his flesh in order to stay alive until they were picked up by the barque *Montezuma* five days later. Two were charged with murder and sentenced to death, a punishment subsequently commuted to six months' imprisonment.

Penlee, Cornwall

203/474270

There is a memorial garden to the crew of the Penlee lifeboat *Solomon Browne* 'who gave their lives in service 19 December 1981' in a gallant attempt to save the crew of the *Union Star* off Boscawen Cliffs. In terrible seas they managed to take four off before both vessels were overwhelmed. Coxswain William Trevelyn Richards was posthumously awarded the Gold Medal of the RNLI and his crew the Bronze Medal. (See *Mousehole*; *Paul*.)

The Sea Cadet Unit at Penrhyn. (Catherine Saunders)

Penrhyn, Cornwall
204/787345

The Sea Cadet Unit here is *T.S. Robert Hichens*, members of which are presented with a short biography of this Second World War hero on their enrolment. His own book, *We Fought them in Gunboats*, provides an excellent account of his long patrols across the North Sea and encounters with German E-boats. He was killed while operating off the Dutch coast on 13 April 1943, when a cannon shell hit the bridge of his gunboat. His record of 148 operations and 14 actions, for which he was awarded a DSO and bar, DSC and two bars, and three times mentions in despatches, speaks for itself. Peter Scott, who served in many similar actions, said: 'He left a rich legacy – the fruits of his energy in the development of the boats, and the fruits of his experience in the way they should be handled and fought, and then that other thing – that example of courage that makes people think, as they go into action, "This would have been a mere nothing to Hich."' (See *London – Hill Street.*)

Penzance, Cornwall
203/473297

A plaque in the Union Hotel reads: 'Here in the Dining Room of this hotel, from its minstrel gallery, was made the first announcement to the British public of the victory at Trafalgar 21st October 1805.' The news had been brought in by the schooner *Pickle.* (See *Falmouth.*)

Perranuthnoe, Cornwall
203/537345

Remembered in the church are Captain Sir

Christopher Cole, who served in the Royal Marines for 34 years and died in 1836, and Francis Cole, commander of the frigate *La Revolutionnaire*, who died aged 38.

Petersham, Surrey
176/182730

Captain George Vancouver's simple tombstone records only that he 'died in the year 1798 aged 40.' However, a commemorative service to celebrate his achievements is held here each May, and there is a plaque to his memory, erected by the Hudson Bay Company, inside the church. His last voyage of discovery in the North Pacific, on board the sloop *Discovery*, with the armed tender *Chatham* in attendance, was of nearly five years' duration, in which time only one of the crew had been lost to illness. Vancouver spent the last years of his short life preparing his journal for publication, work which was largely undertaken in his rooms at the Star and Garter hotel here in Petersham. (See *King's Lynn.*)

Pewsey, Wiltshire
173/164598

The altar rails in the church are made of timber from the French ship *San Josef* (112 guns), boarded by Nelson off Cape St Vincent on 14 February 1797. She became the first gunnery school at Devonport and was not broken up until 1849.

Pimperne, Dorset
195/918102

Beside the road high on the Downs is a small pillar set in a tiny plot known as Collingwood Corner. Here, on the 4 June or thereabouts each year, people gather to remember those of the Collingwood Battalion, Royal Naval Division, who fell in action in Gallipoli on the same day in 1915, when the battalion, which had completed its training on these Downs, was practically destroyed. (See *Crediton*.)

Pirbright, Surrey

186/943559

In the church there is a plaque to Lieutenant Patrick Charles Annesley Brownrigg RNVR, died 6 May 1942 aged 27.

Playden, Sussex

189/920217

A superb window in the church is in memory of Lieutenant-Commander William Brodrick, who was lost when HMS *Barham* was torpedoed in the Eastern Mediterranean on 25 November 1941. (See *London – Westminster Abbey*.)

Plymouth, Devon

201/477538

On the famous Hoe – it could not be anywhere else – is a fine statue of Sir Francis Drake looking out over Plymouth Sound towards the sea. Born near Tavistock about 1540, he 'singed the King of Spain's beard' during numerous actions both in the West Indies and along the coast of Spain. His great circumnavigation of the globe lasted from 1577 to 1580. As a vice-admiral at the time of the Spanish Armada he captured the *Rosario* off Portland. He died off Nombre Dios in the West Indies in 1596.

Nearby is the Armada memorial, a tall pillar with bronze plaques, surmounted by Britannia and a lion. The Royal Navy memorial, like those at Chatham and Southsea, records on plaques around the base the names of the fallen. The lighthouse is the third to have been built on the Eddystone Rock. Finished in 1759, it was dismantled in 1877 when fissures were discovered in the foundations, and re-erected here as a memorial to its builder, John Smeaton (1724–94).

The visit of HRH Prince Philip, Master of Trinity House, to the Eddystone light on 28 July 1982 is remembered on a bronze which 'commemorates the centenary of the rekindling of the Eddystone Light on 18-5-1882 on completion of the tower built by James Douglas. It also marks the commissioning on 28-7-1982 of an unmanned light in that tower standing 14 miles seaward of this place on the notorious Eddystone Reef.' (See *Dartmouth*.)

Pontelands, Northumberland

88/166730

A plaque in the church is to members of the Ogle family, all of whom rose to become admirals, and who 'rendered good services to their country, and history in its impartial and indelible records preserves their names for the emulation of future generations.' First is Sir Chaloner Ogle who died in 1750 aged 70, best remembered as commander of the ship which caught up with the pirate Black Bart. (See *Wales – Little Newcastle*.) A second Chaloner Ogle died aged 87 in 1816. Thirdly there is Sir Charles Ogle, who died in 1858.

Part of the memorial window at Playden dedicated to Willam Brodrick, lost on HMS Barham *in 1941.*

One of his commands was the North American station, where 'he caused the successful search to be made for the dangerous Virgin Banks and determined their position.'

Porchester, Hampshire

196/625045

The marine artist William Wylie is buried in the churchyard of the ancient priory church, his body having been brought from Portsmouth in a cutter manned by Sea Scouts following his death in 1931. Set into the headstone is a scene from the Battle of Trafalgar.

Memorials inside the church include one to Charles Marshman, lost in the transport *Maria* off Holland in 1805. There is the burgee of Rear-Admiral Hugh Smith RN, a commodore of convoys lost when the *Manchester Brigade* was torpedoed off County Donegal in September 1940. The most important memorial is that to James Lind MD (1716–94), 'the father of nautical medicine', who for 25 years was a physician at the Royal Naval Hospital, Haslar. He joined the Royal Navy as a surgeon's mate in 1739 and, while on the *Salisbury*, began to study scurvy, quickly discovering that 'oranges and lemons were the most effectual remedies for this distemper at sea'. In 1757 his *Essay on the Most Effectual Means of Preserving the Health of Seamen* highlighted the effects of disease, observing that 'the number of seamen in time of war, who died by shipwreck, capture, famine, fire or sword are inconsiderable in respect of such as are destroyed by the ship's diseases and the usual maladies of intemperate climates.'

Portesham, Dorset

194/614876

High on the Black Down above the village where he was born is a splendid memorial tower to Nelson's great friend Admiral Sir Thomas Hardy (1769–1839), captain of the *Victory* at Trafalgar. His last service was as Governor of the Greenwich Hospital, where he devoted much attention to the needs of the naval veterans in his care. (See *London — Westminster Abbey.*)

Porthleven, Cornwall

203/623257

To the west of the village is a granite cross 'erected in memory of the many mariners drowned on this part of the coast from time immemorial and buried on the cliffs hereabouts. Also to commemorate the "Grylls" Act'. The Grylls were a prominent local family, and the passing of the Act meant that bodies cast up by the sea could henceforth be buried in consecrated ground.

Portland, Dorset

194/689745

A plaque in the tiny naval church recalls enemy action in the very heart of the anchorage when, on 4 July 1940, some 20 Stuka dive bombers sank the armed merchant cruiser *Foylebank*. The starboard 20 mm pom-pom gun was manned by Leading Seaman Jack Mantle who, early in the attack, had his left leg shattered. Despite this he remained at his post, even when all power was lost, until, suffering further wounds, he fell dead beside his gun. He was posthumously awarded the Victoria Cross. Six ratings lost when the destroyer HMS *Delight* was attacked off Dover at the end of the same month are also remembered. Another memorial is to the 1,338 men of the *Hood*, lost in the Denmark Strait 24 May 1941. (See *Boldre*.) The sailors lost from the pinnace of HMS *Illustrious* in Portland Harbour on 17 October 1948 are remembered, as is the ship's flight of HMS *Glamorgan*, lost in the Falklands on 12 June 1982 when an Exocet missile struck the stern of the ship, causing serious damage to the hangar area. (See *Egerton*.)

At the base of the hill is a memorial to the American assault forces which gathered here in readiness for the invasion of Normandy. The Naval Cemetery, with its splendid views eastwards over the anchorage, is worth a visit to see the names of both men and ships which once sailed from here.

Portsdown, Hampshire

196/610071

On the ridge overlooking Portsmouth Harbour is a tall memorial pillar with a bust of Nelson. The first stone was laid in 1807, with part of the cost being met by sailors and marines who had fought at Trafalgar giving up two days' pay. From where the monument stands it is possible to have an uninterrupted view through the narrow entrance of Portsmouth harbour to Spithead. (See *Burnham Thorpe*.)

Portsmouth, Hampshire

196/628006

There is only one place to start a visit to Portsmouth and that is at HMS *Victory*, Nelson's flagship at the Battle of Trafalgar on 21 October 1805. Nearby are the *Mary Rose*, the *Warrior*, and HMS *Minerva*, the last a small monitor whose service included the Dardanelles operations. There are also ships' figureheads and a statue of Captain Scott. A little further away is the church of Saint Ann.

Here famous and less well-known encounters alike are remembered on ornate memorials and simple plaques. One can mention but a few here.

Who now has heard of Cape Haytien, and the action fought there on 23 October 1865, when the paddle sloop HMS *Bulldog*, guarding British interests in Haiti, skirmished with rebels both ashore and afloat. During the action she ran aground and had to be blown up, though not before she had sunk a rebel steamer. The memorial plaque here lists the five casualties.

Another memorial records the death of Charles Head, Whitehead Officer at HMS *Vernon,* the torpedo base, killed in Great Britain's worst railway accident, when 227 people died at Gretna Green on 22 May 1915. George Harper is remembered here, though he is buried in Constantinople, where he served as captain of a battleship 'in the service of Sultan Abdul Medjid the Sovereign of Turkey.' A plaque to Charles Baker tells how, when HMS *Drake* was wrecked in Newfoundland in 1822, he 'refused to provide for his own safety until the whole of the crew should be previously saved and in pursuance of this generous resolution perished.'

Others commemorated here include Captain William Bate, 'killed under the walls of Canton at the storming of the city' in 1857; Lieutenant W. Montressor of HMS *Euryalus*, 'killed while bravely defending the guns of the naval brigade at the battle of Tamasi in the Soudan'; Rear-Admiral Charles Austen, who 'departed this life off Prome in the River Irrawaddy while conducting the naval part of the attack on the Burmese Empire'; and The Hon Algernon Egerton, a 16-year-old midshipman on HMS *Meander*, killed in 1851 by 'the accidental discharge of a musket while employed on boat service at Guayman.'

Large plaques list those who died on the training frigates *Eurydice*, lost off the Isle of Wight in March 1878 (see *Bosham*) and *Atalanta*, which disappeared in February 1880. Both were returning from the West Indies.

The main font was carved by convicts working in the Dockyard, while a portable font of wrought-iron work with matching candlestands is a memorial to those lost when the battleship *Royal Oak* was torpedoed in October 1939. (See *Scotland – Kirkwall*.) There is a book of remembrance to those lost on the battle-cruiser *Hood* (see *Boldre*), and ensigns that were flown when the German Fleet was escorted to Scapa Flow in 1918, and at St Germain-en-Laye when the German armed forces surrendered in 1945.

A plaque remembers the 67 officers and men of the Free French destroyer *La*

Memorials in St Ann's Church, Portsmouth, to Captain William Bate, killed at the storming of Canton in 1857, and all those lost during the East Indies commission of HMS Ranger *(1884–7).*

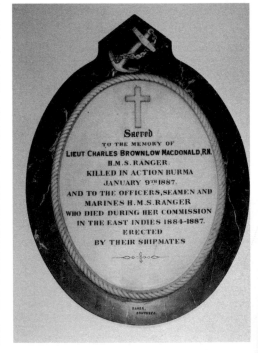

The grave of a seaman from the Mary Rose *in Portsmouth Cathedral.*

Combatante, mined off the East Dudgeon Lightship in February 1945. HMS *Penelope*, nicknamed HMS 'Pepperpot' on account of enormous shrapnel damage, was torpedoed off Anzio in February 1944 with 435 casualties. There is a plaque to the Coastal Forces and, outside, a sundial in memory of Douglas Clare of the 1st Destroyer Flotilla Association

Move now to Portsmouth Cathedral where, beneath a handsome stone of Welsh slate, lies a sailor from the *Mary Rose*, Henry VIII's flagship which sank in the Solent in 1545. Another *Mary Rose* is remembered by the hanging model of *Mary Rose VI*, in which Admiral Kempthorne defeated seven Algerine pirate vessels in 1669. Its hull contains a piece of wood salvaged from Henry VIII's *Mary Rose* in 1836. A memorial to a recent tragedy is to the crew of the fishing vessel *Wilhelmina V*, run down in the Solent in 1991. Those lost are also remembered by a small metal plaque on a corner of Old Portsmouth's Camber Docks.

In a frame of *Victory* oak is a fragment of the White Ensign flown at Trafalgar. Another ensign is that of the cruiser HMS *Hawkins*, flown off the Normandy beaches in 1944. She survived, but the destroyer *Isis*, remembered here by a plaque, was not so fortunate, being lost off Normandy on 20 July 1944

with 154 of her crew. The 233 men from HMS *Fiji*, sunk off Crete in May 1941, are also remembered (see *Haslemere*), as are the 159 from HMS *Cossack*, which foundered in October the same year. The names of those lost on HMS *Glamorgan* during the Falklands conflict are recalled on a plaque, with a window above. (See *Egerton*.) A tragedy recorded from 1915 concerns a husband and wife lost on HMS *Natal*. (See *Scotland – Invergordon*.)

The oldest monument is to Sir Charles Blount, who served on the Cadiz expedition of 1596 and subsequently died at sea. George Villiers, Duke of Buckingham and Lord High Admiral, has a fine monument. He was murdered nearby at 11 High Street, the house of Captain John Mason, and although buried in Westminster Abbey 'My Lord Duke's bowels were buried here'. By contrast the floor stone to John Merrett, a master block-maker of the Dockyard who died in 1708, will need to be searched for. Don't miss the superb *Golden Barque* weather vane of about 1710 in the nave, mounted on some of the original oak from HMS *Victory*. This was blown down from the tower in 1954, a replica being put up in its place.

There are windows to Admiral Ramsey and 'those under his command who were killed' in the Dunkirk evacuation and Normandy landings. Others commemorate Captain R.F.G. Laughton, whose grandfather was the

A memorial in St Ann's Church, Portsmouth, commemorating 36 gallant shipmates from HMS Rattler *who died in the service of their country between 1851 and 1856.*

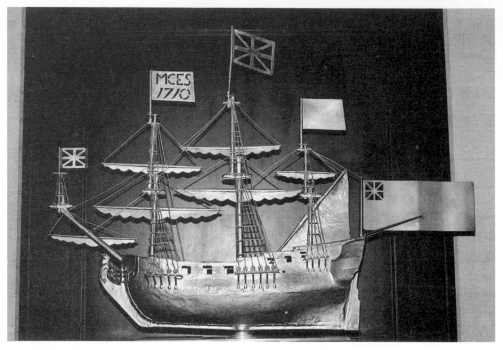

The Golden Barque, *the former weather-vane of Portsmouth Cathedral.*

naval historian Sir John Knox Laughton; Second Officer Doreen Crooks, who served in the Wrens throughout the war, including a period as a cypher officer with Winston Churchill during his foreign tours; and all those lost on Arctic convoys. (See *Liverpool.*)

Timber from a number of different ships has been used to construct some of the furniture and artefacts in the Cathedral. Outside there is a small plaque to those lost in the Falklands conflict, and a circular rose garden dedicated to the memory of Earl Mountbatten. (See *Romsey.*)

A plaque in memory of Admiral Nelson, formerly on the George Hotel, Portsmouth.

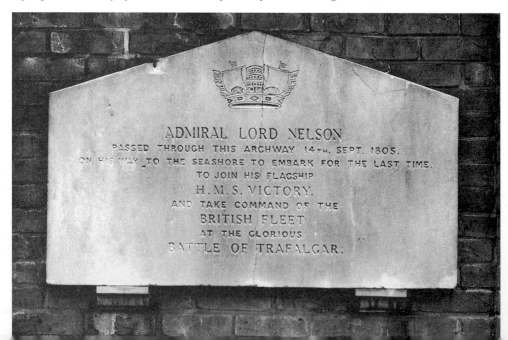

A plaque in the High Street tells how Nelson walked here on 14 September 1805 on his way to join the *Victory*. Just down the road at the Sally Port we read that 'from this place naval heroes innumerable have embarked to fight their Country's battles.' A plaque tells how, in 1587, 91 men 17 women and nine children set sail for North Carolina, where, on Roanoke Island, they established the first English colony in America. Alas, it had disappeared by 1590. The Falklands conflict memorial lists 87 names from the Royal Navy, 27 from the Royal Marines, ten from the Royal Fleet Auxiliary, and six from the Merchant Navy.

Nearby is a large boulder brought back by the crew of HMS *Hecla* from the Crimea. The ship had landed a party of sailors, two of whom had kept the Russians at bay while hiding behind this boulder. The seats on the walkway above include two with plaques of maritime interest, one to the Longhope lifeboat (see *Scotland – Longhope*), the other to Fred Feltham, boat-builder and shipwright of 'Spice Island', as this part of Portsmouth is known.

In the heart of the Cascades shopping centre is a handsome sculpture of HMS *Sirius* of the 'First Fleet'. (See *Ryde*.) The church of St Mary's Portsea must be visited, for here in the grounds are buried many of those lost in the *Royal George* in 1792. A worn plaque inside commemorating those lost in the disaster was 'erected by one who was a stranger to officers and the ships company'. The great west window was also to have been a memorial to those lost, but was dedicated to the First Lord of the Admiralty, W.H. Smith, instead, who gave generously to the church. (See *London – Westminster*; *Ryde*.)

The commissions and the casualties of a number of ships are recorded here – HMS *Boadicea* (1888–91); HMS *Brilliant*, in the West Indies in 1857 when Yellow Fever struck; HMS *Collingwood* (1893–6); HMS *Dreadnought* (1884–7); HMS *Harrier* (1860–65), which included service in the Maori campaign in New Zealand, where Commander E. Hay died of wounds 'received in action at Te Papa'; HMS *Gibraltar* (1896–9); HMS *Severn* (1892–5); and HMS *Trafalgar* (1890–93). Individual memorials include one to William Shepheard, lost when the brig *Confiance* was wrecked at the mouth of the Elbe in 1822.

Do not neglect the memorials in Victoria Park, erected here after removal from other parts of the city. These include one to Admiral Sir Charles Napier (see *Catherington*), while another commemorates men lost from HMS *Active* 1877–9, including W. Aynsley, a signalman killed by the Zulus at Isandhlwana. Other naval brigades remembered include those from HMS *Centurion* and

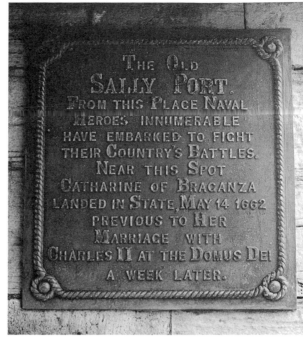

Plaque at the Sally Port, Portsmouth.

HMS *Orlando* which served in North China in 1900, the latter memorial being a bell from the Taku Forts. A brigade from HMS *Powerful* was serving in South Africa at the same date. (See *Lichfield*.)

HMS Sirius *memorial in the Cascades Shopping Centre, Portsmouth. (Maurice Fairall).*

No doubt the various naval establishments boast numerous memorials and deserve investigating. At the Gunnery School a building is named in honour of Petty Officer Evans, who died returning from the South Pole with Captain Scott. Inside are his skis. Twice a year a bust of Evans is given to the best gunnery instructor on passing out. (See *Wales – Rhossili*.)

Prenton, Cheshire
108/308865

A fountain in the War Memorial garden is in 'recognition of the gallant services rendered by the Merchant Marine during the Great War.'

Prestwood, Buckinghamshire
165/863020

Close to the roadside is a monument to John Hampden (1594–1643), whose refusal to pay the Ship-Money tax that Charles I extended to inland counties was one of the causes of the Civil War, in which he died as a result of wounds received at Chalgrove Field.

The twin towers of the church at Reculver, retained as a landmark for shipping on the Thames.

Queenborough, Kent
178/909723

Several tombs in the churchyard are of maritime interest, including those of the wife of Thomas Smith, a gunner in the Royal Navy, and Mr Phillimon Phillips, late master of the man-of-war *Royal Sovereign*, who died in 1744.

Racton, Sussex
197/779093

A small plaque in the church records that, except when away on service, Admiral Robert Hornby worshipped here from childhood to old age.

Ramsgate, Kent
179/383647

Outside the Royal Oak public house at the harbour is a fine plaque commemorating the RAF's 27 Air-Sea Rescue, based here from 1942 to 1945. 'Their combined actions during World War II often in extreme adverse conditions helped save the lives of over 13,000 British, Allied and Enemy aircrew.' Beneath a relief of a rescue launch are the words: 'The Sea Shall Not Have Them.'

Ratby, Leicestershire
140/513059

A rather handsome memorial, with a relief of a cruiser, is to John Richardson, an electrical artificer killed at Coronel 1 November 1914. (See *Catherington*.)

Rawden, Yorkshire
104/220393

HMS *Panther* was lost in the Scarpanto Strait in October 1943, with the loss of 36 of her crew. These are commemorated by a plaque in the crematorium chapel, presented in 1982 by the family of one of the casualties.

Reculver, Kent
179/227694

All that remains of a once massive church are its towers, a plaque recording how they and the cliffs on which they stand were purchased by Trinity House in 1810 and maintained as a conspicuous landmark for shipping.

Redcar, Yorkshire
94/602251

The wooden plaque to Leo Coltman in St Augustine's Church, lost with the crew of the *Derbyshire* on 9 September 1980, includes a relief of his ship. (See *Burnley*.)

Redhill, Surrey
187/278502

In the offices of the Furnace Withy Shipping Line is a stainless steel memorial 'to commemorate all those members of past and present companies in the Furnace Withy Group who made the supreme sacrifice in the service of their Country.' It thus honours more than 4,000 men and women, 3,975 passengers and crew having died in the 244 ships lost to enemy action in addition to others lost in vessels that were only damaged. Ten vessels were lost with their entire crews: *Rappahannock* (1916), *Whorlton* (1918), *Pacific President* and *Bibury* (1940), *Siamese Prince* and *Zealandic* (1941), *Manaqui*, *Culebra* and *Somme* (1942), and *Lancastrian Prince* (1943). There was a single survivor from the *Ceramic* out of the 657 on board, while 863 crewmen, prisoners-of-war and guards were lost on the *Nova Scotia*.

Reigate, Surrey
187/251502

Charles Howard, Earl of Nottingham, lies in the vaults of St Mary Magdalene's Church. He was 'Admyral of Englande Generall of Queen Elizabeth's Royale Navey at Sea against the Spanyards invinsable navye in the year of Our Lord 1588.' A gravestone refers to Lieutenant Farquhar, lost in the wreck of HMS *Racehorse* at Lung-mun Bay, North China, in 1864. (See *Scotland – Gourdon*.)

Ripon, Yorkshire
99/314713

In the Minster is a plaque in memory of Lieutenant Ingleby Jefferson RN, who was in command of submarine *C-34* when, in July 1917, she was surprised on the surface off the Shetlands and sunk by *U-52*. There was just one survivor.

Rochester, Kent
178/744686

A plaque on a handsome building in the High Street tells that it 'was erected at the sole charge and expense of Sir Cloudsley Shovell, Knight, AD1706. He represented this City in three Parliaments in the Reign of King William the Third and in one Parliament in the Reign of Queen Anne.' His naval career included actions against the Dutch and in the Mediterranean, returning home from where his squadron ran aground on the Scilly Isles on 22 October 1707. There were no survivors. (See *St Mary's*.)

In the Cathedral is the bell presented to the sloop HMS *Rochester* on her commission in 1932. There are plaques to Commander

Henry Robinson RN, who died aged 40 in 1872, and Edward Kelly, late Admiral Superintendent of HM Dockyard, Chatham, who died in 1892. As a first lieutenant he was commended for his services when the *Bombay* burnt out off Montevideo in 1864. Look for the window in memory of those from HMS *Vanguard* lost at Scapa Flow in 1917, which includes a portrait of Nelson and a reference to the Nile, 1798. (See *Scotland – Lyness*.)

Rockbeare, Devon
192/020952

A plaque in the church is to Lieutenant Wilfred Stirling RN, navigating officer of HMS *Monmouth* 'when that ship was sunk off the coast of Chile gallantly fighting against overwhelming force' on 1 November 1914. (See *Catherington*.)

Romsey, Hampshire
185/351212

A floor slab in the Abbey records the death 'In Honour Bound' of Admiral of the Fleet Earl Mountbatten of Burma. A great-grandson of Queen Victoria, he went to sea just too late – much to his disappointment – to participate in the Battle of Jutland. His command of the 5th destroyer flotilla 1939–41 was noteworthy for a series of spectacular actions on board HMS *Kelly*, eventually sunk in the Mediterranean during the evacuation from Crete. (See *Hebburn*.) He was Chief of Combined Operations 1941–3, and then Supreme Allied Commander South-East Asia until 1945. Between the end of the war and a

Plaque in Romsey Abbey to Arthur Ward, an engineer on the Titanic.

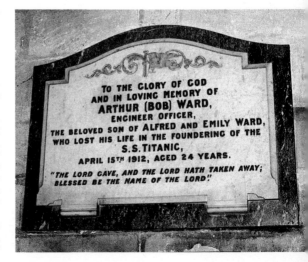

return to naval duties in 1947 he was the last Viceroy of India. Appointed First Sea Lord in 1955, Admiral Mountbatten's final office was as Chief of Defence staff from 1959–65. (See *London – Westminster Abbey*; *Newport*.)

Arthur Ward, an Engineer on the *Titanic* is remembered on a plaque here. (See *Winchester*.)

Ross on Wye, Herefordshire
162/598242

We are told in St Mary's Church how James Green died on board HMS *Flora* on 9 May 1906 'on the journey home.'

Rushbury, Shropshire
137/514918

In the graveyard are remembered two sisters, Constance and Evelyn Brown, aged 31 and 28, 'who lost their lives in the sinking of the SS *Lusitania*.' (See *Barnston*.)

Ryde, Hampshire
196/600927

Unveiled by Earl Mountbatten in 1965 is a memorial to 'the many officers and men of the Royal Navy and Royal Marines who lost their lives when the *Royal George* sank at Spithead on the 29th of August 1782 and lie buried along this sea-front. And here by friends unknown, unmarked, unwept they rest.' Though the 100-gun *Royal George* had been being readied to sail to the relief of besieged Gibraltar a tremendous holiday spirit had prevailed on board, where the 500 officers and men had been joined by some 300 women and children. Such a number in itself would not have been sufficient to capsize the ship, but it seems likely that she was being heeled over to effect repairs close to the waterline when, in the words of William Cowper, 'a land breeze shook the shrouds, and she was overset.' She sank within moments, taking the vast majority of those on board with her, including Admiral Kempenfelt. (See *London – Westminster Abbey*; *Portsmouth*.)

Nearby on Appley Park sea-front is a handsome memorial to HMS *Sirius*, flagship of Admiral Phillip and the 'First Fleet', which sailed from Portsmouth for Australia on 13 May 1787. (See *Bathampton*.)

Rye, Sussex
189/922203

In the parish church a plate records that Thomas Meryon was washed off submarine *C-21* and drowned at the mouth of the Tay, 1913. Also commemorated are Lieutenant James Procter, lost when in command of HM Schooner *Sea Lark* in 1809, and a returning Boer War veteran who died on board the *Tintagel Castle* in June 1901. The White Ensign of the minesweeper HMS *Rye* also hangs here. At the entrance to Rye Cemetery is a memorial to the crew of the steam trawler *Margaret*, six of whom died, leaving just one survivor, when she struck a mine in Rye Bay, 17 December 1916.

Rye Harbour, Sussex
189/938191

Dominating the western edge of the church-

Memorial at Appley Park, Ryde, to the sailing of HMS Sirius *for Australia.* (Maurice Fairall)

Lifeboat memorial at Rye Harbour.

yard is a large memorial 'to the memory of 17 brave men, the crew of the *Mary Stanford* lifeboat who perished in a heavy gale while gallantly responding to the call for help from the SS *Alice* of Riga on the morning of 15 November 1928.' The names of all 17, from just nine families, are recorded here.

St Agnes, Cornwall
203/876084

A plaque in the parish church is in memory of AB Leslie Legg, aged 17, of *MTB 671*, missing after an action with German E-boats near the coast of France, April 1942. Another Legg remembered here is Grenfell, drowned off Annett in July 1968. The lifeboat rescue boards include reference to the loss of the largest pure sailing-ship ever built, the seven-masted *Thomas Lawson*, which ran aground on the Western Rocks during a storm in December 1907 with the loss of 18. There were two survivors.

St Albans, Hertfordshire
166/148073

In the streets of the Abbey parish a unique series of plaques records the names of those who fell in 1914–18, including nine pairs of brothers. Originally there were ten plaques, but one has been removed, while that in Lower Dagnall Street has been defaced, so that AB George Peacock's name is no longer

legible: he served on the *Princess Irene*, which blew up at Sheerness on 27 May 1915. Only a handful of the 131 crew and workmen on board survived. The other seaman commemorated on the plaques is Petty Officer C.E. Wheeler of the submarine *P-46*, whose name is on the Verulam Road memorial.

The porch of the Salvation Army head-quarters in Victoria Street contains a Second World War memorial with the names of three men, all of whom served at sea: Kenneth Dare on the minesweeper *Hussar*, sunk together with the *Britomart* in a ghastly error by our own aircraft off Cap d'Antifer in August 1944; Donald Fake, a Royal Marines bandsman lost on board HMS *Charybdis*, sunk in October 1943 (see *Wales – Castlemartin*); and Lieutenant-Commander William J. Pritchard, Fleet Air Arm, lost at sea March 1945.

St Gennys, Cornwall
190/149972

A memorial in the church records the loss of the *William*.

St Helen's, Hampshire
196/637895

All that remains of the old church is the tower, and used as a seamark. Sailors from ships waiting offshore regularly removed

The 'Holystone' church tower and seamark at St Helen's. (Maurice Fairall)

stones from here for scouring the decks, hence the term 'holystoning.'

St Ives, Cornwall

203/521408

A memorial stone at the lifeboat station records the loss of seven men when the lifeboat *John and Sarah Eliza Stych* was capsized three times while attempting to reach a ship in distress, probably the coaster *Wilston*. There was just one survivor, William Freeman, who managed to scramble ashore when the lifeboat was dashed onto Godrevy Point.

St Just in Roseland, Cornwall

204/848357

In the grounds of this delightful estuary-side church is a seat dedicated to Adrian Stott, and all those lost with him on the MV *Derbyshire*. (See *Burnley*.)

St Keverne, Cornwall

204/791213

The church lies inland from Manacle Point and its off-shore rocks, the Manacles (the *Maen eglos*, 'rocks of the church'), a ghastly hazard to shipping, especially vessels entering or leaving Falmouth and failing to keep far enough offshore. Small wonder that numerous shipwrecks are remembered here. There is the memorial cross to the officers and men of the 7th Hussars on board

Despatch, 1800, lost 'on their return from the Peninsular War'. A similar occurrence took place nine years later to the day, when 126 were lost from the brig *Primrose.*

A memorial at St Keverne incorporating a gudgeon from the brig Primrose, *lost on the Manacles in 1809. (Catherine Saunders)*

A gravestone memorial to 120 buried here following the wreck of the barque *John* in May 1855 was erected by one of the survivors. The *John* was bound for Quebec from Plymouth with 282 on board when she sailed right on to the Manacles. One boat reached the shore, but help was not sent until the following morning, by when the *John* was breaking up. All the crew were saved, but 196 of the passengers were drowned, including many children.

A tall Celtic cross with the single word *Mohegan* may not mean much to the casual onlooker, but this is one of several memorials to those on a luxury liner which struck the coast on the night of 14 October 1898. The *Mohegan*, bound for New York with 149 passengers and crew, remained afloat long enough for several boats to be launched, but only 43 were saved. There are several individual memorials, while inside the church is an inscribed bell presented by the King family of Cincinatti, and a fine stained glass window from the vessel's owners, the Atlantic Transport Company.

John Jones of the Post Office, lost on the *Titanic*, is remembered on a brass plate inside the church by the Postal and Telegraph Services. (See *Southampton*.) On a churchyard grave a disaster from the other side of the world is remembered, John Williams having been lost in the wreck of HMS *Orpheus* at Manukau Harbour, North Island, New Zealand, in February 1863. On another grave there is a reference to a grandson, Richard Retallack, lost on HMS *Barham* 25 November 1941, aged 19. (See *London – Westminster Abbey*.)

St Kew, Cornwall
200/021768

A church plaque to the Reed family includes a reference to Royal Marine John Reed, aged 20, who died 'at the reduction of Cayenne 1809 . . . and is buried in the ocean.'

St Leonards on Sea, Sussex
199/800090

The new church, dedicated in 1956 to replace an earlier one destroyed by a flying bomb, has a pulpit shaped like the bow of a boat used on the Sea of Galilee, made by a Jewish craftsman with timber from the forest of Baasham. The lectern is in the form of a ship's binnacle.

St Levan, Cornwall
203/380223

Close to the south face of the church tower is a plaque to the memory of Captain Henry Rothery of the *Khyber*, and his crew. This sailing ship of the Galgate Shipping Company, Liverpool, was on the final stage of a voyage from Australia when she was driven ashore just inside Gwennap Head. She soon broke up, with the loss of 23 lives. There were three survivors.

St Margaret's at Cliffe, Kent
179/374452

On the cliff-top stands an obelisk to the men of the Dover Patrol. The Patrol was established in the Second World War to prevent German surface ships harrying cross-channel traffic, and U-boats from passing through the Straits of Dover.

A window in the church is in memory of three local men, part of the crew of the *Herald of Free Enterprise* who lost their lives in the tragedy at Zeebrugge in 1987. (See *Dover*.)

St Martin's, Cornwall
203/928156

Among the churchyard stones is one to a Dane, Julius Hoyer, lost when the *Lars Kruse* was torpedoed in February 1917.

St Mary's, Cornwall
203/906106

In thick fog on 7 May 1875 the German liner *Schiller* ran aground on the Retarrier Reef with the loss of 314, lives including Louise Holztmaister, a German millionaire heiress. The huge east window of the parish church in memory of all who died that night was dedicated by her husband, while there is a further memorial in the Old Town churchyard. There is also a memorial window to the 'men who serve Lighthouse and the Royal Naval Lifeboat Institution in these islands.'

At Porth Hellick, on the east coast, a small weathered memorial marks the spot where the body of Admiral Cloudsley Shovell came ashore after the wreck of his flagship, the *Association*, in October 1707. (See *Rochester*.)

St Mawgan, Cornwall
200/872659

A churchyard stone, a replica of their longboat stern, remembers 10 seamen 'who were drifted on shore frozen to death at Tregurrian Beach in this Parish' on 13 December 1846. Their ship, the barque *Hope*, had been abandoned several days earlier off the Welsh coast. Inside the church a plaque recalls the loss of the *Hodbarrow Miner*, whose master was knocked overboard, after which, in heavy seas, the crew abandoned ship with the loss of three more lives.

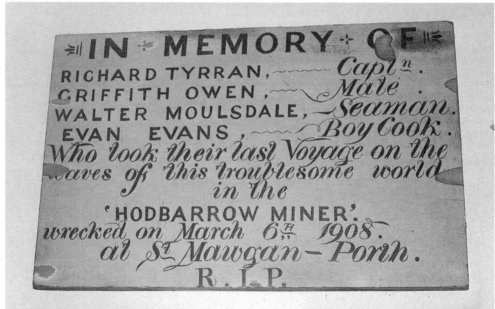

Top *A shipwreck grave in the churchyard of St Mawgan in Pydar.* (M. Garland)

Above *The* Hodbarrow Miner *plaque in the church at St Mawgan in Pydar.* (M. Garland)

St Michael's Mount, Cornwall
203/515298
A seat for the visitor is made of teak from the wreck of HMS *Warspite*. (See *Marazion*.)

St Michael Penkevil, Cornwall
204/857422
Remembered in the church is Admiral

Boscawen – 'Old Dreadnought', as he was known to his sailors – who had distinguished himself at Portobello as well as later victories over the French, including Lagos Bay in 1759.

St Osyth, Essex
168/123155
A fine window in the church recalls how 'in

the month of October 653 a band of Danes under Ingvar and Hvbba landed in the neighbourhood and ravaged the country'.

Salcombe, Devon
202/740392

A crest in the Maritime Museum is to HMS *Leda*, the town's adopted warship, a fleet minesweeper sunk by a German submarine as she returned from escorting a convoy to Russia on 20 September 1942. The war memorial contains a panel to the 13 lifeboatmen lost on 27 October 1916 as they crossed the harbour bar going to the rescue of the schooner *Western Lass*.

Salford, Lancashire
109/797986

A pew in St Joseph's Church is dedicated to the memory of Ted and all the crew of the *Derbyshire*. (See *Burnley*.)

Salisbury, Wiltshire
184/144294

Maritime memorials in the Cathedral include one to Captain Willoughby who 'perished in the *Satellite* which he commanded off Cherbourg' in 1810. Another recalls the loss of the destroyer HMS *Cobra*, which broke in two off the Outer Dowsing Shoal in heavy weather while on trials in September 1901. There were just 12 survivors. Her commander, Alan Bosworth Smith, 'remained steady on the bridge with his arms folded to the last, and went down with his vessel.'

Sandown, Hampshire
196/600846

Christchurch churchyard contains the grave of seven sailors lost on board the *Eurydice*, which sank offshore on 24 March 1878. (See *Bosham*.) A window of the Princess Royal Chapel inside the church is in memory of Lieutenant Edward Boxer, lost with HMS *Captain*, 7 September 1870. (See *Anwick*.) In St Helen's churchyard a tombstone concerns a smuggler, Richard Mathews, shot by a revenue man in November 1816.

Sandwich, Kent
179/330582

A plaque in St Peter's Church refers to William Clowes of the Royal Navy who 'fell a victim to climate in the island of Jamaica on the 20 September 1814 at the early age of 23 years.' There is also a plaque to Admiral Sir Edward Rich Owen (1771–1849). The White Ensign hanging in St Clement's Church belonged to HMS *Robertson*, the

nearby landing craft base paid off in 1946. An elaborate wall memorial is to Admiral Peter Rainier, who saw much service in the East Indies, although it was in the West Indies that he was severely wounded while in command of the sloop *Ostrich*.

Sandy, Bedfordshire
153/174403

In the church is a fine life-size statue of Captain Sir William Peel RN, KCB, VC. His home was The Lodge, on the nearby hill, now the headquarters of the Royal Society for the Protection of Birds. He entered the navy at 13, rising to command the *Daring* in 1847 and promoted to captain the following year. He commanded a battery of the naval brigade

This fine statue in Sandy Church is to Captain Sir William Peel RN, who was awarded the Victoria Cross for his bravery during the Crimean War.

at Sebastopol, where for his acts of bravery he was awarded the CB and the Victoria Cross. During the Indian Mutiny he formed a Naval Brigade, which pulled 10 eight-inch guns to Lucknow where, on 9 March 1858, he was fatally wounded, dying at Cawnpore, aged 33, on 27 April. (See *Southsea*.)

Scarborough, Yorkshire
101/051886

In August 1941 convoy OG-71, en route from Liverpool to Lisbon and Gibraltar, was attacked by submarines and aircraft. Ten ships were sunk, including two of the escorts and the commodore's ship, the SS *Aguila*, with the loss of 336 lives, 157 of them on board the *Aguila*, including 21 Wrens and a QARNNS nursing sister. A bench on the lighthouse pier is dedicated to their memory, for no fewer than 12, all Chief Wrens, were from Scarborough. The Wrennery was situated in the then Hotel Cecil (now private flats), where a brass plaque to the *Aguila* Wrens was unveiled in 1991. A year later the DEMS Association dedicated a tapestry in their memory in St Mary's Church.

The Tindall family have several memorials in St Mary's, including that to William who 'lost his life while nobly attempting to save some of the crew of the Scarborough lifeboat during the storm on 2nd November 1801.' Other memorials are to John Burton, drowned from the lifeboat in 1861, and Frank Dalton, bowman of the lifeboat 'who died in service 9 December 1951.' Three others remembered in the churchyard lost their lives when the lifeboat overturned on 17 February 1836. At St Martin's-on-the-Hill there is a memorial to James Moody, sixth-officer of the *Titanic*. (See *Southampton*.) The obelisk on Oliver's Mount recalls the bombardment of the town by German warships in 1914.

Scropton, Derbyshire
128/192302

Admiral Sir Arthur Cumming (1817–93), who lived nearby, is remembered by a small window in the south wall of the church. In 1843 he had captured a slave brigantine off Brazil.

Seal, Kent
188/551567

A plaque on the Recreation Ground pavilion tells how its erection in 1950 was financed by contributions made by the crew of HM Submarine *Seal*. The submarine had been adopted by the villagers, and early in May 1940, during a minelaying patrol in the Kattegat, she was captured on the surface after being badly damaged, and all her crew made prisoners of war. The villagers main-tained contact, sending them parcels of food and clothes via the Red Cross, and on their return after the war the men handed over a cheque in grateful appreciation of the support provided during their long years in captivity. A further plaque was added in 1988 to commemorate a visit by seven survivors of the crew, including her commanding officer, now Canon Lonsdale.

Seale, Surrey
186/897479

The church contains a plaque to Edward Noel Long, an ensign in the Coldstream Guards, who on a voyage to Spain in 1809 'with others of his regiment perished during a fatal accident caused by the *Isis* man of war falling on board the transport on which he was embarked.' The verse on the memorial was written by Ensign Long's school-friend, the poet Byron. Near the church door a plaque records Lieutenant Charles Woodrow, killed in HMS *Hardy* at Narvik, 10 April 1940. (See *Wales – Whitewell*.)

Selby, Yorkshire
105/616325

A memorial on the wall of the Abbey nave is to a shipowner of the town, Thomas Staniland, who died on 6 January 1799 aged 34.

Sefton, Lancashire
108/356013

The fine window memorial to Midshipman Cecil Richard Molyneux, a son of the 7th Earl of Sefton, includes the name HMS *Lion*, on which he lost his life at the Battle of Jutland. (See *Brooksby*.) The flagship of Admiral Beatty, *Lion* received 12 hits, one of which struck the midships turret. It was here that Major Harvey of the Royal Marines, despite having lost both legs, was able to ensure the magazines were flooded to prevent a catastrophic explosion. For this deed he was posthumously awarded the Victoria Cross.

Shadoxhurst, Kent
189/970377

Buried in the churchyard and with a fine memorial in the church is Sir Charles Molloy (1684–1760), one time captain of royal yachts and an Elder Brother of Trinity House.

Shaftesbury, Dorset
183/863229

The organ in St Peter's was renovated in memory of Commander Richard Harris, 'born and laid to rest in Shaftesbury 1899–1958.'

Shalfleet, Hampshire
196/414892

A lovely memorial beneath a stained glass window is in memory of Lieutenant Alistair Kindersley RN, Fleet Air Arm, who was killed in action 'defending the Malta Convoy against enemy air attack on Friday 25 July 1941 while serving in HMS *Ark Royal*.' This was during Operation Substance, in which 'much was owed to the determination and experience of the veteran fighting pilots of the *Ark Royal*'.

Sharpness, Gloucestershire
162/672029

A plaque in the church is in memory of the many boys who trained for the Merchant Navy on the *Vindatrix* during the Second World War and who gave their lives for their country.

Seventeen villagers lost on the emigrant ship Cospatrick *are remembered on the fountain in Shipton-under-Wychwood.* (Maurice Fairall)

Shenton, Leicestershire
140/386003

Admiral Sir Alexander Arbuthnott, who as a midshipman served on HMS *Mars* at Trafalgar, is remembered on a plaque inside the church. In 1807 he was at Copenhagen and from 1808 to 1811 served in the Baltic and off north-west Europe. During the expedition against Algiers in 1824 he commanded the bomb-ship *Terror*. During the Carlist wars in Spain he served in the British Auxilary Legion, and later he served with the Turkish army. He died at Shenton, aged 82, on 8 May 1871, 'after serving his country with true devotion'.

Sherborne, Dorset
183/637165

Hanging in the abbey church is the colour once proudly held by the 54th Foot (West Norfolk Regiment), later the 2nd Battalion Dorsetshire Regiment. In 1857 some 368 officers and men of the regiment, together with their families, were embarked upon the steam transport *Sarah Sands* for India. On the afternoon of 11 November, several days after leaving Cape Town, a fire broke out on board. The women and children were got away in the boats, and the regimental colours were got ready in case the ship had to be abandoned. Eventually, however, the fire was extinguished and everyone taken back on board.

Shipton-under-Wychwood, Oxfordshire
163/280175

On the village green is an obelisk and drinking fountain in memory of 17 parishoners, from just two families, lost on board the 1,200-ton *Cospatrick* during a voyage to New Zealand. She had left Gravesend on 11 September 1874 with 433 passengers and 42 crew, her voyage uneventful until 17 November, when she caught fire about 300 miles to the south-west of the Cape of Good Hope. The fire rapidly took hold, smoke and flames enveloping the whole vessel as she suddenly swung into the wind. Only two boats got launched, with four seamen, the baker, the emigrant's cook and 23 male passengers in one, commanded by Second Officer Henry McDonald, and 32 men and women and a baby on the other, commanded by First Officer Charles Romaine. During the night of the 21st they became separated and Romaine's boat was never seen again. With no supplies on board, only five men on McDonald's boat survived to be rescued by the *British Sceptre* on 27 November, and two of these died shortly afterwards.

Shirehampton, Gloucestershire

172/531769

John Shaw Haven is buried here; he died in 1796, aged 80. As captain of the 44-gun *Lion*, with a crew of 168 men, he engaged the French *L'Orient* (74 guns and 800 men) in the Bay of Biscay in December 1778, driving her off after a fierce engagement in which the French lost 137 killed and 244 wounded. The *Lion*'s casualties amounted to 22 killed and 19 wounded.

Shoeburyness, Essex

178/929846

In the Garrison Church is a memorial to the 5th Marine Royal Artillery Regiment, bearing 139 names in all. (See *Scotland – Lochwinoch*.)

Shotley, Suffolk

169/252342

The 143-foot tall mast, now a listed monument, of the boys' naval training school HMS *Ganges* still stands here. The lower part came from HMS *Cordelia*, the rest from the HMS *Agincourt*. It was last manned on 15 May 1973, in the presence of HRH the Duke of Edinburgh.

Shrewsbury, Shropshire

126/492125

Above a door in St Mary's Church is a large ornate memorial 'erected by public subscription to commemorate the service of John Benbow Esq Vice Admiral of the Blue, a skilful and daring seaman whose heroic exploits long remembered him the boast of the British navy and still point him out as the Nelson of his times. He was born at Caton Hall in this parish and died at Kingston in Jamaica November 4th 1702 aged 51 years of wounds received in his memorable action with a French squadron off Carthengena in the West Indies fought on the 19th and five following days of August in that year.'

In the King's Shropshire Light Infantry Museum is the bell from the private chapel on board the *Ville de Paris*, flagship of the French fleet captured by Rodney at the Battle of the Saints, 12 April 1782. (See *Old Alresford*.) Afterwards she was used as a transport, a sad end for a ship which, when built, had been decribed as a 'leviathan of ships' and the 'finest and largest first-rate in the world.'

Sidmouth, Devon

192/126873

The war memorial at the church provides, in addition to the names of the fallen, a list of their ships. As well as familiar names these include others which would be forgotten but for such memorials, such as the *Greavesash*, a collier sunk by a submarine off Cape Barfleur in February 1918, and the hospital ship *Llandovery Castle*, sunk without warn-

War graves in a corner of the cemetery at Shotley.

ing by *U-86* some 114 miles west of Fastnet on 27 June 1918. The submarine subsequently fired on the lifeboats, leaving 24 survivors from 258. (See *Dawlish*.) A plaque on the wall of the nearby Bedford Hotel records that the Royal Marines Library of John Wallis, Bookseller, was established here in 1813.

Sissinghurst, Kent
188/795375

The church, which was a gift from Captain A. King RN and was consecrated in 1838, contains a memorial window to engineer Rear-Admiral William Deans CB (1880–1947).

Slimbridge, Gloucestershire
162/740036

A plaque in the church records that James Watts, surgeon on HMS *Tweed*, died 'of malignant fever while on the Jamaican station the 17th day of March 1808 in the 25th year of his age.'

Snargate, Kent
189/991287

On the north wall of the church is a remarkable terracotta coloured painting of a sixteenth century ship, a four-masted vessel of about 800 tons.

Sneaton, Yorkshire
94/894078

A plaque in the church tells that Commander Dyer Bond served in many actions 'under the following named gallant leaders: Admirals Wm. Browne, Hon Wm. Waldegrave, Sir John Jarvis and Horatio Lord Nelson.'

Snodland, Kent
178/705617

Interred near the vestry door in 1850 was Thomas Waghorn. After serving in the Royal Navy (1812–17), the merchant navy, and the Bengal marine pilot service, he pioneered the overland route between Cairo and Suez whereby travellers and freight were transported across the desert, thus linking shipping on the Mediterranean and the Red Sea and greatly cutting the passage time to India. (See *Chatham*.)

Soham, Cambridgeshire
154/594732

A plaque on the pulpit recalls the wreck in September 1869 of the P&O mail-boat *Carnatic* off Shadwan Island in the Gulf of

Memorial in Somerton Church to Commander Tremlett who, when he died in 1865, aged 97, was the oldest officer in the Royal Navy.

Suez, with the loss of 27 lives from the 230 passengers and crew. These included George Warren and his daughter Helen, just three years old, who is remembered here by the lectern.

Somerton, Somerset
193/490286

The war memorial in the church includes Matron Cicely May West, Queen Alexandra's Imperial Military Nursing Service. With other nurses she was on board the *Kuala* which, packed with refugees fleeing from Singapore in February 1942, was bombed off Banka Island. A plaque tells how less than a month later Lieutenant-Commander Giles Robert Pretor-Pinney of the destroyer HMS *Stronghold* was lost with 69 officers and men off Java.

Also remembered in the church are Admiral William Henry Brown Tremlett, who died in 1865 aged 94, and Commander George Neat Tremlett, who died the same year aged 97, having joined the Royal Navy in 1780. There is also plaque to John Jacob 'who met with a premature death in his 13th year while serving as midshipman on board HMS *Hero* of 74 guns.' The whole ships company were lost in a storm off Holland in 1811. (See *Fareham*.)

Southam, Warwickshire

151/417617

The south chapel in the church is dedicated to the memory of Midshipman Alexander Lattey, aged 17, lost on board HMS *Hawke* in October 1914. (See *Oundle*.)

Southampton, Hampshire

196/417112

Although there is, unsurprisingly, a greater concentration of *Titanic* memorials here than anywhere else in the country, one can nevertheless be forgiven for commencing with a reference to the fountain at the western end

The crew memorial to those lost on the Titanic, *in the ruined church of the Holy Rood, Southampton.*

of Town Quay, erected to honour the memory of Stewardess Mary Anne Rogers of the *Stella,* a Channel ferry which ran aground on the Casquets in March 1899. Although several of the lifeboats got away, 112 passengers and crew were drowned. (See *London – Aldersgate*.)

Just to the east is the *Mayflower* memorial with its several plaques. The *Mayflower*, in company with the *Speedwell,* which subsequently turned back, sailed from here with the Pilgrim Fathers on 15 August 1620 to establish their colony in New England. (See *Lincoln*.)

A memorial in the Old Cemetery recalls the Royal Mail steamships *Rhone* and *Wye*, lost off the Virgin Islands during a hurricane in 1867 which claimed some 60 ships and over a thousand lives. Nearby is another Royal Mail memorial, this time to the *Douro,* rammed by a Spanish vessel, the *Yrurac Bat*, off Cape Finisterre on 1 April 1882.

A plaque in St Michael's Church records the loss of the wooden paddle-steamer *Amazon,* which caught fire on her maiden voyage to the West Indies in 1852, sinking with the loss of 102 lives. At St Julian's Chapel is a memorial to Philip Carteret, who sailed round the world with John Byron, and then repeated the feat in the *Swallow* in 1766. Among his discoveries was Pitcairn Island.

In St Mary's Church, with its seamen's chapel, is the bell from the *Hantonia*, which sailed between Southampton and Le Havre. It is rung whenever people are called to prayer in connection with an event at sea, good or bad. There are many other items of maritime interest here, including model ships and the house-flags of major shipping companies. A superb memorial window shows a number of vessels closely associated with Southampton, together with the emblems of five oceans.

However, memorials to those lost on the *Titanic* on 15 April 1912 dominate any visit to Southampton, for 549 of the 688 crew and 815 of the passengers who died were from the port. Perhaps best-known of all is the Engineers' Memorial situated at the north-west corner of East Park, unveiled in the presence of an estimated 100,000 people on 22 April 1914. The inscription reads: 'To the memory of the engineer officers of the RMS *Titanic* who showed their high conception of duty and their hero-

Top right *Outside the main post office in Southampton is a plaque in memory of musicians lost on board the* Titanic.

Middle right *Plaque in the church of the Holy Rood, Southampton.*

Right *Falklands plaque at the ruined church of the Holy Rood, Southampton.*

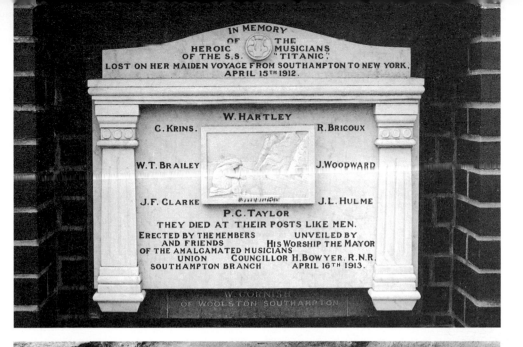

IN MEMORY

OF THE
HEROIC MUSICIANS
OF THE S.S. "TITANIC",
LOST ON HER MAIDEN VOYAGE FROM SOUTHAMPTON TO NEW YORK,
APRIL 15TH 1912.

W. HARTLEY

C. KRINS.   R. BRICOUX

W.T. BRAILEY   J. WOODWARD

J.F. CLARKE   J.L. HULME
P.C. TAYLOR
THEY DIED AT THEIR POSTS LIKE MEN.
ERECTED BY THE MEMBERS   UNVEILED BY
AND FRIENDS   HIS WORSHIP THE MAYOR
OF THE AMALGAMATED MUSICIANS
UNION   COUNCILLOR H. BOWYER. R.N.R.
SOUTHAMPTON BRANCH   APRIL 16TH 1913.

W. CORNISH
OF WOOLSTON SOUTHAMPTON

THE MERCHANT NAVY MEMORIAL
IS MAINTAINED WITH THE AID OF
A GENEROUS BEQUEST IN MEMORY OF
CHARLES PARTRIDGE
WHO WAS BURIED IN THE WAR CEMETERY
ON THE ISLAND OF HOY, ORKNEY,
IN 1918.

THE FALKLAND ISLANDS
MAY - JULY 1982
This tablet marks the invaluable
and heroic service of the
MERCHANT NAVY
operating out of the
PORT OF SOUTHAMPTON
in the campaign to recover
THE FALKLAND ISLANDS
from occupation by ARGENTINE FORCES

ERECTED by SOUTHAMPTON CITY COUNCIL on BEHALF of the CITIZENS of the CITY

ism by remaining at their posts 15 April 1915.'

In 1993 a new memorial, in the form of a low plaque, was unveiled in the grounds of Ocean Gate by Miss Millvina Dean. Just a few weeks old at the time of the sinking, she, her brother, and her mother had all survived the disaster, but her father was lost with the ship.

The crew's memorial stands in the bomb-damaged church of the Holy Rood in High Street, now a memorial to the Merchant Navy Service. The main Post Office holds a bronze tablet recording two British and three American Post Officers who were lost. This is made out of metal taken from the *Titanic*'s reserve propeller, kindly donated by her builders, Harland and Wolff. Two wooden plaques in the care of the Southampton Museum Service record the names of trimmers, firemen, and greasers from the neighbourhood who were lost, including one, Richard Hosgood, who only joined the *Titanic* as she was about to sail. At Millbrook, in Holy Trinity Church, is a plaque with the names of 12 men lost from the parish, together with a plaque to Richard Barker, an assistant purser.

The original musicians' memorial was destroyed when the library was bombed in 1940, but a replacement was unveiled at the site in 1990. The *Titanic*'s musicians had continued to play as the lifeboats were loaded, and were all lost. (See Index under *Titanic* for numerous other memorials.)

South Charlton, Northumberland
75/164202

A plaque in the church is in memory of Sarah Elizabeth Dixon, a sister in the Queen Alexandra's Imperial Military Merchant Service who 'was lost at sea by enemy action' in January 1942.

South Harting, Hampshire
197/784195

At nearby Ditcham was the home of Captain Cowper Coles, designer of the ill-fated *Captain*. He was amongst those who died when she sank in 1870, and is remembered in the church here. (See *Anwick*.)

Southill, Bedfordshire
153/146422

The Byng family vault contains memorials to Admiral George Byng, who died in 1732 aged 70, and to his son John Byng, whose tomb stone reads: 'To The Perpetual Disgrace of Publick Justice The Honble John Byng Esq Admiral of the Blue Fell a Martyr to Political Persecution March 14th in the Year 1757 when Braverey and Loyalty were Insufficient Securities For the Life and Honour of a Naval

Officer.' He had joined the Navy in 1704 at the age of 14, and risen to become Admiral of the Blue. Following an indecisive encounter against a French fleet and his failure to relieve besieged Minorca, Byng was arrested. A court-martial found him guilty of neglect of duty, and he was executed by firing squad on the deck of the *Monarque* in Portsmouth Harbour.

South Perrot, Dorset
193/472066

The church is dedicated to the memory of the naval Hoods. (See *Butleigh*.)

Southport, Lancashire
108/334173

On the Promenade stands a tall pillar set on a fine plinth, with plaques which record both the generosity of the Misses Macrae in presenting a new lifeboat – the *Edith and Annie* – and the services of earlier vessels here: the *Rescue*, which saved 175 lives from 20 vessels between 1840 and 1861; the *Jessie Knowles* of 1861, which saved 75 lives from nine vessels; and the *Eliza Fernley*, which between 1874 and 1886 saved 52 lives from nine vessels before she was lost with 14 of her crew of 16 during the attempt to reach the

One of the plaques on the Southport Lifeboat memorial which records some of the early boats on station here.

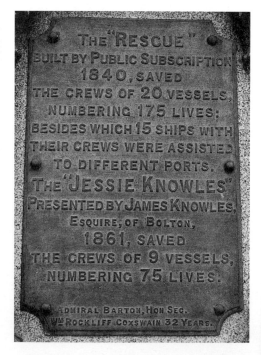

The Tyne, *a memorial to the lifeboat pioneers Greathead and Wouldhave at South Shields.* (Denis Wright)

barque *Mexico* on the night of 10 December 1886. There is a large memorial in the Southport cemetery, where they are buried, to 13 of the crewmen, surmounted by a broken mast. (See *Lytham St Anne's.*)

Standing against the outside south wall of Holy Trinity Church is the gravestone of William Rockcliffe, who died in 1873, 'thirty years coxswain of the Southport lifeboats during which period he was instrumental in saving three hundred lives.'

Inside is a wooden wall-plaque in memory of '448 officers, NCOs and gunners of the 4th Regt Maritime Royal Artillery who gave their lives during the Second World War.' These constitute nearly a third of the total fatalities suffered by the MRA during this conflict. (See *Scotland – Lochwinnoch.*)

Southsea, Hampshire
196/638985

On the sea front, from where one looks out past the Spithead Forts, or hard right towards Old Portsmouth, the entrance to Portsmouth Harbour and the Naval Base, stands the great naval memorial to those who died serving in the Royal Navy during the world wars, whose only grave is the sea. (See *Chatham*; *Plymouth.*)

Close by is a series of small memorials, each recalling a fragment of maritime history. A well-weathered white pillar is in memory of 48 officers and men who died during 'the epidemic of yellow fever on board HMS *Aboukir* at Jamaica in 1873–74.' Another records the deaths of 49 officers and men of HMS *Trident*, who 'died of yellow fever in the short space of six weeks during the

unusual epidemic at Sierra Leone, 1859.'

A square pillar surmounted by a trophy made from a gun captured at Lucknow is in memory 'of the *Shannon*'s Naval Brigade who fell whilst employed in the NW Provinces of India during the Mutiny AD 1857–8.' All the casualties are listed, as are the details of the services rendered during their marches and battles in what was subsequently described as 'a most trying campaign.' (See *Sandy.*)

A statue of Nelson in the gardens of Clarence Esplanade includes the words: 'Near this memorial on the 14th September 1805 Admiral Lord Nelson embarked for the last time, being killed on the following 21st October at the victorious battle of Trafalgar. (See *Burnham Thorpe.*)

Just east of Southsea Castle an information board tells passers-by of the wreck of HMS *Invincible*, which ran aground here in 1758. The remains of the ship were discovered by divers in 1980.

South Shields, County Durham
88/372676

A prominent and ornate clock tower close to the sea front is a memorial to the designer and builder of the first lifeboat – Henry Greathead and William Wouldhave respectively – at South Shields in 1790. Hard by in a covered shelter is the second-oldest preserved lifeboat, which differs little from that designed by Greathead some 40 years earlier. Named appropriately *Tyne*, it was built in 1833 and in a service which spanned 60 years saved 1,028 lives. There are memorials to both Greathead and Wouldhave in St Hilda's Church.

At St Stephen's Church a plaque refers to the pilots who acted as coxswains of the Tyne lifeboats. Some lived to well-earned retirement, but 20 were lost 'by the capsizing of the lifeboat *Provide* when attempting to rescue the crew of the *Betsy* on 4 December 1849.' Two other pilots were washed overboard from the lifeboat *Northumberland* when attempting to rescue the crew of the brig *Gleaner*, 18 December 1872.

Another plaque is in memory of those lost when the pilot cutter *Protector* was mined off the mouth of the Tyne on 30 December 1916. In addition to the master and his crew of four, including cabin-boy Benjamin Rumney, no fewer than 14 pilots were lost. Pilot assistants were also lost when the *Spennymoor* was sunk in the English Channel on 28 May 1915, and the *Phare* off Scarborough on 31 October 1917, both by torpedoes.

St Aidan's Church contains a number of memorials, including one to Henry Heatley, aged 21, 'whose life was lost at sea by the supposed foundering of the SS *Lovaine* of North Shields in the Atlantic, April 1887.' Another youngster, Stephen Archdale Geary aged 20, was killed by falling from aloft in the *Cromton* in the South Pacific, 26 July 1898. His elder brother, William Henry Geary, aged 27, was lost just a year later when the SS *Laleham,* of which he was

The fine plaque at the Southwold Reading Room.

master, foundered with all hands during a hurricane off the coast of America. Also remembered is Henry Douglas Rudd DSC, who 'gave his life in a British convoy returning from Russia November 1942.'

Overlooking the Tyne is a statue of Dolly Pell, fishwife and notorious smuggler, who died in 1857. She was 'a determined fighter against the press-gang, and is said to have hid fugitives beneath her vast petticoats until the coast was clear. When her husband was caught by the gang, Dolly followed him to sea and served in the ship's "cockpit" – the part of the ship where crude surgery was performed on the wounded sailors.'

Not far away at Mill Dam is a memorial to 'the thousands of merchant seamen who sailed from this port and lost their lives in World War II.' Someone who made 'tireless efforts to improve the wages and conditions of British seafarers' was Jim Slater CBE, General Secretary of the National Union of Seamen, who is remembered at the Customs House by a plaque unveiled in 1994. Nearby at the Missions to Seamen is a plaque to the crew of the *Derbyshire*. (See *Burnley*.)

Southwell, Dorset
194/687702

Avalanche Road in this most southerly of the Portland villages may sound a little strange, but not once you have visited the tiny church, dedicated to memory of the three-masted clipper *Avalanche*, lost off Portland Bill on the evening of 11 September 1877. The *Avalanche*, sailing to New Zealand, collided with the larger *Forest* shortly after dusk and sank immediately, just three crewmen managing to scramble to apparent safety on to the forecastle of the *Forest* as she drifted clear. However, this proved to be but a brief respite, for the *Forest* was sinking too. Though she was able to get away three boats two were lost during the night. The third, with nine survivors – including the three from the *Avalanche* – succeeded in reaching Chesil Beach.

Overall casualties in this disaster totalled 94 from the *Avalanche* and 12 from the *Forest*. Relatives and friends of those lost contributed £2,000 to the building of the church, which was consecrated in 1879. The memorials include stained glass windows, plaques listing those lost, flags, a fine model of the *Avalanche* made by an inmate of the nearby prison, and artefacts brought up from the wreck, including one of the anchors.

Southwold, Suffolk
156/510761

On the cliff-top is the splendid Sailors' Reading Room, packed with many maritime artefacts and mementoes. Outside a small plaque is to Captain D. Simpson, who, at the age of 70, lost his life while commanding the *Empire Merlin*, sunk to the west of the Outer Hebrides in 1940 with just one survivor.

Spalding, Lincolnshire
131/250225

This fenland town, now some 11 miles from the Wash, boasts possibly the only local ship wrecked sailors society in the country still in operation, now 150 years old. In the parish church is a memorial to John Perry, who in 1693 commanded HMS *Cygnet*. For several years he was controller of the maritime works of Czar Peter in Russia and on his return home was 'employed by ye Parliament to stop Dagenham Breach which he affected and thereby preserved the navigation of the River Thames and rescued many private families from ruin.'

During the Second World War the town adopted the submarine HMS *Taku*, and her White Ensign hangs here. Among the maritime graves in the cemetery there is a reference to John Knott, lost at sea off Scarborough in December 1837, and his three sons: Henry, lost off Dimlington in 1842; Thomas, lost in the Bristol Channel in 1852; and John, drowned in the Thames in 1869.

Spilsby, Lincolnshire
122/402661

Standing at the centre of the town is a statue of Sir John Franklin, 'discoverer of the North West Passage, born at Spilsby April 1786 died in the Arctic regions June 1847.' Nearby is the Franklin House Bakery, upon the wall of which is a plaque with the words: 'Captain Sir John Franklin RN, KCH, KR, DCL, the Arctic navigator and explorer was born in this house 16 April 1786.' The church contains a wall-plaque, and also a fine chair in memory of Franklin, made of timber from the *Royal George*. (See *Ryde*.) A plaque to Franklin's first wife, Eleanor, tells how, in 1825, although 'smitten by mortal illness yet speeded her husband on his second Arctic expedition and surviving his departure only six days.' (See *Gravesend*.)

Stamford, Lincolnshire
141/032071

His family and shipmates erected a plaque in St George's Church to Frederick Wilson, who died at sea in 1910, aged 17, on HMS *Donegal*.

Steeple Claydon, Buckinghamshire
165/705267

A marble tablet in the church is in memory of

A statue of the Arctic explorer Sir John Franklin stands close to his birthplace in the town square, Spilsby.

A plaque in Spilsby Church also commemorates Sir John Franklin.

Edward Chaloner who was 'Lieutenant in the Navy above 50 years and shewed his courage in his exertions in the Eastern, Western, Northern and Southern Seas. Nor did he want the gentle virtues of a good friend and Husband. He retired from a military to a private life for want of health and to prepare for a state of eternal peace.' He died in 1776, aged 78.

Stoke Poges, Buckinghamshire
176/976827

At the western edge of the churchyard are four graves, a reminder of the tragedy at Land's End on 6 May 1985 when Robert Ankers, James Holloway, Nicholas Hurst, and Ricci Lamsden were washed into the sea while on a school visit to Cornwall.

Stoke Prior, Herefordshire
149/520565

A plaque in the church porch is to the memory of Sarah Sussanah Wyatt, who died on 10 March 1830 while on her way to visit

A poignant gravestone in Stoke Poges churchyard, of a schoolboy swept away at Land's End.

her husband John Wyatt Watling, then commanding HMS *Hyperion* lying at Newhaven.

Stone, Staffordshire
127/904338

Behind the church is a large stone mausoleum within which 'lie the mortal remains of Admiral John Jervis, Earl of St Vincent'. Inside the church there is a fine marble bust of the admiral, a painting of him as a young man, and a wall-memorial. The lengthy inscription on the last reveals that he was born at nearby Meaford Hall on 20 January 1735 and at 'the early age of thirteen he entered The Royal Navy, and remained during a long and active life, one of the brightest ornaments.' Greatest of his actions was the victory over the Spanish at Cape St Vincent 'on the ever memorable 14th of February 1797'.

Storrs, Westmorland
97/391941

Situated on the shore of Lake Windemere is a stone summer house erected in memory of Nelson. The inscriptions on the landward side are to Admirals Vincent and Duncan; presumably there are others on the lake side.

Stoughton, Leicestershire
140/640021

Anne Beaumont had a plaque erected here to her brother Admiral Basil Beaumont, 'who was lost in the Great Storm to ye inexpresable grief of his relations.' Born in 1669, his vessel, the *Mary*, was overwhelmed on the Goodwin Sands in November 1703. Everyone on board was lost, and a biographer has since observed that 'the circumstances of his death have given Admiral Beaumont's name a wider repute than his career as an officer would otherwise have entitled it to.'

Stow, Lincolnshire
121/882820

The massive church, a landmark for miles around, was commenced in about 975. Just visible on the south pier of the chancel arch is the famous scratched drawing of a Viking ship. When and by whom this was left here are not known, but it is an important reminder of the Norse invaders who dominated this part of England for so long.

Stowe, Buckinghamshire
152/675369

To the north of the Octagon Lake is a monu-

Memorial to Nelson and his admirals at Storrs on the shore of Lake Windermere.

ment to Captain Cook, which was originally topped with a globe. (See *Great Ayton*.)

Stow-on-the-Wold, Gloucestershire
163/191258

Plaques in the church are to members of the Chamberlayne family. One refers to Admiral Chamberlayne who 'after long and arduous Services to his King and Country died in the bossom of his own family' in 1810. His sons were not so fortunate. The eldest, George, captain of the sloop *Busy* in the West Indies, died in 1802 aged 22; Charles had died three years previously, just 16, on his return from sea, 'a Naval Officer in the service of his Country'; and Edwin, a post captain, died aged 37 in 1821. A descendant, Midshipman Rupert Henry Ingles-Chamberlayne, was killed in action on HMS *Hawke* on 15 October 1914, aged 17. (See *Oundle*.)

Stowting, Kent
179/125418

Several members of the Jenkin family who served in the Royal Navy are buried here, while in the church is a memorial to Conrad Jenkin, a lieutenant who died at Scapa Flow on Christmas Eve 1916 in 'the 23rd of his joyous life after serving his country with distinction in His Majesty's Ships *Cornwall*, *St Vincent*, *Cornwallis*, *Invincible*, *Inflexible*, *Iron Duke* and *Warspite*.'

Stubbington, Hampshire
196/555030

A plaque in the church lists the names of four

A midshipman lost on HMS Hawke *is remembered in Stow-on-the-Wold Church.*

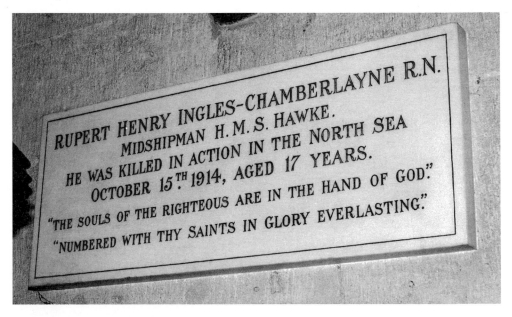

IN LOVING ⚓ MEMORY OF

**BOB FAGAN
MIKE TILL 🍃
ADRIAN WELLSTEAD
LT. CDR. JOHN WOODHEAD DSC**

WHO GAVE THEIR LIVES
SERVING THEIR COUNTRY ON BOARD
H. M. S. SHEFFIELD
OFF THE FALKLAND ISLANDS
4TH MAY 1982

Memorial in Stubbington Church to four seamen from HMS Sheffield *who lost their lives in the Falklands.*

of those killed on HMS *Sheffield* during the Falklands conflict in May 1982. (See *Guisley*.)

Studland, Dorset
195/036825

The village war memorial includes coastguard Henry Tupper, who was among those lost on HMS *Monmouth* on All Saints Day 1914 (see *Catherington*), and Lieutenant Denys Wright, who served on board HMS *Triumph*.

Sunderland, County Durham
88/398567

In Mowbray Park is a statue of Jack Crawford, the young sailor who at Camperdown in 1797 nailed the colours of Admiral Duncan to the mast of the *Venerable* after they had been shot away. He was afterwards feted, presented to King George III, and awarded a pension. A hero from a more recent war is buried in Bishopwearmouth Cemetery. He is Bombardier H. Reed of the Maritime Anti-Aircraft Regiment, who, while sailing on the SS *Cormount* in an East Coast convoy, suffered fatal wounds in action against enemy planes, for which he was posthumously awarded the George Cross and the Lloyd's Medal for Bravery at Sea. (See *Scotland – Lochwinnoch*.)

Sunderland Point, Lancashire
102/423559

Close to the entrance to the River Lune is Sambo's Grave, where 'Poor Sambo a faithful Negro' lies buried. He was a ship's master's servant who, having thought he had been deserted, refused all food and died in the loft above the inn about 1736.

Sunninghill, Berkshire
175/939685

The fine memorial near the church hall is to Rear-Admiral Sir Home Popham (1762–1820), and lists the engagements at which he was present – Copenhagen, Cape Town, Buenos Aires, and the north coast of Spain. Once described as 'a damned cunning fellow', he was 'well versed in the more scientific branches of his profession and was known as an excellent surveyor and astronomical observer.'

Swanage, Dorset
195/032787

A sea front memorial commemorates the great naval battle fought in Swanage Bay by Alfred the Great in 877. One of the murals in St Stephen's Hall, Westminster, depicts Alfred's longships attacking the Danish invaders at Swanage. King Alfred observed that: 'There is no advantage in living on an island unless your navy holds undisputed sway over the waters that surround it.'

Swarland, Northumberland
81/174029

The roadside monument to Nelson was erected by his prize agent, Alexander Davison, to commemorate their close friendship. In his nearby estate he planted trees to represent the Battle of the Nile, when the French fleet was decimated in 1798. (See *Felton*.)

Swindon, Gloucestershire
163/935249

In the church a plaque includes references to Sir Tristram Ricketts, Vice-Admiral of the Blue, who died in 1842; Commander Simpson Ricketts RN, who died in 1858; and Admiral Cornwallis Ricketts, who died in Florence in 1885. Also remembered here is Captain Edward Stopford RN, 'who after a lingering illness which he bore with exemplary firmness and resignation departed this life at Cheltenham 17 March 1837 in the 53rd year of his life.'

Tatsfield, Surrey
187/417562

A plaque is 'in proud and loving memory of my dear husband Captain Ambrose Langley Hunt RNR who was killed at his post on October 5 1915 aged 46 while navigating Admiralty transport ship to Mudros Base during operations on Gallipoli.'

Taunton, Somerset
193/229246

The fine church of St Mary Magdalene contains a number of maritime memorials. That to Admiral Nicholson, who died in January 1932, was erected by the Naval Fellowship of Taunton, Bridgwater and Wellington, which he had founded five years previously. Others commemorate John Onebye Bliss, a lieutenant in the sloop *Acorn* lost 'together with the whole ship's company in a hurricane between Bermuda and Halifax', April 1828; Henry Chichester, first lieutenant on HMS *Venus* and only son of Rear Admiral Hart, 'cut off in the execution of his duty at Carlisle Bay, Barbados' on 30 June 1813; and Captain C.I. Prowse, who went down with his ship, HMS *Queen Mary*, at Jutland on 31 May 1916. (See *Brooksby*.)

On the south side of the nave is a memorial to Sir Robert Seppings, who was apprenticed at Plymouth and rose to become Surveyor of the Navy 1813–32. Choir seats show his

home in Mount Terrace, Taunton, and the *Royal George*, on board which he was knighted by the Prince Regent in 1817.

Tenterden, Kent
189/884333

A plaque in the church is to Admiral Sir Charles Carter Drury, born in New Brunswick, Canada, who 'after serving his country for 52 years in the Royal Navy' died in May 1914.

Terrington St Clement, Norfolk
131/552205

A wall-monument to the memory of Sir Andrew Snape Hammond, who died in 1828, records that he was a captain in the Royal Navy, an Elder Brother of Trinity House, and twice Member of Parliament for Ipswich. Born at Greenwich in 1738, he is remembered particularly for 'his gallantry and activity while commanding His Majesty's ship *Roebuck* during the contest with America from 1773 to 1780.'

Tetbury, Gloucestershire
163/890930

A plaque in the church is to Captain Walter Pike, a lieutenant who served on the frigate *Euryalus* at Trafalgar and died in 1849. Also here are John Dacres, aged 37, who died at Mozambique in 1848, while in command of the sloop *Nimrod*; and Commander Alfred John Paul, aged 15 when he entered the Royal Navy, who served on the *Dartmouth* at Navarino and was flag lieutenant in the *Wellesley* at the taking of Chusan and the operations against Canton in 1841.

Tewkesbury, Gloucestershire
150/890324

At the west end of the Abbey is a reminder that not all sudden deaths of seamen took place at sea, for here is recorded the death of Lieutenant Robert Brydges RN, who drowned in the River Severn in February 1818 with his 13-year-old brother, Charles.

Thornbury, Gloucestershire
172/634906

A memorial table in the church is to the 6th Maritime Royal Artillery Regiment, based at nearby Kynton House during the Second World War. (See *Lochwinnoch – Scotland*.)

Thursley, Surrey
186/899359

A roadside memorial is to 'a generous, but

unfortunate Sailor, Who was barbarously murdered on Hindhead On Sept 24th 1756 By three Villains After he had liberally treated them And promised them his farther Allistance On the Road to Portsmouth.' His was as lonely a death as if he has been at sea, for the memorial concludes with the words: 'No dear Relation or still dearer Friend, Weeps my hard Lot, or miserable End; Yet o'er my sad Remains (my Name unknown) A generous Public have insrib'd this Stone.'

Thurstaston, Cheshire

108/248842

The lych gate is in memory of Thomas Ismay, chairman of the White Star Line 1867–92, while inside the church a plaque refers to his chairmanship for nearly 30 years of the training ship *Indefatigable*. (See *Maryport*.)

Tintagel, Cornwall

200/050884

The grave of Domencio Catanese, a cabin-boy, is in the shape of a lifebelt mounted on a cross. He died when the barque *Iota* ran into heavy seas and drifted ashore near Lye Rock in the late afternoon of 21 December 1893.

Titchfield, Hampshire

196/542058

A plaque in the church tells of Edward Ives, surgeon of the *Kent* about 1760, 'an instruc-

A fine lych gate memorial to Thomas Ismay at Thurstaston.

tive and cheerful Companion.' A window is in memory of Captain William Hoare, who died in 1886.

Torcross, Devon

202/824420

A Sherman tank, looking out over Start Bay, is a memorial to the loss of no fewer than 946 servicemen, mostly from the United States, on the night of 27 April 1944, when nine German E-boats intercepted and sank a convoy of tank landing craft exercising in preparation for the D-Day landings.

Treen, Cornwall

203/397220

Close to the coast is Logan Rock, a rocking stone weighing over 60 tons, which in 1824 a naval lieutenant managed to lever out of position, much to the distress of the local inhabitants who forced the Admiralty to exact £130 from the miscreant so that the stone could be replaced.

Truro, Cornwall

204/827448

In the Cathedral is a memorial to those lost in the Penlee lifeboat tragedy of December 1981 (see *Paul*), and a plaque to Samuel Wallis, during whose circumnavigation of the world on board HMS *Dolphin* in 1766–8 Tahiti was discovered.

Tunstall, Lancashire

97/614739

A plaque in the church to Lieutenant Miles North, who died in 1837, depicts a shipwreck.

Tweedmouth, Northumberland

75/995523

Vice-Admiral William Grive, who died in 1891, and Captain Francis Osborne, who died in 1924, are remembered in the church, where the roll of honour includes several naval casualties on vessels which include the *Royal Oak* (see *Scotland – Kirkwall*) and HMS *Grenville*, 1943. A recent addition is the name of Paul Henry, second engineer on *Sir Galahad*, killed during the Falklands conflict, 8 June 1982. His actions in the inferno at Bluff Cove earned him a posthumous George Medal. (See *Marchwood*.)

Tynemouth, Northumberland

88/373688

An information board concerning the Black Middens reads: 'These exposed rock formations once a notorious shipping hazard claimed 5 ships in 3 days of blizzards November 1864. 34 passengers and crew perished within sight of the shore.' As a result the Tynemouth Volunteer Life Brigade was formed, and their building still stands on the cliff-top above.

Nearby is the massive memorial, surmounted by a 23-foot high statue, of Admiral Collingwood. Born in Newcastle-upon-Tyne in 1750, he entered the Navy at the age of 11. His naval career reached its highest point when he took command of the fleet at Trafalgar following Nelson's death, though it has been opined that 'what he did under Nelson's directions he did gallantly and splendidly; [but] what he did after Nelson's death left him commander-in-chief has been considered more doubtful.' He continued in the service, though failing health led to his death in March 1810. He was described as a 'brave and capable sailor, a good officer, an admirable second in command, but without the genius fitting him to rise to the first rank as commander-in-chief.' (See *Newcastle*.)

At the Tynemouth Amateur Rowing Club two strake boats are memorials to seven club members who fell in the First World War.

Ulverston, Lancashire
97/295791

High on Hoad Hill the prominent tower, shaped like a lighthouse, is a memorial to one of the town's greatest sons, John Barrow. Born in June 1764, in a cottage which now serves as a lock-up shop, he started work in a Liverpool foundry, then went to sea on a whaler. Later he travelled to China and South Africa before being appointed Second Secretary to the Admiralty in 1804, a position he was to hold until 1845. He helped promote a number of the Polar voyages and was remembered by explorers, who named Barrow Sound, Barrow Strait and Point Barrow in the Arctic, and Cape Barrow in the Antarctic, after him. In addition he has a 'living memorial', a fine diving duck of Arctic regions named Barrow's goldeneye.

Up Marden, Sussex
197/795141

A plaque in this isolated church is in memory of Midshipman James Warner Thomas, who died of yellow fever while engaged in survey work in West Africa from HMS *Aetna* in 1834.

Upper Sheringham, Norfolk
133/145419

A plaque in the church records the death of

The tower in memory of Sir John Barrow overlooking Ulverston.

Commodore King when his yacht was wrecked in Cornwall in August 1930.

Upton-upon-Severn, Worcestershire
150/851407

In the shadow of the clock tower stands a fine bronze bust of Admiral Sir William Tennant, one of the last cadets to join the training ship *Britannia*. During the First World War he served in a variety of ships including the cruiser *Chatham* at the Dardanelles, and later the *Nottingham* until she was sunk by *U-52* in the North Sea in August 1916. In 1940 he was the Senior Naval Officer at Dunkirk and was awarded the CB for his services in organizing the embarkation of troops, himself being one of the last to leave. In 1941 he was commander of the *Repulse* when she was sunk by Japanese dive bombers off Kota Bahru on 10 December. Fortunately he was among the survivors, and later helped organize the construction of the 'Mulberry' harbour for the invasion of Normandy.

Wallasey, Cheshire
108/288931

Closest church to the sea is St Nicholas's, built by the Harrison family as a memorial to James and Jane Harrison and those who served with the Harrison Line sailing out of Liverpool. There is a plaque to John MacKenzie Jones, second engineer on the *Empress of Ireland* when she was sunk in the Gulf of St Lawrence, May 1914. The war memorial at the rear of the church includes the name of Frank Brade, killed during the coastal motor boat attack on Kronstadt harbour on 18 August 1919. Others served on the *Queen Mary*, sunk at Jutland; the *Tiger*, which was damaged in the same action (see *Devonport*); and the liner *Laurentic*, which, serving as an auxiliary cruiser, hit a mine and sank in Lough Swilly on 23 January 1917.

The cemetery at St Hilda's contains a number of maritime graves, including one to Captain Henry Rowles 'who was killed during a gale on board the SS *Rathmore* near Baltimore on the 20th November 1879', and his stepson Harford Giles Hargreaves, third officer of the same SS *Rathmore* 'which foundered at sea January 1880.'

At the United Informed Church in Seabank Road is a plaque to William Bullock 'who gave his life when his ship the SS *Canadian* was torpedoed by an enemy submarine, April 5th 1917 having first by his skill and courage secured the safety of all on board.' Nearby a pew in memory of Joseph MacCaig is 'set apart for the use of Aged Mariners.'

A visit to the Town Hall will be instructive, for there are a number of memorials including a plate marking the inauguration of the world's first hovercraft service between Wallasey and Rhyl, 20 July 1962. Below is a copy of the rough log kept during the first proving voyage a few days earlier.

The offices of the Mersey Ferries at Seacombe hold splendid plaques relating to the Zeebrugge Raid of St George's Day 1918, removed from the ferries *Daffodil* and *Iris*, which subsequent to taking part in the operation were granted the prefix 'Royal' by King George V. (See *Dover*.) A plaque on a boulder in the park above the promenade, unveiled in 1993 on the fiftieth anniversary of the Battle of the Atlantic, is dedicated 'in honour of all seafarers who served in the war of 1939 to 1945. They held their course.'

Walmer, Kent
179/366504

Memorials in the old parish church include Rear-Admiral Henderson, who had been 'present at many actions, Trafalgar, Lissa, in arduous and successful boat service at Regosniza, Guadaloupe, and commanded HMS *Edinburgh* in the operations on the coast of Syria in 1840.' By contrast Henry Royse, also remembered here, had a short career, dying in China aged 23 'from fever, brought on by exposure, fatigue and anxiety, in the faithful discharge of his duty' in 1861. Captain Richard Vincent is buried here, who, in command of the sloop *Arrow*, fought the two French frigates *L'Hortense* and *L'Incorruptible* in February 1805. Two sons of Admiral Harvey – Henry, who fell overboard from HMS *Rose* off Newfoundland in 1788, and Richard, killed when the *Ardent* blew up six years later – are just some of the many other naval persons commemorated.

Walsall, Staffordshire
139/015986

Outside the library is a bust of Ordinary Seaman John Henry Carless VC, and a plaque

The inscription on the John Henry Carless VC memorial in Walsall town centre.

Graves at Walton-on-the-Naze of men lost from HMS Conquest.

which tells us that he was born at Walsall on 11 November 1896 and killed in action at Heligoland Bight, 17 November 1917: 'Awarded the Victoria Cross for most conspicuous bravery and devotion to duty. Although mortally wounded in the abdomen he still went on serving the gun at which he was acting as rammer, lifting projectiles and helping to clear away the other casualties. He collapsed once, but got up, and tried again, and cheered on the new gun's crew. He then fell and died.' His death occurred during the last 'big ship' engagement of the First World War, when the light cruiser *Caledon*, on which Carless was serving, was straddled and hit by salvoes from the battleships *Kaiser* and *Kaserin*.

Walton-on-the-Naze, Essex

169/252216

In the memorial ground a set of headstones together with two slightly larger memorials recall seamen lost from HMS *Conquest* in 1916 when returning by boat to the ship anchored offshore.

Walton on the Wolds, Leicestershire

129/592197

Admiral Hobart, the son of the Reverend Augustus Hobart, was born here in 1822. He led an adventurous life, the many exploits of which earned him the nickname Hobart Pasha. Although there is no memorial, a tall cedar in the grounds of the former vicarage is said to commemorate him.

Warblington, Hampshire

197/728054

A fine tombstone to William Bean, aged 20, tells us that after being pressed into the Navy he lost his life when the *Torbay* exploded in Portsmouth Harbour in September 1758.

Wareham, Dorset

195/925872

In St Mary's Church are memorials to the Coad family, including Robert Coad, who while serving on HMS *Redwing* against slavers in West Africa died of a malignant fever on 16 March 1826, aged 32. His grandson Charles James Coad served in no fewer than 22 ships and became Paymaster in Chief.

Warnford, Hampshire

185/622227

Like many communities this village adopted a ship during the Second World War – HMS *Duncton*, a Hills class trawler; a plaque in the church provides details.

Warsash, Hampshire

196/489061

A fine model of the 36-gun frigate *Hotspur* was presented to the church in 1973 by its builder, Peter Clissold. A memorial on the waterfront tells how Naval and commando units sailed from here on the night of 5 June 1944 for the D-Day landings.

Model of the frigate Hotspur *in Warsash Church.*

Warwick, Warwickshire
151/282650

A plaque in St Mary's Church is in memory of 'Arthur Prattinson Turner, Captain SS *Matiana* BISNC and late Lieutenant RNR who lost his life at sea December 1898.' An Ensign flown on HMS *Warwick* at Zeebrugge, St George's Day 1918 hangs nearby.

Waterperry, Oxfordshire
164/629063

Midshipman Henley, lost 'in the foundering of HMS *Victoria* in June 1893' is remembered by his 'bereaved parents. (See *Bulwick*.)

Wellington, Herefordshire
149/497483

The church war memorial records Lieutenant T.E.A. St John RNR of HM Submarine *E-9*. She was the second British submarine to enter the Baltic, being brought in by Max Horton in October 1914, having previously sunk the light cruiser *Hela* off Heligoland.

Wells, Somerset
182/551458

On a plaque inside the Cathedral, to the Freemasons of Somerset lost 1914–18, are two merchant seamen, Captain W.G. Price and Chief Steward E. Knight, both of the SS *Feltria*, which was torpedoed some eight miles off Mine Head, County Waterford.

Wells-next-the-Sea, Norfolk
132/916437

Beside the harbour stands a memorial to the lifeboat disaster of 29 October 1880, when 11 of the crew of the *Eliza Adams* lost their lives. Their names, and those of the two survivors, are recorded here. The lifeboat had already effected a rescue from one ship and was making its way to another when it capsized.

Wentworth Woodhouse, Yorkshire
110/389947

The 100-foot high Keppel's Pillar is a monument to Augustus Keppel, who went to sea in 1735 and five years later sailed around the world with Anson. (See *Elvedon*.)

West Bromwich, Staffordshire
139/004913

A sailor from Nelson's time is remembered in All Saints' Church. The prominent gravestone of Captain James Eaton, who died in 1857 aged 71, records that he was a signal midshipman at the Battle of Trafalgar, and 'had the honour of repeating from *Victory* Nelson's last immortal signal "England expects that every man this day will do his duty".'

Westerdale, Yorkshire
94/664058

A memorial in the garden of his house, Arkangel, tells the story of the sailor Thomas Bulmer.

West Kirby, Cheshire
108/222866

The column was erected by the Trustees of the Liverpool Docks in 1841 as a beacon for mariners on the Mersey.

West Meon, Hampshire
185/640241

The grave of Captain Burgess, who entered the Royal Navy in 1897 and died in 1924, contains in addition the ashes of his son, Guy, who had attended the Royal Naval College, Dartmouth, and with Donald Maclean defected to Russia in 1951.

Weston-under-Lizard, Staffordshire
127/806106

A fine plaque with a picture of a sailing ship records that The Hon Richard Bridgeman DSO RN 'laid down his life in the Great War when flying over the Rufigi River in East Africa Jan 9 1917.'

West Walton, Norfolk
131/471133

Although now some nine miles from the Wash, but barely 12 ft above sea-level, a board in the church recalls three great floods: 'One First of November 1603 the Sea broke in and overflowed all Marshland, to the grate danger of Mens lives, and lose of goods; One the three and twentieth day of March 1614 this Country was overflowed with the fresh. And one the twelveth and thirteneth of September 1670 all Marshland was again overflowed by the Violence of the Sea.'

Whippingham, Hampshire
196/511936

A tablet in the church recalls William Arnold, late collector of customs at Cowes, 'a man who by his amiable as well as faithful discharge of his duty to his public station and private character justly entitled him to the warmest esteem and affection of all.'

Whitby, Yorkshire
94/895115

Unveiled in 1968, on the bicentenary of his first voyage, stands a statue of Captain James Cook, which bears the words 'For the lasting memory of a great Yorkshire seaman this bronze has been cast and is left in the keeping of Whitby, the birthplace of those good ships that bore him on his enterprises, brought him glory and left him at rest.' (See *Great Ayton*.) Close by is a whalebone arch in memory of the famous whaler William Scoresby, father of the explorer and chronicler of the same name.

A memorial in St Hilda's Church recalls the lifeboat disaster of February 1861, when, after effecting five rescues in one day, the boat was swamped with the loss of 12 of her 13 crew. Another memorial, in the cemetery, concerns the loss of the liner *Rohilla* and some 83 of the 233 on board, in October 1914, the survivors being rescued by the Whitby, Redcar, and Upgang lifeboats.

Whitchurch, Shropshire
117/541418

A plaque in the church is in memory of a grand-daughter of Captain John Richards Lapenotiere, who as captain of the *Pickle* delivered the despatches to the Admiralty after the Battle of Trafalgar. (See *Falmouth*.) Another plaque is to Commander Alfred Peel Athelston of HMS *Powerful*, who was killed at Graspan 1899. (See *Devonport*.)

Whitchurch Canonicorum, Dorset
193/396955

A plaque in the church records that Admiral Sir George Somers was a shipmate of Sir Walter Raleigh. He had discovered the Bermuda islands when he was wrecked there in 1609. Returning the following year, he died of a 'surfeit of eating hogs.' Nearby Lieutenant-Commander Edgar Cookson VC is remembered. He had entered the Royal Navy in 1883 and on 28 September 1915, in command of the armed paddle-steamer *Comet*, sailed up the Tigris to force a passage through a barrier of sunken boats connected by heavy cables, just downstream of Kut. Even the power of the *Comet* was unable to break through, so Cookson scrambled on to a sunken dhow and endeavoured to cut the supporting cables with an axe. Shot during this gallant attempt, he was dragged back on board and died shortly afterwards. Two days later the Turks fled and the river was cleared.

Whitstable, Kent
179/106665

We are told in the church of William

Edwards, 'for many years a respected inhabitant and ship owner of this town. He died while serving his country as a submarine engineer in the Crimea during the late war.' The bells were restored in memory of Lance-Corporal James Burrough of The Buffs, drowned at sea in 1943.

Elsewhere in the town there is Starvation Corner, where poverty-stricken unemployed seamen waited in the hope of work. By contrast, the house in Dollar Row is named from the fortune recovered by Whitstable divers from the wreck of the slave-ship *Enterprise* near the Copeland Islands, Northern Ireland, in 1834. Whitstable divers were then in great demand, one of the most famous being Weasel Rigden, who is buried in the churchyard.

Whittington, Worcester
150/877529

The memorial in the church to Admiral Powell, who died in 1857, tells how he was present at the Battle of Algiers in 1816 when 'three thousand Christians were liberated from slavery.' His house in London Road, Worcester – Heron Villa, now Heron Lodge – was named after his first command, HMS *Heron*.

The grave of Captain Wildman-Lushington at Widley. (Fleet Air Arm Museum)

Whitworth, County Durham
93/236347

The Hall was the home of the Shafto family between 1652 and 1981, the most famous member of which was Robert (1732–97), better known as 'Bonnie Bobbie', who, in the words of the nursery rhyme, with silver buckles on his knee went 'running off to sea.'

Wickersley, Yorkshire
111/476917

A fine memorial to the Coastal Forces, erected by their comrades in the North Midlands Branch of the Coastal Forces Volunteer Branch, stands in the car park of the Companions Club. The plaque on the base shows a D-Class MTB. (See *Gosport*.)

Widley, Hampshire
196/668065

Buried in the churchyard is Gilbert Wildman Lushington, Royal Marine Artillery and Royal Naval Air Service, who in 1913 was teaching Winston Churchill to fly. On 2 December he was killed at Eastchurch in the first fatal flying accident to be suffered by the RNAS.

Another grave is that of the Phillips family, of which the father, three sons, and a grandson all served in the Royal Navy. One, Albert Markham Hood Phillips, was commander of HMS *Bulwark* when she blew up at Sheerness in 1914. (See *Blakeney*.)

Wilmington, Kent
177/538725

In the graveyard a stone marks the resting place of Lieutenant David Mitchell-Dawson RN, who died at Chatham in 1912.

Winchelsea, Sussex
189/905174

In the ancient church, pillaged several times by French invaders in the 14th century, is a fine tomb believed to be that of Gervase Alard, Admiral of the Western Fleet of King Edward I, while close by lies Stephen Alard, Admiral of the Cinque Ports and the Western Fleet. A window commemorates the loss of the Rye lifeboat during the great storm of 15 November 1928. (See *Rye Harbour*.)

Winchester, Hampshire
185/483293

The statuette in the retrochoir is a reminder of the work by the diver William Walker which saved the cathedral. Through his single-handed efforts, working in flooded

Memorial in Winchester Cathedral for the first lieutenant of HMS Doterel, *lost when the ship's magazine exploded.*

IN LOVING REMEMBRANCE OF
WILLIAM CARMICHAEL FORREST,
1ST LIEUT. H.M.S. DOTEREL,
SON OF
CAPTAIN FORREST,
CHIEF CONSTABLE OF THIS COUNTY,
AND OF **SELINA** HIS WIFE;
WHO LOST HIS LIFE BY THE ACCIDENTAL
EXPLOSION OF THE SHIP'S MAGAZINE
AND CONSEQUENT FOUNDERING OF THE SHIP
OFF SANDY POINT IN THE STRAITS OF MAGELLAN
ON THE 26TH DAY OF APRIL 1881,
HIS BODY WAS RECOVERED,
AND BURIED IN THE CEMETERY AT
SANDY POINT ON THE 4TH DAY OF JULY.

giving was held the following year with King George V and Queen Mary being present on St Swithun's Day, the patron saint of the Cathedral. Each year on the same day a petition is made for William Walker.

A memorial in the south aisle is to Lieutenant William Forrest, first lieutenant of the sloop HMS *Doterel*, which sank in a violent explosion off Punta Arenas in the Straits of Magellan, 26 April 1881. There were just 12 survivors, 143 officers and men being lost. Another event in the southern hemisphere is also remembered, in which Captain Pearson, when navigating officer of HMS *Calliope* in 1889, helped bring his ship out of Apia harbour, Samoa, during a hurricane which sank three American and three German ships at their moorings with much loss of life.

The bell of HMS *Iron Duke,* flagship of Sir John Jellicoe at Jutland, hangs at the south-west corner of the dais as a memorial to his flag captain Frederick Dreyer 'who in a naval career of over fifty years made an outstanding contribution to the gunnery of the Fleet and of the Merchant Navy.' A window and plaque are to Edward Bligh of the Drake Battalion, Royal Naval Division, who died of wounds at Gallipoli on 10 September 1915 and is buried in Lancashire Landing Cemetery. A plaque in memory of Arthur Ward, engineer officer of the *Titanic*, is suplemented by another placed by 'a few of his fellow townsmen and friends. (See *Romsey*.)

Outside, the war memorial includes a reference to HMS *Hampshire*. (See *Scotland – Marwick Head*.) While in Winchester do not neglect to visit the superb group of mili-

tunnels from 1906 until 1911, he was able to shore up the foundations and so prevent their collapse. A week-long service of thanks

The inscription on Winchester war memorial commemorating those lost on board HMS Hampshire *when she was sunk in June 1916.*

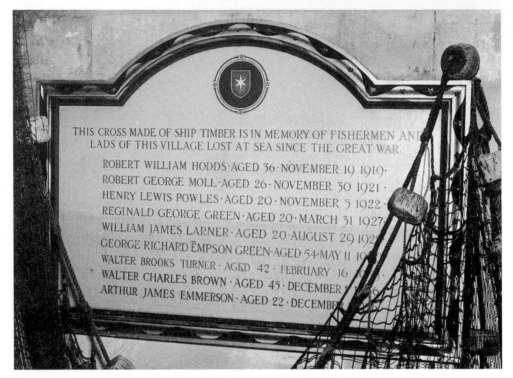

THIS CROSS MADE OF SHIP TIMBER IS IN MEMORY OF FISHERMEN AND LADS OF THIS VILLAGE LOST AT SEA SINCE THE GREAT WAR

ROBERT WILLIAM HODDS·AGED 36·NOVEMBER 19 1919·
ROBERT GEORGE MOLL·AGED 26·NOVEMBER 30 1921·
HENRY LEWIS POWLES·AGED 20·NOVEMBER 5 1922·
REGINALD GEORGE GREEN·AGED 20·MARCH 31 1927·
WILLIAM JAMES LARNER·AGED 20·AUGUST 29 192
GEORGE RICHARD EMPSON GREEN·AGED 54·MAY 11 19
WALTER BROOKS TURNER·AGED 42· FEBRUARY 16
WALTER CHARLES BROWN·AGED 45·DECEMBER
ARTHUR JAMES EMMERSON·AGED 22·DECEMBE

Fishermen's corner at Winterton, with the names of villagers lost at sea.

tary museums in the Peninsular Barracks. In that to the Gurkha Regiment there is a fine display, with photographs, battle honours, and a model, of the third HMS *Gurkha*. The destroyer *Larne* became the first HMS *Gurkha* after every man in the Gurkha Regiment contributed a day's pay in order to replace the previous HMS *Gurkha*, sunk off Bergen in April 1940. Two years later her successor was torpedoed and sunk off Libya. The bell of the fourth *Gurkha* is also here.

At St Bartholomew, Hyde, a tablet tells of 'Edm. Norton, Gent', an Armada veteran, 'Who had 2d a day pencion for his good service By Seae in Ano Dni 1588.'

Windlesham, Surrey
175/930637

A memorial in the church is to one of those lost on the *Eurydice*. (See *Bosham*.)

Winterton, Norfolk
134/491195

The church contains a fine memorial corner to fishermen, which includes a cross made from ships' timbers, and the names of 'Fishermen and Lads of this village lost at sea since the Great War', nine names in all. A model boat hangs in memory of Robert

Haylett BEM (1903–83), the sexton here for nearly 50 years.

Wolverhampton, Staffordshire
139/916986

In a roadside garden at the very heart of the town is a head and shoulders bronze of Able Seaman Douglas Morris Harris, below which a plaque shows him slumped over the wireless table from which he had continued to send messages when the drifter *Floandi*, together with others guarding the anti-submarine nets in the Straits of Otranto, were attacked by three Austrian cruisers on 15 May 1917.

Nearby in St Peter's Church a fine statue of Sir Richard Levenson, who as a young man had served against the Armada, once formed part of a much larger memorial destroyed by soldiers during the Commonwealth. The statue survived by remaining hidden until the restoration of Charles II in 1660.

The Lady Chapel of St John's Church contains a plaque to the memory of Petty Officer Alfred Edward Sephton VC. He was operating a gun director on the anti-aircraft cruiser *Coventry* providing protection for the hospital ship *Aba* during attacks by Stuka dive-bombers south of Crete on 18 May

1941. Although in great pain after being fatally wounded, Sephton continued at his post until the attack was over. Admiral Cunningham was later to write: 'Sephton's action may well have saved the *Coventry* and the *Aba*, and for his magnificent example he was awarded a posthumous Victoria Cross.' (See *Coventry*.)

At Willenhall Road School there is a plaque in memory of Boy Seaman Harry Parr-Temple of HMS *Royal Oak*, who drowned rescuing two out of three boys from a frozen pool in 1927.

Woodchester, Gloucestershire
162/842011

A plaque records the death in Flanders in October 1914, while serving with the South Staffordshire Regiment, of George Archer Shee. As a boy he had been sent to Osborne as a naval cadet and while there was wrongly convicted, and expelled, for stealing a 5s postal order. The case was a *cause célèbre* at the time, and eventually the family were given £3,000 compensation by the Government for the wrongful expulsion. The story formed the basis for Terrence Rattigan's play *The Winslow Boy*.

Wool, Dorset
194/847865

A framed 1914–18 war memorial in the church lists Walter and Richard Cobb, who died at sea in submarines, and Ralph Butler, assistant paymaster on HMS *Hampshire*. (See *Scotland – Marwick Head*.)

Woolacombe, Devon
180/456437

The memorial stone overlooking the beach records that in 1944 Americans trained both here and at nearby Saunton Sands for the Normandy invasion.

Worthing, Sussex
198/146045

A plaque in St Mary's Church is 'sacred to the memory of the eleven unfortunate fishermen who lost their lives by the oversetting of a boat in an attempt to render assistance to the distressed crew of the barque *Lalla Rookh* off Worthing during a storm on 25th November 1850.' The sum of £5,000 was raised to provide relief and support for the eight wives, 37 children and other dependents left to mourn following the tragedy. Among churchyard graves is a reference to Frederick Croad, who perished when the *Cleopatra* was lost between Bombay and Singapore in 1847.

Wouldham, Kent
178/713644

Each Trafalgar Day local schoolchildren come to lay flowers on the grave of Walter Burke, who was purser on HMS *Victory* at Trafalgar and 'in whose arms the immortal Nelson died.' He himself died, aged 70, in 1815. Two cannon-balls in the church are said to have come from HMS *Victory*.

Wraxall, Somerset
172/490719

The memorial in the churchyard at All Saints to members of the Coathupe family includes Henry Thornton Coathupe, aged 22, medical officer on board the *Morning Star*, who died at sea 8 June 1856; his brother Gilbert, captain of the Pacific Steam Navigation vessel *Eten*, which, sailing between Valpariso and Panama, she was driven on to rocks near Cape Ventanas on the coast of Chile; and Frederick, an RNR lieutenant, who died at Clifton in 1881, aged 42, after a career spent on ships of both the Union and the Castle lines.

Outside the church is a fine teak seat which includes the crest of HMS *Snapper*, a submarine lost in the Bay of Biscay on her thirteenth patrol, February 1941. Her commander was Lieutenant Geoffrey Prowse, whose father Captain Cecil Prowse had been lost at Jutland. (See *Brooksby*.)

Wyke Regis, Dorset
194/662777

Just inside the church door is a plaque in memory of Charles Hickes, a cadet on HMS *Britannia* when he died, aged 14, in 1862. Another is to Nathaniel Arbuthnot, Admiral of the Blue, who died 31 January 1794. It is well worth looking around the churchyard for other maritime memorials.

Yarmouth, Hampshire
196/355897

An unfinished statue of Louis XIV of France was being conveyed on board a ship captured by Sir Richard Holmes, who then compelled the sculptor to finish it by carving Holmes' own head onto the body. It was erected in the parish church following Holmes' death in 1692.

Yeovilton, Somerset
183/546230

The Fleet Air Arm Church contains a poignant memorial to the nine pilots murdered by the Japanese in Changi Jail, Singapore, after the end of the war in August 1945. They had flown from the carriers *Indomitable*, *Illustrious*, and *Victorious*, in the raid on oil refineries at Palembang,

Plaque in Wyke Regis Church to a naval cadet from HMS Britannia.

Plaque in the Fleet Air Arm Church at Yeovilton to those lost during the Falklands conflict.

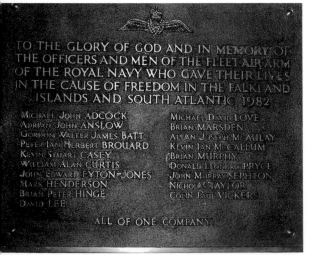

Sumatra, the previous January, and had been held at Changi ever since. Make note of the inscription: 'None of us should forget.'

A plaque tells of Peter Gordon, an aircraft artificer lost in August 1966 while helping a fellow member of the Royal Navy's East Greenland Expedition. Others are in memory of six men of 845 Naval Air Commando Squadron, lost on operations in Sarawak in 1964–5, and ten from RNAS Howden who died in 1917–18. There is also a plaque commemorating those 'who gave their lives in the cause of freedom in the Falklands and South Atlantic 1982'.

York, Yorkshire
105/603523

The Minster contains a superb marble wall-monument to Admiral Craddock, including a head-and-shoulders relief. The inscription reads: 'To the Glory of God and in Memory of Rear Admiral Sir Christopher Craddock Knight Commander of the Royal Victorian Order, Companion of the Most Honourable Order of the Bath who gallantly upholding the high traditions of the British Navy led his squadron against an overwhelming force of the enemy off Coronel on the coast of Chile and fell gloriously in action on All Saints Day 1914. This monument is erected by his grateful countrymen.' (See *Catherington*.)

Another is to Henry Medley, Commander in Chief in the Mediterranean when he died at Savona, 5 August 1747. Lieutenant-Colonel Willoughby Moore of the 6th Inniskilling Dragoons is also remembered here, along with those who perished with him when the transport *Europa* was lost by fire. She had been making for the Crimea in May 1854 with a crew of 44, 60 men of the Dragoons, a servant, two women, and 57 horses, when the fire broke out. In addition to Colonel Moore, veterinary surgeon James Kelly and 16 men were also lost.

Yoxall, Staffordshire
128/142190

A large tomb in the church, with a reclining figure, is that of Admiral Henry Meynell.

Zennor, Cornwall
203/454385

Famed for the mediaeval carved 'Mermaid Chair'; a mermaid being said to have lured Matthew Trewhella, a local man whose singing she admired, down into the sea at nearby Pendour Cove. A fine model of a Cornish two-masted schooner hangs in the church in memory of W.A. Procter, lost somewhere in the Pacific on a single-handed voyage in 1956, and all the unnamed sailors who lie buried in the churchyard.

Isle of Man

Ballabeg
95/247705

Captain John Quilliam, who served as first lieutenant on the *Victory* at Trafalgar and is depicted at the far right of the surrounding group of officers in the famous painting of *The Death of Nelson* by Benjamin West, lived in Castletown, where his house is marked by a wall plaque. His remains are interred in Arbory parish church where annually on Trafalgar Day a service is held by the burial vault, and throughout the day the church flies a White Ensign, the only church in the Isle of Man allowed to do so.

Bishopscourt
95/333923

Over the decades Bishopscourt Glen near the north-west coast has been extensively planted with trees and shrubs. Bishop Hildesley had a large mound shaped here, Mount Aeolus, on which the bowsprit of the French ship *Belle Isle* was placed to commemorate the capture by the *Aeolus*, *Brilliant*, and *Pallas* of the French privateers *Blonde*, *Marechal de Belle-Ile*, and *Terpsichore* off the Isle of Man in 1760. Two cannons placed at the same time survive, but the bowsprit has long disappeared.

Cornaa
95/467897

A plaque on the east wall of the bridge remembers William Kennish, 'poet, inventor, engineer, explorer', born 'close by the foot of the Bridge of Cornaa' in 1799. He joined the Royal Navy and rose to become master carpenter of the Mediterranean fleet. Among his inventions was one to concentrate the fire of a broadside from a man-of-war. He even produced a plan to cut a canal across the isthmus of Panama, though it was never adopted.

Cregneash
95/189672

A memorial stone in the boundary wall of Kirk Christ tells the sad story of a disaster that occurred during an attempt to salvage the brig *Lily*, which had run aground on Kitterland Rock in Calf Sound in 1852, carrying a mixed cargo that included 61 tons of gunpowder. While the salvage team sent by Lloyds were at work on the wreck it disappeared in a huge explosion, killing 29 out of 30 men, who between them left 22 widows and 77 orphans. (See *Kitterland*.)

Douglas
95/388755

The tower of refuge in Douglas Bay takes the form of a castellated shelter, built by Sir William Hilary for the use of mariners who might be wrecked on Conister Rock. Hilary is better remembered for his founding of the Royal National Lifeboat Institution, the first meeting of which took place at the City of London tavern early in 1824. The previous year he had published a pamphlet entitled *Appeal to the British Nation on the Humanity and Policy of forming a National Institution for the preservation of Lives and Property from Shipwreck*. Not only did he found the Institution but he took part in many rescues, helping to save 305 lives, and was three times awarded the Gold Medal for great gallantry. He died in 1847 and is buried in St Mary's churchyard. On the wall of the lifeboat-house is a bronze in his memory.

At Broadcasting House on Douglas Head there is a plaque in memory of those from HMS *Valkyrie*, a training base established here for radar operators during World War Two. Another training station, HMS *St George*, which was situated at what was formerly a holiday camp, is remembered by a plaque on the sole remaining building. At the crematorium church there is a plaque to 'the ship's company and the boys of HMS *St*

George who died whilst this establishment was on this Island September 1939 – December 1945.'

On the wall of the South Quay there is a plaque commemorating the great tragedy which befell the herring fleet on 21 September 1787, overtaken by a tremendous storm as it returned to port. It is thought that 58 boats were swamped or smashed on the rocks, with the loss of 161 fishermen.

A drinking fountain, formerly on the Victoria Pier but now situated on Loch Promenade, is in memory of David Kewley, 'as a tribute of admiration for his bravery in saving at various times 23 lives from drowning.' He worked on the quayside as a mooring man for the Isle of Man Steam Packet Company and was a member of the lifeboat crew. The Royal Humane Society awarded him their bronze medal and a 'purse of gold' containing £58. He died aged 54 in 1904.

A tablet and window formerly in the demolished St Barnabas' Church are now in the offices of the Steam Packet Company and commemorate those members of staff who laid down their lives in the Second World War.

Kitterland

95/173667

A fine memorial to the *Lily* disaster was unveiled in May 1994, overlooking Calf Sound. The congregation included several

The simplest of memorials, inscribed on a rock at Langness. (D. Rose)

descendants of those lost in December 1852. (See *Cregneash.*) Nearby is a Cross of

The Thousla Cross, overlooking Calf Sound, Kitterland. (D. Rose)

Lorraine, a memorial to the schooner *Jeune St Charles* wrecked on Thousla Rock in November 1858. The six crew scrambled on to the rock, but the two cabin boys were washed away before help arrived. Originally the cross was on the rock itself as part of a warning beacon, since replaced by an obelisk and light.

Langness
95/288660

Roughly-carved it may be, on the rocks above the shore, but at least the crew of the *Provider*, 'all lost 1853', are not forgotten, though no other details are given.

Peel
95/242846

Inside the lifeboat house is the figurehead of the Norwegian schooner *Saint George*, washed ashore after she sank off Peel in a violent storm on 7 October 1889. All 23 people on board, including the captain's wife and nine-month-old daughter, were rescued by the Peel lifeboat, whose crew received silver medals from the Norwegian Government for their bravery. At a centenary celebration of the rescue in 1989 a guest of honour was Mrs Karen Nordli, granddaughter of the baby who was rescued.

At the corner of East Quay and the Promenade, known as Weatherglass Corner, are two plaques. One is in memory of those in HM Patrol Service who gave their lives in World War Two. The other is simply 'in Memory of the seamen of this island lost at sea in war and peace. *Ays cooinaghtyn jen ny marrinnee voish yn ellan shoh cailit ayns y cheayn ayns caggey as atns shee.'*

Ronaldsway
95/282688

Two plaques in the main concourse of the airport remind one of the time when this was HMS *Urley*. One refers to its use as a Royal Navy Air Station and the training of crews in Barracuda torpedo reconnaissance aircraft. Another is 'in memory of those of HMS *Urley* who were trained on the Isle of Man who gave their lives during the Second World War 1939–1945.'

Northern Ireland

Armagh, County Armagh
8/887450

A Naval Brigade casualty from Sebastopol remembered in the Cathedral is Lieutenant Thomas Kidd, who, while serving ashore from HMS *Albion,* was shot on the Redan while endeavouring to recover some wounded men, so that 'Her Majesty's service has lost one of its most promising young officers'. The scene is depicted on the memorial.

Ballycastle, County Antrim
1/121414

The fact that the first transmission of wireless messages across the sea took place here in 1898, over the six miles to Rathlin Island, is recalled by a memorial near the harbour. The information, concerning shipping movements, was then passed to Lloyd's in London.

Banbridge, County Down
9/124458

An impressive statue flanked by polar bears in Church Square is to Captain Francis Crozier, who had first visited the Arctic as a midshipman on Parry's second and third expeditions. In 1839 he sailed in command of the 340-ton *Terror*, with James Clark Ross, on the greatest of the nineteenth century Antarctic voyages. Among the many discoveries made was Ross Island, its eastern-most point being the black volcanic cliffs that Ross named Cape Crozier. Once again on the *Terror*, he sailed with Franklin on the ill-fated attempt to seek the North-West Passage in 1845, and after Franklin's death he commanded the unsuccessful march south. (See *England – Spilsby*.)

Belfast, County Antrim
6/338739

In front of the City Hall is a statue of Sir Edward Harland, who came to Belfast from Yorkshire and in 1858 founded the famous shipbuilding company which bears both his name and that of his German partner, Gustav

The Titanic *memorial outside Belfast City Hall.* (E. Lendrum)

Wolff. Close by is the memorial 'erected to the imperishable memory of those gallant Belfast men whose names are here inscribed and who lost their lives on the 15th April 1912 by the foundering of the Belfast built RMS *Titanic*.'

At the Botanic Gardens stands a statue of William Kelvin, the Scottish physicist born in Belfast in 1824, whose many discoveries and innovations included the first submarine cables, improvements to ships' compasses, and tide predictors. Sinclair's Seamen's Church in Corporation Square has a pulpit which is made from a ship's prow and bears port and starboard lights.

Carncastle, County Antrim

3/359075

In the graveyard lies Robert McCalmont of the *William and George*, who died at Larne in 1775.

Carrickfergus, County Antrim

6/414873

The statue of King William III, unveiled in 1990, commemorates the landing here of the Prince of Orange on 14 June 1690, on his way to victory over the Jacobites at the Battle of the Boyne.

Holywood, County Down

6/396794

At the bottom of Church Street stands a mast with a weather-vane, the latest of a succession of masts that have stood here since about 1700, when a Dutch ship was wrecked just offshore.

Larne, County Antrim

3/414022

Two plaques at the harbour recall the events of 24–5 April 1914, when the SS *Clyde Valley* brought a shipment of arms here to be used by the Ulster Volunteer Force in the event of an armed struggle being necessary to maintain the union with the United Kingdom. The emigrants' memorial in Curran Park is dedicated to those who left these shores in May 1717 upon the *Friend's Goodwill*, bound for Boston. One other memorial must not be missed, that to the MV *Princess Victoria* which foundered in the North Channel with the loss of 133 lives in January 1953, 27 of whom were inhabitants of Larne. (See *Scotland – Stranraer*.)

Londonderry, County Londonderry

2/434165

A particularly fine memorial in St Columb's Cathedral is in memory of Captain John Boyd, who lost his life while in command of HMS *Ajax*, which had gone to the rescue of the *Neptune* off Dun Laoghaire during the hurricane of February 1861. The Browning memorial and a window are reminders of the raising of the siege of Londonderry in 1689, when Michael Browning, master of the *Mountjoy*, was killed as the 105-day siege was brought to an end. This event is also remembered by a memorial on the city walls between the Magazine and Shipway gates.

Portrush, County Antrim

1/861403

A memorial to Captain Alexander Clark was erected by his brother in the churchyard, and refers to some 40 years in command of vessels around the coasts of Great Britain 'distinguished by many acts of heroism and humanity', including, in the last year of his life, the rescue of 64 persons from the steamer *Armenian*, which ran aground on the Arklow Bank in January 1865.

Scotland

Aberchirder, Aberdeenshire

29/629526

In St Marnan's Church is a plaque, the frame of which is timber from HMS *Vindictive,* in memory of Angus Maclachlan, who, aged just 18, had served on this destroyer during the attack on Zeebrugge on 23 April 1918. He later died at his post, in the after control position, during the operation to block Ostend on 10 May, when the *Vindictive* grounded in the harbour entrance. (See *England – Dover.*)

Memorial in Hazelhead Park, Aberdeen, to those lost in the Piper Alpha disaster.

Aberdeen, Aberdeenshire

38/895054

In the grounds of Hazelhead stands a powerful memorial, surrounded by a large rose garden, to the 167 men lost when the Piper Alpha oil platform exploded on 6 July 1988. It comprises three seven-foot high figures, of a mature oilman (the oldest casualty was Raymond Mahoney, aged 60), a youthful figure (the youngest was Mark Ashton, aged 19), and a roustabout. The names and ages of all the casualties are listed here.

Set in a warehouse wall on Blakie's Quay is a simple granite memorial 'in memory of the dock labourers who gave their lives for King and Country.' At Pocra Quay, Footdee, a granite obelisk erected as a war memorial by local inhabitants includes a bronze panel depicting a seaman, commemorating the men of the Royal and Merchant Navies.

Aberdour Bay, Aberdeenshire

30/884646

A memorial designed by her great grandson commemorates the heroism of Jane Whyte, who in October 1884 managed to catch a lifeline thrown from the steamer *William Hope,* ashore in heavy seas. She was awarded an RNLI Silver Medal for her bravery, which resulted in 15 men being saved.

Anstruther, Fife

59/567036

A memorial room in the Fisheries Museum contains nearly 190 brass plaques which record fishing tragedies around the Scottish coast and those who lost their lives. Here are remembered vessels like the *Devotion, Guiding Star, Honey Dew, Ocean Lover,* and *Star of Hope.* The oldest fisherman I could see commemorated was George Slater, 69, of the *Caledonia* of Portnockie, while the youngest was George Mair of the *Lapwing,* aged 15. Lifeboats are also remembered here:

the *Mona* at Broughty Ferry (see *Broughty Ferry*); the *Robert Lindsay* at Arbroath (see *Arbroath*); the *TGB* at Longhope (see *Longhope*); and the two Fraserburgh lifeboats – *John and Charles Kennedy*, 9 February 1953, and the *Duchess of Kent*, 21 January 1970.

Nearby in the High Street a plaque tells of Captain John Keay (1828–1918), who lived here for many years and was 'master of many clipper ships', including the famous *Ariel*.

Arbroath, Angus
54/644413

The south transept of the ruined Abbey Church has a circular window known as the 'O' of Arbroath, which was formerly lit and used as a beacon for mariners. In the Old Church there is a plaque to the six crew of the Arbroath lifeboat lost on 27 October 1953, erected by Charles Cargill and his wife, who lost two sons in the disaster.

The Arbroath Lighthouse Musem contains a sign removed from the Bell Rock Tavern of Grimsby, now demolished, which shows the famous Inchcape Bell, which, on the Inchcape Rock some 11 miles to the southeast, served as a warning to mariners. A lighthouse now stands there, on what is now less romantically called the Bell Rock. It was here, so we are told in the famous poem, that Rolf the Rover foundered after he had cut loose the bell some time previously. A wooden plaque in the Museum is to the fishing vessel *Maggie Smith* and her crew of three lost near to the Bell Rock, probably after hitting a mine, in February 1918.

Ardnoe Point, Argyllshire
55/772945

A tall gravestone on the Point is that of John Black, 'Feuar and Fish Curer of Grenock who died of cholera on board his Schooner *Diana* and was interred here 28 July 1832.'

Ardrossan, Ayrshire
70/233421

In the late afternoon of 27 March 1943 the escort-carrier HMS *Dasher* was passing offshore, when aviation fuel exploded. She sank almost immediately with the loss of 379 crew. There were just 149 survivors. Fifty years later the people of Ardrossan came together to honour those lost by dedicating a memorial on a pink granite boulder close to the sea front.

Balcary, Kircudbrightshire
84/820496

Balcary House, now a hotel, was built origi-

Plaque to the memory of Captain John Keay, on his house in Anstruther.

nally by smugglers, as their local headquarters and contraband store.

Barra, Outer Hebrides
31/648981

Captain Roderick MacKinnon, a resident of Barra, was so moved by the absence of a monument to the 129 men of the island, and of neighbouring Vatersay, who had lost their lives during the war, that he instigated a campaign to raise funds for a memorial, which was unveiled in 1993. All but a handful of the names recorded were of men who served in the Merchant Navy.

Blackness, West Lothian
65/056803

The local inhabitants had been told by the English to build a ship, to protect the nearby port of Bo'ness, but instead they built a castle in the shape of a mediaeval warship.

Boarhills, Fife
59/562136

Against the north wall of the churchyard is a memorial stone to the nine crew of the brig *Napoleon*, including Charles Odman, the master's son, lost offshore during a severe storm in October 1864.

Broadford, Inverness-shire
32/642235

Several of the 338 casualties from HMS *Curacoa* lie in the churchyard. She was an anti-aircraft cruiser cut in two in a collision

The brig Napoleon *memorial at Boarhills.*

Plaque on the lifeboat house at Broughty Ferry commemorating the loss of the crew of the Mona.

IN HONOURED MEMORY OF THE CREW
OF THE ROYAL NATIONAL LIFEBOAT "MONA"
STATIONED AT BROUGHTY FERRY
WHICH FOUNDERED, WITH THE LOSS OF ALL HANDS,
IN A GALE IN THE FIRTH OF TAY
ON 8TH DECEMBER 1959,
WHILE RESPONDING TO A CALL FROM THE
NORTH CARR LIGHTSHIP WHICH WAS
ADRIFT IN THE NORTH SEA.
RONALD GRANT   GEORGE WATSON
GEORGE B SMITH   JAMES FERRIER
ALEXANDER GALL   JOHN T. GRIEVE
JOHN GRIEVE   DAVID ANDERSON

with the *Queen Mary* off the Bloody Foreland, 2 October 1942.

Broughty Ferry, Angus
54/460306

A plaque on the lifeboat station wall is in memory of the eight crew of the *Mona*, which foundered on 8 December 1959 'while responding to a call from the North Carr lightship which was adrift in the North Sea.'

Buckie, Banffshire
28/425656

A gallery in the Maritime Museum is devoted to the life and works of Peter Anson (1889–1975). After a period as a monk in the Anglican Benedictine community on Caldy Island, Pembrokeshire, he became interested in the fishing industry. His books, and perhaps even more his drawings and water colours, which are housed here, are a unique record of the fishing communities around our coast. The Fishermen's Memorial Chapel in New Street has numerous plaques in memory of fishermen lost at sea.

Chapel Hill, Aberdeenshire
30/068356

A memorial in the churchyard is to those from the steamship *Wistow Hall* which ran ashore in a gale in January 1912 with just four survivors from her crew of 57.

Collieston, Aberdeenshire
38/042285

The rocky cove known as St Catherine's Dub takes its name from the Spanish galleon *Santa Catherina*, wrecked here in 1594. (See *Slains Castle*.) The war memorial in the churchyard has just one naval name, that of William Mitchell of the Royal Naval Division, who died at Alexandria, August 1915, though Staff Sergeant J. Ritchie died on the hospital ship *Valdivia*.

Coldingham, Berwickshire
67/904658

Remembered in the church here is Lieutenant Andrew Jenkins RNR, master mariner, 'an honour conferred upon him by King George V in recognition of special service, zeal and devotion to duty shown during the Great War in carrying on the trade of the Country while he was in command of the Prince Line steamer *Japanese Prince*. He died on board at Philadelphia in May 1917.'

Deerness, Orkney

6/570087

The cliff-top memorial on Scarva Taing is to some 200 Covenanters wrecked here in 1679.

Drummore, Wigtownshire

82/134367

In the churchyard of this, the most southerly church in Scotland, is a grave in the shape of a lighthouse erected to James Scott, a lighthouse keeper from the Mull of Galloway who died in 1852.

Dunbar, East Lothian

67/678793

A large monument which formerly carried a barometer was 'presented to the Fishermen of Dunbar to whose Perilous Industry the Burgh owes much of its Prosperity' in 1856. The provision of a barometer was the inspiration of William Brodie, who was subsequently told by an old sailor at Eyemouth further down the coast that: 'Many a coarse blast, and many a life it has saved. We counted ourselves guid judges o' the weather when we got it, but this is the best ane. If ye was comin' here at twa o'clock i' the mornin' ye wad see them burning lucifer matches, keekin' at it, in case any change had ta'en place durin' the nicht.'

Dundee, Angus

54/409302

With her masts showing above nearby buildings the *Discovery* now rests here in her home port, from where she was launched in 1901 for the Antarctic Expedition commanded by Captain Scott. Her next three years were spent in the Antarctic, much of the time beset by ice in McMurdo Sound. Subsequently she was bought by the Hudson's Bay Company and later, from 1925 to 1931, made several oceanographic research voyages to the southern oceans. Upon her retirement she was taken over as a headquarters training ship for the Sea Scouts, and for a time during the 1939–45 war served as the establishment for Sea Scout Signalmen. In 1955 the Admiralty assumed responsibility for the *Discovery* and she was moored on the Thames, attached to the London Division of the Royal Naval Reserve. Then in 1979 she was handed over to the Maritime Trust for restoration to her 1925 configuration and eventually returned to Dundee, a most fitting memorial to the great age of Polar exploration.

Camperdown Park and House on the northern edge of the city were built by the son of Admiral Duncan, commander of the British fleet during the brilliant victory over the Dutch at Camperdown in 1797. The Howth, an old cemetery, contains a number of graves of maritime interest and deserves exploration.

Dunoon, Argyllshire

63/173770

Two plaques in Holy Trinity Church tell of losses at sea. William Davey, an apprentice aged 16, was drowned in 1900 on a voyage from New York to Melbourne, while nine years later William Hart was lost in the wreck of the *Hestia* off Nova Scotia. The lighting in the church was installed in memory of the officers and men of HMS *Curlew*, the cruiser sunk off Norway in May 1940 and subsequently the Harbour Defence Depot at Inellan, just down the coast where the Firth of Clyde narrows.

Edinburgh, Midlothian

66/252735

The Scottish National War Memorial stands in the highest part of Edinburgh Castle. The section devoted to the Royal Navy includes both the principal battles of the Second World War, and some of the individual actions and the names of the enemy ships captured or destroyed, among them HMS *Carmania* and the *Cap Trafalgar*, HMS *Sydney* and the *Emden*, HMS *Severn* and *Mersey* and the *Konigsberg*, and HMS *Achilles* and *Dundee* and the *Leopard*. Inside the shrine are figures including a midshipman, a submarine rating, a petty officer gunner's mate, a stoker, and a WRNS officer.

On Calton Hill is a 106-foot high tower in the shape of a spy-glass, the city's memorial to Nelson, completed in 1815. Above the entrance are two panels, one bearing the year of Trafalgar, the upper containing Nelson's crest with the reference to the *Sans Josef*, which he captured at St Vincent in 1797. (See *England – Pewsey*.) Nearby is an unfinished monument to the dead of the Napoleonic Wars.

In St Giles' Cathedral there is a memorial to Lieutenant-Colonel Seton and the men of the 74th Highlanders lost on the *Birkenhead*. (See *England – Beckingham*.) A fine model of the tea clipper *Ariel* can be seen in St Mary's Cathedral. (See *Anstruther*.)

Ednam, Roxburghshire

74/735362

The obelisk on Dove Hill commemorates James Thomson (1700–48), who was born in Ednam, best-remembered for the words of *Rule Britannia*, though these are also claimed by David Mallett, with whom he worked on

Alfred: a Masque, which contains the song. A memorial inside the church is to Patrick Edmonstoune (1698–1793), one of the few survivors of the Darien Expedition.

Eyemouth, Berwickshire

67/945643

On the morning of 14 October 1881 a storm swept the east coast, catching many fishing boats unawares. Some managed to ride out the high seas and a few reached harbour, but no fewer than 129 men were lost, including 60 from the nearby villages. The Eyemouth Tapestry hanging in the museum includes a list of all the boats and crews lost that day. There is also a broken mast memorial in the churchyard, where some of the men are buried.

Forres, Morayshire

27/044591

The 70-foot high octagonal Nelson Tower was built to commemorate the victory of Trafalgar. For many years it was the meeting place of the Trafalgar Club, which had a spittoon made in the form of Napoleon's head.

Fraserburgh, Aberdeenshire

30/995666

In St Peter's is a remarkable 15-foot long

The fine memorial to the Free French naval forces at Gourock. (Mac MacKay)

model of a two-masted line fishing vessel. This originally hung in a church at Torry on the edge of Aberdeen before being brought here in 1983. The number '153' refers to the fishes caught by the disciples Peter and Andrew in the Sea of Galilee.

Glasgow, Lanarkshire

64/604656

On Glasgow Green stands a tall obelisk in memory of Nelson. (See *England – Burnham Thorpe*.) In the Cathedral is a book of remembrance formerly in the RNVR Club, the SV *Carrick*. Those who fell in the Falklands campaign are remembered here.

Glen Prosen, Angus

44/371606

Formerly a rather fine fountain commemorated Captain Robert Scott and Dr Edward Wilson. Both knew this area well, Wilson having lived near here – in what is now known as Scott Lodge – when studying red grouse diseases. The original fountain was accidentally destroyed in 1979, and now a simple stone cairn marks the spot where it stood.

Gloup, Shetland

1/507045

A memorial at the old fishing station at the north end of Yell, depicting a wife looking out to sea, with a child at her shoulder, is a poignant reminder of the tragedy of July 1881 when 10 boats were overwhelmed in a storm and 58 men lost. Six of the boats and 36 men were from Gloup, the rest were from Fethaland, Haroldswick, Havera, and Ronas Voe. Their names are all recorded here, as are those of their crofts, and, where known, their boats, the famous Shetland 'sixerns' used to catch cod and ling.

Gourdon, Kincardineshire

45/826707

Beside the harbour is a memorial in memory of Lieutenant William Farqhuar, who died when the gunboat *Racehorse* ran aground in thick weather near Chefoo, northern China, in November 1864. Only nine from her crew of 108 were rescued. A barometer on the memorial, dated 1871, is 'to the seafaring men of Gourdon.' (See *England – Reigate*.)

Gourock, Renfrewshire

63/255774

On Lyle Hill the Cross of Lorraine and anchor is dedicated 'to the memory of the sailors of the Free French Naval Forces who sailed from Greenock in the years 1940–1945 and gave their lives in the Battle of the Atlantic for the liberation of France and the success of the Allied cause.' Specifically mentioned are the corvettes *Alysse* and *Mimosa*, and the submarine *Surcouf*.

In 1622 Mary Lamont was burnt as a witch on a charge of intending to throw the stone known as Granny Kempock's Stone into the sea, to cause shipwrecks. It now stands in Kempock Street close to Kempock Point.

Govan, Lanarkshire
64/546657

A drinking fountain in Elder Park was erected by the Fairfields Shipping Company in memory of those lost when HM Submarine *K-13* failed to surface in the Gairloch during trials, 29 January 1917. Some 80 persons were on board – the crew, plus engineers from the shipyard – when she made her third dive, leaving a hatch open which caused the after section to flood with the immediate loss of part of her crew. Despite much effort it proved impossible for the survivors to bring the submarine to the surface. A desperate plan was then embarked upon whereby two officers would enter the conning-tower, which would then be partly flooded. Air was then pumped in to keep further water out and the hatch opened. Unfortunately Commander Goodheart was killed when his head struck the superstructure, but his companion, Commander Godfrey Herbert, who had originally intended to remain below after closing the hatch, was forced to the surface by the air pressure. The information he brought with him enabled a rescue operation to proceed, the bows of the submarine being raised to the surface so that a hole could be cut for the survivors. Six shipyard workers and 26 naval personnel died in this disaster.

Great Cumbrae, Buteshire
63/182593

A monument on the shore records the drowning of two young naval officers in 1844 while engaged upon the original Admiralty survey of the area.

Greenock, Renfrewshire
63/279763

A plaque on 57 The Esplanade tells that Lieutenant 'Birdie' Bowers was born here in 1883. (See *Rothesay*.) A Sailors' Gallery in the West Church includes a model frigate.

Helensburgh, Dumbartonshire
56/285833

In the Hermitage Park are set up the flywheel of the *Comet*, Europe's first steam-driven craft, and the anvil used by its inventor, Henry Bell, while a tall obelisk to Bell stands in the town centre. (See *Neilston*; *Port Glasgow*; *Rhu*.)

Hownam, Roxburghshire
80/777193

A sailor remembered here is John Douglas, who died on board HMS *London* off Sebastopol on 10 June 1855. Admiral of the Fleet Sir Henry Oliver, who died aged 101 in 1965, is also commemorated here. His obituary in *The Times* described him as a 'man of few words and great achievements'.

Inverary, Argyll
56/078061

A plaque in a caravan park reminds visitors that this was HMS *Quebec*, the original training camp for Combined Operations. Nearby at Cherry Park, in the grounds of Inverary Castle, is the Combined Operations Museum, with a history of commando assaults from the sea on the Lofoten Islands, in north-west Europe, and in the Far East.

Inverbervie, Kincardineshire
45/833727

Near the bridge on the north side of the town is a memorial to Hercules Linton (1836–1900), designer of the *Cutty Sark* (a 'cutty sark' being a scanty nightie), launched at Dumbarton in 1869 and now preserved at Greenwich. Shaped like the figurehead, the memorial was unveiled by Sir Francis Chichester in 1969.

Invergordon, Ross & Cromarty
21/711684

Formerly an important naval base. A plaque not far from the lifeboat station is in memory of those lost when the cruiser HMS *Natal* exploded shortly after a fire broke out on 30 December 1915, killing some 405 sailors and guests on board for a reception. (See *Wales – Pembroke*.) Near to the yacht club is a memorial to the naval mutiny here of 1931, when seamen refused to take the Atlantic Fleet to sea. Among the plaques in St Ninian's Church is one to the officers and men of HMS *Shark*, which gallantly attacked German light cruisers in the early evening of the Battle of Jutland and was sunk with the loss of all but six of her crew, including her captain, Commander Loftus Jones, who was posthumously awarded the Victoria Cross. The lectern and communion rails are in memory of Sub-Lieutenant Patrick Vance, another of those lost.

Shipwreck memorials at Irvine. (John Hall)

Irvine, Ayrshire
70/323387

White obelisks in the churchyard commemorate two tragedies. One, dating to 1860, is the grave of 'seven sailors who lie together here drowned and washed ashore from the schooner *Success* of Nantes'. The other is to Joseph McPhail senior, aged 45, and Joseph McPhail junior, aged 13, together with five companions, 'drowned by the upsetting of a small boat near Irvine Bar' in 1876.

Kelso, Roxburghshire
74/729337

Remembered on gravestones in the grounds of the Abbey are George Paul, a master mariner who died at 'Kurrachee, East India', in 1869, and Robert Purves, one of the three surgeons on board HMS *Captain* when she

foundered in September 1870. (See *England – Anwick.*)

Kilmory, Argyllshire
62/703753

A splendid fifteenth century carved stone which includes a picture of a galley can be seen in this remote Knapdale church.

Kilmory, Arran
69/963218

Five men from the schooner *Bessie Arnold* are buried here. Sailing from Millom to Glasgow in December 1908, their vessel came ashore during a storm, with just the mate, Thomas Byrne, managing to swim ashore. Despite heroic efforts by the Campbeltown lifeboat it proved impossible to rescue the rest of the crew. For many years the schooner's figurehead stood above the grave, but to prevent deterioration this was later moved into the church, and subsequently to the Heritage Museum at Brodick.

Kinghorn, Fife
66/272870

The model warship known as HMS *Unicorn* has been in the church for over 350 years, reputedly having been made by prisoners on Inch Holm in the nearby Forth.

Kircudbright, Kircudbrightshire
84/680507

The ancient tollbooth is now a memorial to John Paul Jones, who was once imprisoned here. (See *Kirkbean.*)

Kirkbean, Kircudbrightshire
84/979592

The font was presented by the United States Navy in memory of John Paul Jones, born in a nearby gardener's cottage on the Arbigland Estate. He became an American citizen and during the War of Independence cruised in the *Ranger*. Later, while commanding the *Bon Homme Richard*, he fought the British frigate *Serapis* off Flamborough Head.

Kirkcaldy, Fife
59/283915

A plaque on the sea-wall tells how this was constructed in 1922–3, to relieve unemployment.

Kirkwall, Orkney
6/450110

In St Magnus' Cathedral is a memorial plaque

to those from the battleship HMS *Royal Oak* who died, not in action on the high seas, but while moored in the great anchorage of Scapa Flow. Here, on the night of 14 October 1939, the German submarine *U-47* slipped through the narrow passage of Kirk Sound and fired a salvo of torpedoes, sinking the *Royal Oak* with the loss of 810 officers and men. To prevent further such incursions blockships were sunk at the four Sounds on the eastern side of Scapa Flow, upon which roadways – today known as the Churchill Causeways – were subsequently built.

Also in the Cathedral is a fine reclining figure memorial to John Rae, born at Stromness in 1813, who became a doctor to the Hudson Bay Company. Following two expeditions of his own in Arctic Canada, he participated in two of the searches for Franklin, on the second of which he discovered the first clues to the fate of this expedition. (See *England – Spilsby*.)

Kylesku, Sutherland
15/223337

A stone cairn memorial to the memory of the men of the 12th Submarine Flotilla – the midget submarines, or 'X-craft' – 39 of whom died during the war. Much training was carried out here, including that for the attack on the *Tirpitz*, which, lying in Altenfjord, was attacked by three midget submarines in September 1943. Two others were assigned to the *Scharnhorst*, and one to the *Lutzow*.

Alas, two vanished on passage while a third developed defects and abandoned her attack on the *Scharnhorst* which unbeknown had left her berth shortly before. Of the others, one was lost on the final approach to the *Tirpitz*, while the remaining two successfully laid charges which crippled the great battleship. Their two crews were decorated for gallantry, with their commanders Donald Cameron and Godfrey Place receiving the Victoria Cross.

Largs, Ayrshire
63/207577

The obelisk, locally known as 'The Pencil', recalls the battle here in 1263 when Norwegian forces under King Hakon IV were defeated by the Scots, as a result of which Norway lost control of the Hebrides and the Isle of Man.

Leadhills, Lanarkshire
71/885147

A monument below the churchyard is to William Symington, born here in 1763, whose many inventions included one of the

The memorial fountain at Lerwick harbour commemorating whale-ship captain John Gravill. (Shetlands Museum Service)

first steamboats ever built, the *Charlotte Dundas*, launched at Grangemouth in 1802.

Lendalfoot, Ayrshire
76/133903

Between the road and the sea, with Ailsa Craig in the distance, is a memorial to Archibald Hamilton and his crew, natives of Arran, who were drowned here in September 1711. The inscription requests passers-by to 'Disturb ye not this small respect, Thats paid to sailors clay.'

Lerwick, Shetland
4/477414

Close to the harbour is a fountain in memory of the providential return of the whaler *Diana* in 1867. (See *England – Hull*.)

Loch nan Uamh, Inverness-shire

40/720844

'Bonnie Prince Charlie' landed on the north shore on 5 August 1745, returning the next year as a fugitive following the Battle of Culloden. From here he was eventually taken into exile on board the French frigate *L'Heureux* on 20 September 1746, a cairn marking the spot of his final departure.

Lochranza, Arran

69/918508

Close to the shore west of the village is a low cairn with a plaque, which records that John McLean, who died in August 1854, lies here. He had died from cholera on board ship, but was not allowed to be buried at the cemetery for fear of the disease.

Lochwinnoch, Renfrewshire

63/353586

A memorial plaque in the church lists all the casualties from the 1st Maritime Royal Artillery Regiment who lost their lives between 1940 and 1945. The regiment was formed in 1940 to man guns on merchant ships plying Great Britain's coastal waters. A year later it had over 9,000 soldiers serving at sea in every theatre, and by November 1942, when the title Maritime Royal Artillery was adopted, this number had risen to nearly 14,000, of which over 1,300 gave their lives. (See *England – North Shields*, *Shoeburyness*, *Southport*, and *Thornbury*.)

Longhope, Orkney

7/333894

The figure of a lifeboatman stands on a cairn in the cemetery, overlooking Kirk Sound and the Pentland Firth, where the Longhope lifeboat *TGB* was overwhelmed on the night of 17 March 1969 going to the aid of the tanker *Irene* in difficulties off Halcro Head. Coxswain Kirkpatrick and his crew of seven were lost in mountainous seas in Brough Sound. (See *England – Portsmouth*; *Anstruther*.)

Lower Largo, Fife

59/420026

Alexander Selkirk, born here in 1676, ran away to sea, joined up with buccaneers, and following a quarrel while serving as William Dampier's sailing-master was put ashore at his own request on Juan Fernandez, where he lived for four years and four months. He died aged 47, when lieutenant of HMS *Weymouth*. A fine statue on a house standing on the site of his birthplace records these facts. Selkirk's adventures provided the inspiration for

Alexander Selkirk's house in Lower Largo.

Daniel Defoe's *Robinson Crusoe*. (See *England – Hull*.)

In the church lies Sir Andrew Wood, a Scottish admiral who, in his ship *Yellow Caravel*, led the Scots to victory over the English in 1489. His castle, of which only a tower remains, lies a little distance away.

Lyness, Orkney

7/303946

In the cemetery, with its graves of sailors from two wars, is a special memorial, a Celtic cross with the name *Vanguard,* for here are remembered 668 men of the battleship of that name which blew up in the nearby anchorage of Scapa Flow in July 1917. There were just two survivors. (See *England – Rochester*.)

Marwick Head, Orkney

6/226252

The tower above a clamorous seabird colony is to Lord Kitchener, who was lost on 5 June 1916 when the the cruiser HMS *Hampshire* struck a mine in heavy weather just north of the Head. The ship, which was carrying the seven man Kitchener Mission to Russia, had a crew of 655, of whom just 12 survived.

Maybole, Ayrshire
70/295110

Near Cargilston Farm is a monument to six of the Covenanters drowned while prisoners in a slave-ship off Orkney in 1679. (See *Deerness.*)

Montrose, Angus
54/720570

Among the dunes bordering an industrial estate is a remarkable memorial cross which has stood here since 1944. It marks the resting place of Bamse, a St Bernard dog, the 'largest dog of the Allied naval forces', who lived on the Norwegian ship *Hjord*, where he was a 'faithful friend to all on board.'

Morebattle, Roxburghshire
74/773250

Robert Handyside, engineer, is remembered in the village churchyard. He was lost on the SS *Carmona*, which sailed from Barrow for New York in February 1887.

Mull of Oa, Argyllshire
60/270415

In 1918 two ships were sunk within sight of Islay, both carrying American servicemen: 166 lives were lost on the *Tuscania*, torpedoed in February carrying 2,235 passengers and crew; and 431, of whom 351 were servicemen, died when the *Otranto* collided with the liner *Kashmir* in October. The lighthouse-shaped tower standing on the cliffs was presented by President Wilson 'to the memory of his fellow citizens who gave their lives for their country in nearby waters – 1918.'

Neilston, Renfrewshire
64/480573

In the churchyard is an obelisk in memory of John Robertson who manufactured engines for the steamship *Comet*. (See *Helensburgh.*)

Nigg, Aberdeenshire
38/946032

A model of a frigate in the parish church, the *Phesdo*, was made by craftsman James Welsh about 1829.

North Queensferry, Fife
65/131803

The curious six-sided lighthouse tower, built about 1810, helped guide ships to the Old Ferry Pier at night.

Oban, Argyllshire
49/857303

A lifebelt and picture on one of the nave pillars in the church commemorates the officers and men of the torpedo gunboat *Jason*, mined off Coll in April 1917. The mine, laid by *U-78*, claimed 25 lives from the crew, which had worshipped in the Cathedral. Another memorial is to Lieutenant Donal Campbell, lost when the submarine *A3* sank following a collision off the Isle of Wight in 1912. (See *England – Gosport.*)

Otterwick, Shetland
1/529854

Standing on the shore is the 'White Lady', the figurehead of the German sail training-ship *Bohus*, wrecked here in 1924. Three of those who died rest in the churchyard at Mid Yell.

Panbride, Angus
54/572357

A fine font in the church commemorates Captain William Oudney. Born in Dundee in 1846, he served in sailing ships like the *Cochin* and *Hiddekel* and died in 1923. His son and grandson both became ships' masters in turn.

Peterhead, Aberdeenshire
30/126460

Servicemen buried in unmarked graves in the churchyard are listed on a central memorial. Thirteen maritime names are given from the First World War; the names of a further two seamen are unknown, as is that of the single maritime casualty from the Second World War. Most served on requisitioned fishing vessels, but two were from the sloop HMS *Lilac*.

Pittenweem, Fife
59/549026

Buried in the churchyard is Andrew Hughes, a seaman gunner who died on HMT *Refundo* in December 1940. High on the exterior wall of the church is a plaque to members of the Henderson ship-owning family.

Port Edgar, West Lothian
65/117787

The marina and water sports area was formerly HMS *Lochinvar*. There is a fine memorial to the men and ships of the

The Algerines memorial at Port Edgar.

minesweeping service which operated from here 1939–75, erected by the Algerines Association ('Algerines' being a class of fleet minesweepers).

Port Glasgow, Renfrewshire
63/320747

The *Comet*, which was built here in 1812, is remembered outside the Municipal Hall. (See *Helensburgh*.)

Prestwick, Ayrshire
70/347258

A memorial which includes the Polish coat of arms commemorates 'the Polish sailors who lost their lives in the Battle of the Atlantic 1939–1945.'

Rhu, Dumbartonshire
56/267840

On top of a massive plinth in the churchyard sits a statue of Henry Bell, who invented the steamboat *Comet*. (See *Helensburgh*.)

Rothesay, Buteshire
63/089645

A fine plaque in St Ninian's Church is 'sacred to the memory of Henry Robertson Bowers a Lieutenant of the Royal Indian Marine who lost his life in the Scott Antarctic Expedition on the return journey from the Pole on or about 27 March 1912, aged 28 years.' Together with Edward Wilson and Apsley Cherry Garrard, Bowers had made the mid-winter journey to Cape Crozier to study the emperor penguins, and his strength and skills made him a natural choice to go south with the polar party, though it was only in the final stages that Scott asked him to become the fifth member of the team with which he would push on to the Pole. Later, snowbound in their last camp, Scott would write to Bowers' mother that her son had 'come to be one of my closest and soundest friends . . . and he has remained cheerful, hopeful, and indomitable to the end.'

A special panel on the war memorial refers to the 12th Submarine Flotilla, which trained here. (See *Kylesku*.)

St Abb's, Berwickshire
67/920673

A small plaque at the car park to the memory of George Colven BEM, harbour master 1966–86, was erected by Alsager BSAC Branch 887 'on behalf of all divers who heeded his advice and enjoyed safe diving around St Abb's.'

St Andrews, Fife
59/509166

In Holy Trinity there is a fine series of stained glass windows to the services, including individual regiments as well as the Royal Navy. Hanging in All Saints Church in memory of the novelist Sir Hugh Walpole, who died in 1954, is a model Dutch man-of-war dating from the early eighteenth century. A plaque in the Episcopal Church is to Leading Seaman William Newnham, 'who gave his life while on duty in HM Submarine *H3* in the Adriatic, 16 July 1916', which struck a mine off the Austrian naval base at Cattaro in present-day Montenegro.

St Monance, Fife
59/524017

Captain Marr RN had a model of his frigate built and presented it to the church, where it hangs under the south transept arch. Another model hanging here is that of a locally-built fishing boat, and there is a memorial to 37 men of the village lost during the storm of 1875.

Saltcoats, Ayrshire

70/245413

William Dunlop, a gunner's mate, gave the fine model of a warship to St Cuthbert's Church in 1804. It is today called the *Caledonia,* even though the first of this name was not built until 1808. There is a strong suggestion that the model was actually based on the the *San Josef,* the prize taken at St Vincent in 1797. (See *England – Pewsey.)*

Slains Castle, Aberdeenshire

30/052301

A cannon here is said to have come from the Armada ship *Santa Catherina,* wrecked close by in 1588. (See *Collieston.)*

Spean Bridge, Inverness-shire

41/208824

Standing prominently at the road junction is a dramatic memorial to the commandos who trained on the mountains and around the lochs here during the Second World War.

Stonehaven, Kincardineshire

45/885874

A memorial records the names of the four crew of the lifeboat *St George* who were drowned at the entrance to Aberdeen harbour after attempting to render assistance to the *Grace Darling* of Blyth in February 1874.

Stornoway, Outer Hebrides

8/445305

The memorial standing close to the cliff-edge is a reminder of a terrible shipping tragedy. The yacht *Amalthea,* having been requisitioned by the Admiralty and renamed *Iolaire,* was being used to transfer 261 naval personnel on leave from the Kyle of Lochalsh to Stornoway on New Year's Eve 1918. Shortly before 2 am the following morning she ran onto the Beasts of Holm at the entrance to Stornoway Harbour. Some of those aboard managed to reach the shore and one, Seaman John MacLeod, took a heaving line with him, by means of which a hawser was pulled across. However, only 79 lives were saved, the heavy seas swiftly claiming the *Iolaire* and the rest of those on board, 'the blackest day in the history of the island for on it 200 of our bravest and best perished on the very threshold of their homes'. In St Peter's Church is a painting in memory of one of those lost, John MacAskill RNVR.

Stranraer, Wigtownshire

82/054615

On the shore of Loch Ryan is a cairn of boul-

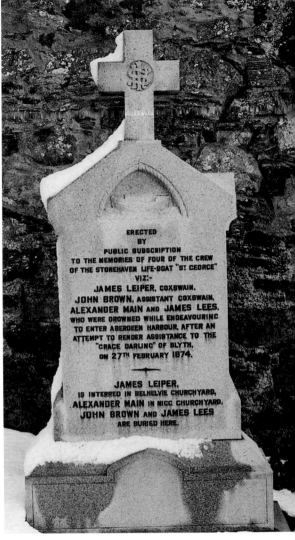

A lifeboat memorial in Stonehaven church-yard.

ders topped with an anchor, a memorial to the 133 lives lost, 23 of whom were from Stranraer, when the ferry *Princess Victoria* sank in a gale on 31 January 1953 while crossing to Larne. (See *N. Ireland – Larne.)*

Close to the harbour is the North West Castle Hotel, built in the shape of a ship, once the home of Sir John Ross, the Arctic explorer who was born nearby in 1777. He served with distinction in the Napoleonic Wars, and in 1812 led an expedition to the White Sea and the Arctic. In 1818 and again in 1823 he searched for the North-West Passage, the latter expedition being financed by Sir Felix Booth of gin fame, whose name

The Princess Victoria *memorial at Stranraer.* (Mac MacKay)

is commemorated by the Boothia Peninsula in Arctic Canada. Later he also took part in one of the Franklin search expeditions.

Stromness, Orkney
7/252084

A plaque at Login's Well says it was used by Hudson's Bay Company ships as a source of fresh water between 1670 and 1891. There is much else here concerning the Company, including houses and offices formerly used by its employees. A house near the northern edge of the town is sometimes referred to as the 'Lieutenant's House' because it was built by Lieutenant James Robertson, who had commanded the gunboat *Beresford* at the Battle of Plattsburg in 1812. Not far away another lieutenant, James Millar, is remembered by 'The Millar's House', his most famous encounter being an action against the French in the Bay of Naples on 26 June 1809 while commanding the *Cyane*, part of a force which captured or destroyed 22 Neapolitan gunboats.

Taynuilt, Argyllshire
50/005311

Just north of the church stands the first monument to be erected to Nelson after his death. Even before his body had been brought back to England, a granite pillar weighing

about four tons, was dragged for over a mile to its present situation, where it stands some 12 ft high with the inscription: 'To the memory of Lord Nelson this stone was erected by the Lorn Furnace workmen 1805.' (See *England – Burnham Thorpe*.)

Tongue, Sutherland
10/573592

During a storm in the early hours of 8 January 1945 the tramp steamer *Ashbury* foundered at the entrance to the Kyle of Tongue. Despite great efforts by the Canadian frigate *Ste Therese* to effect a rescue, all 42 of her crew were lost. Of these 14 were subsequently buried at Thurso, and two, Third Engineer J.T. Addicott and a Maltese seaman, here at Tongue. The tragedy highlights one of the great injustices to our merchant seamen and their dependents. Although on war service, and part of a convoy travelling from Loch Ewe to the Tyne, the next of kin were unable to claim a war pension as they had not died as the result of enemy action. Many years later the tragedy brought together Peter Barber and George Monk, who were independently carrying out research on the vessel. The outcome was the compilation of a memorial register of all 1,400 or so radio operators lost at sea during the Second World War.

Vatersay, Outer Hebrides

31/630952

An obelisk on the dunes is in memory of the *Annie Jane*, wrecked with the loss of 348 lives in September 1853. Most were emigrants for Canada who had orginally sailed from Liverpool a month previously. Rough weather caused the *Annie Jane* to put back to port for repairs, though when the voyage recommenced further damage was received before she ran aground during the night and was quickly overwhelmed. Most of the 102 saved came ashore on wreckage.

West Wemyss, Fife

59/320947

In a private burial ground lie members of the Wemys family, including Admiral of the Fleet Roslyn Wemyss, who died in 1933. 'In dear Rosy,' wrote King George V, 'I have lost one of my best and oldest friends of 56 years standing'. He had entered the Royal Navy in 1877, with his most distinguished services being at Gallipoli in 1915 and then on the East Indies and Egyptian stations. He became First Sea Lord in 1917.

Whalsay, Shetland

2/536624

The Pier House has been restored and renamed the Hanseatic Booth as a tribute to the links between the islands and the Hansa merchants who traded here in the seventeenth and eighteenth centuries, bartering fishing tackle, tobacco and illicit gin for salt fish and knitwear.

Wick, Caithness

12/376510

The memorial tower on the north side of Wick Bay, unveiled in 1908, commemorates 'the Patriotism of those natives of Caithness who served their Country on Land and Sea.' It contains a casket with their names. On the South Head stands the Bremner Memorial, James Bremner being a naval architect and harbour builder who died in 1856. A plaque reports that 'Wick Harbour is sheltered by one of 18 yet efficient breakwaters constructed on these northern coasts by his skill. He saved scores of wrecked mariners' lives at the risk of his own. He refloated 236 stranded or sunken vessels, including the largest ship of his day, the *Great Britain*.'

Wigtown, Wigtownshire

83/437556

An unusual memorial is found on the shore, where the Wigtown Martyrs – Margaret McLauchlan and Margaret Wilson – are said to have been tied to stakes and drowned for their Covenanter beliefs in 1685. They are also remembered in the churchyard.

Windwick, Orkney

7/459868

A roadside memorial overlooking the bay on South Ronaldsay recalls the 188 men lost when the destroyers *Narborough* and *Opal* ran aground on the nearby Hesta Rocks during appalling weather on 12 January 1918. (See *England – New Brighton*.)

Wales

Aberaeron, Cardiganshire
146/456627

Commander Oswald Harcourt Davies, who died on board HMS *Triumph* and was buried off the coast of Portugal on 1 January 1911, is remembered in the church.

Aberdaron, Caernarvonshire
123/173263

A stone in the cemetery recalls that John Jones, aged just 13, was 'unfortunately drowned in the melancholy shipwreck of the *Monk Steamer* on the Carnarvon Bar' on 7 January 1845. (See *Llanfairpwllgwygyll*.) Nearby lies an unknown sailor from the armed boarding steamer *Stephen Furness*, torpedoed in December 1917 with the loss of 101 officers and men.

Aberdyfi, Merionethshire
135/615960

Surprisingly for such a maritime area, the war memorial just below the church has but a single naval name from the First World War – Lieutenant John Phillips RNR – and two from the Second World War – commando Max Laddie and cadet Vincent Parry MN.

Abergele, Denbighshire
116/946779

The emigrant ship *Ocean Monarch* sailed for Liverpool in August 1848 with 42 crew and 396 passengers, one of whom was discovered lighting a fire in a ventilator while the ship was off the Great Orme. Heroic efforts were made to control what quickly became a major conflagration, and despite rescue efforts by ships in the vicinity 178 lives were lost, either in the fire or after falling into the sea when the masts collapsed. Nine were buried here at St Michael's Church.

Aberporth, Cardiganshire
145/256511

A brass in the church to Commander Thomas Jenkins, HEIC Maritime Service, who died in 1853, records that he 'was a man of action, daring and resolution who was repeatedly commended and rewarded for distinguished conduct in action on land and sea.'

Aberystwyth, Cardiganshire
135/581816

Tucked away in the main church is a tiny plate 'in happy memory of John Purton Morgan 3rd Officer SS *Watarah* lost at sea July 1909.' The fate of this liner, which vanished without trace while travelling between Durban and Cape Town, is one of the mysteries of the sea. Despite extensive searches no trace of the vessel or the 219 souls on board was ever found.

The adjacent churchyard contains a number of headstones of maritime interest, though probably none more so than that standing against the wall of a tower at the southern boundary, this being to David Lewis 'alias the old Commodore', who died in 1850. He had served on board the *Conqueror* at Trafalgar.

Amllwch, Anglesey
114/442929

A plaque records that the electric lighting in the church was installed in memory of a commando, Captain Edwin Williamson, killed on the Normandy beaches on D-Day. Another plaque commemorates Charles Paynter, lost on the *Lusitania*, 7 May 1915. (See *England – Barnston*.) Among the gravestones arranged around the churchyard walls is one to members of the Jones family: Thomas, a ship's carpenter at Liverpool, and his nephews Thomas, master of the barque *Zillah*, who died in Tahiti in 1866, and Thomas Lewis of the *John Bunyan*, drowned off the Bell Buoy the following year.

Amroth, Pembrokeshire

158/164078

An early U-boat attack is recalled on a tombstone to Francis Baldwin, one of 103 who lost their lives when the steamship *Falaba* was torpedoed west of The Smalls by *U-28*. When first observed the U-boat was flying a White Ensign, and it eventually managed to sink the *Falaba* before her lifeboats could be lowered.

Angle, Pembrokeshire

157/866028

Hidden behind the church is a tiny Seamen's Chapel which was originally used as a mortuary for bodies washed up on local beaches.

Bangor, Caernarvonshire

115/581721

Among those buried here are John Parry and his wife, who were among the 127 lost when the 75-ton wooden paddle-steamer *Rothesay Castle* foundered on the Dutchman's Bank at the eastern entrance to the Menai Straits during heavy weather, August 1831.

Barry, Glamorgan

171/115677

Plans are well advanced for a long-overdue memorial to the merchant seamen who sailed from here, to be situated opposite the Post Office. Meanwhile a local resident, Fred Hortop, has prepared his own tribute, in the form of detailed rolls of honour. These unique memorial books to the merchant seamen of Barry lost in two world wars, include his brother, Robert, a carpenter on the *Baron Dechmont* when she was torpedoed by *U-507* off Brazil in January 1943. A fine model of the ship is held by the Town Council as an example of the merchantmen which sailed from this port during both world wars.

A plaque in the wheel-house of the Arran Class lifeboat stationed at Barry Dock refers to the radio carried in the inflatable rescue craft being in memory of Susan Penfold, who had sailed from here during her time at University in Cardiff. (See *Lawrenny*.)

Borth, Cardiganshire

135/602886

Included in the list of First World War names on the cliff-top war memorial are three who 'lost their lives salvaging in Borth Bay.'

Bosherston, Pembrokeshire

158/966948

A tiny stained-glass window in the church, depicting St Nicholas, is in memory of George Evans, petty officer on HMS *Tipperary*, sunk at Jutland. It was erected by his widow, the village schoolmistress. (See *England – Clayton West*.) Nearby is a plaque in memory of Richard Howells, 'killed in the execution of his duties as a Coastguard by a mine on Broad Haven beach', January 1943.

Brecon, Breconshire

160/045285

Douglas Goodger, formerly a chorister at the parish church, is remembered by a wooden plaque which tells of his loss while serving as a petty officer on HMS *Faulkener* in January 1943.

Breidden Hill, Montgomeryshire

126/295144

Rodney's Pillar, erected in honour of the admiral 'by subscription of the Gentlemen of Montgomeryshire 1781', is a superb landmark for miles around. (See *England – Old Arlesford*.)

Caernarvon, Caernarvonshire

115/481632

In the Garrison church is a plaque to Llewellyn Turner, who was commodore of the Royal Welsh Yacht Club in 1873. He died in 1903 and is remembered for bringing the water supply to the town.

Cardiff, Glamorgan

171/183761

This was Captain Scott's last port of call on the *Terra Nova* before his voyage south in 1910. His farewell banquet at the Royal Hotel on 13 June is still celebrated in style by the Captain Scott Society, which has regular meetings in the Terra Nova Room, and an exhibition case contains many mementoes of the expedition. In Roath Park there is another unique memorial to the expedition, in the shape of a lighthouse standing in the lake. A further link with the *Terra Nova* was the gift of beds to the Royal Hamadryad Hospital in memory of two of her crew – Lieutenant Commander Rennick, lost on HMS *Hogue*, and Commander Pennell, lost on HMS *Queen Mary*.

Paid for by public subscription is a gravestone in the Cathays Cemetery, now rather worn, which includes a carving of HMS *Iphigenia*, one of the blockships used at Zeebrugge during the famous raid on St George's Day 1918. Here lies Stoker John Cleal, who died of wounds received there. (See *England – Dover*.)

Cardigan, Cardiganshire
145/181460

The churchyard is rich in maritime inscriptions, including one to Midshipman Ronland Ronlands, aged 20, who died of yellow fever on board the *Swiftsure* in the West Indies in 1796. Another commemorates both Thomas Jones, aged 19, who in 1850 'perished with all the crew at sea in the schooner *Pomona* of Cardigan on the coast of Scotland', and his 16-year-old brother, 'who shared the same fate' on the brig *Hope* in 1856. Many shipwrights, sailmakers, and other craftsmen can also be found buried here.

Carregwasted Point, Pembrokeshire
157/927405

A lichen-covered stone marks the spot where the last invasion of Great Britain took place, when some 1,400 French soldiers and convicts were landed in 1797. (See *Fishguard*.)

Castlemartin, Pembrokeshire
158/910988

A row of headstones marks the graves of five of the seven crew-members lost when the *Ionian* ran aground near Linney Head after being torpedoed. In the church a small plaque erected by parishioners and friends remembers Stoker P.O. Thomas Morris 'who gave his life whilst serving on HMS *Charybdis* 23 October 1943.' (See *Llandyssul*.)

Chepstow, Monmouthshire
162/533938

Although there is no direct connection, the gun taken from a captured German U-boat makes a fine memorial to Seaman William Williams, whose Victoria Cross was awarded for his gallantry at the landings from the *River Clyde*, at V Beach, Gallipoli, on 25 April 1915. There is a small memorial display, which includes a painting of the landings, in St Mary's Church, where the bell of HMS *Chepstow*, a minesweeper in 1914–18, and the crest of HMS *Warwick*, adopted by the town in 1942, can also be seen.

Church Bay, Anglesey
114/306896

A particularly poignant inscription concerns David Lloyd Master and his crew, of the schooner *Osprey*, who were lost in April 1853 'by endeavouring to land in their boat near Porthwan after having been run down by the schooner *Ann & Mary* of Newquay the night previous off Holyhead Harbour leaving a Widow and two Children to mourn his sudden departure. If the Captain of *Ann & Mary* had the humanity to lie by the poor Sufferers for a short time it is thought their lives would be saved.'

Cilgerran, Pembrokeshire
145/191431

Members of the Gower family, including Admiral Sir Erasmus, who died June 1914 (see *England – Hambledon*), are remembered in the church. Just inside the entrance is a detailed memorial to Griffith Griffith, surgeon on HMS *Confiance*, which foundered off Ireland in April 1822. His previous service included the ships *Franchise*, *York*, *Serapis*, and *Shearwater*

The U-boat gun to be seen in Chepstow constitutes a memorial to Seaman Williams VC.

which had helped guard St Helena during Napoleon's exile.

Cowbridge, Glamorgan
170/994746

A plaque in the church commemorates Alick Stockwood, aged 20, who fell from the rigging of the *Penrhyn Castle* in a gale off Cape Horn in 1899.

Criggion, Montgomeryshire
126/296152

George Phillips of the Hood Battalion, Royal Naval Division, is listed on the war memorial inside the church. He died while a prisoner of war in Germany, a week after the Armistice of 1918.

Dolgellau, Merionethshire
124/728179

The war memorial in the church includes Meredith Williams, who was on board the Anchor Line's *Cameronia* when she was torpedoed about 150 miles east of Malta on 15 April 1917 while carrying 2,630 troops to Egypt. Fortunately the sea was calm and only 128 troops and 11 crew were lost.

Dulas, Anglesey
114/477894

A solitary stone marks the resting place of 'Six men and a Youth names unknown who were cast ashore from the wreck of the *Royal Charter* Oct 26th 1859'. (See *Llanallgo*; *Moelfre*.)

Fishguard, Pembrokeshire
157/958370

Outside St Mary's Church is the grave of the town's most famous citizen, Jemima Nicholas, 'the Welsh Heroine who boldly marched to meet the French invaders who landed on our shores in February 1797.' She died in 1832, aged 82. Close by, a sign above the door of the Royal Oak public house records that the 'last invasion of Britain peace treaty was signed here.' (See *Carregwasted Point*.)

A plaque in the church provides details of the eventful career of Thomas Roblyn, who 'had served under Lords St Vincent, Keith, Nelson, Sir Sydney Smith and other Admirals during an eventful period.' He died in 1855, aged 75, at Cairo Lodge, Weston-super-Mare. In the Customs Hall at the ferry terminal is a memorial to those who gave their lives on the *St Andrew*, the *St David*, which was sunk at Anzio, and the *St Patrick*, bombed and sunk in 1941 in St George's Channel.

Granston, Pembrokeshire
157/896342

An unknown man washed ashore in 1916 on a nearby beach is buried in this remote churchyard.

Haverfordwest, Pembrokeshire
157/951155

A small stained-glass window in the porch of St Mary's asks you to 'of your charity pray for the good estate of Harold Rhys Jenkins, Midshipman HMS *India* now an interned prisoner in Norway.' The auxiliary cruiser *India* had been torpedoed off Bodo with the loss of 160 crew in August 1915.

A link with Nelson is provided in Hill Street, where two houses are known as Trafalgar House and The Lord Nelson, the former once being a public house owned by John Owen, a sailor wounded at Trafalgar.

Not far away is Cromie Avenue, commemorating submarine commander Francis Cromie, who had attended the local grammar school. In 1903 he was one of the first to volunteer for service in submarines and by 1914 was in command of three C-class vessels on the China Station. In *E-19* he forced his way into the Baltic, where he was described as a leader in the John Buchan style with carefully groomed side whiskers and always wearing a spotless white scarf. Among his successes was the sinking of the light cruiser *Undine* in November 1916. When our submarines became trapped as a result of the Russian Revolution he became naval attaché at the British Embassy in Petrograd, where, on the afternoon of 31 August 1918, he was killed when armed men broke in. He was buried in the Smolensky cemetery. In addition to the avenue, Barn Street School boasts Cromie House, and there is a plaque in Tasker Milward School, successor to the grammar school.

Outside Prendergast Church is the grave of Admiral John Stokes, who died in 1885. As a young man he had sailed with Darwin on the *Beagle* and was later to become noted for his surveying of the coasts of Australia and New Zealand. He lived during his reirement years at nearby Scotchwell House.

Henfynyw, Cardiganshire
146/447612

A plaque in the church records that Steward Gwilym Jones was lost when the steamship *Stanholme* was 'torpedoed between Cardiff and Barry, Christmas Day 1939.' In the churchyard there is a grave of two unknown sailors buried in January 1945, while a stone refers to Thomas Jones, master mariner, lost with all hands when the brig *Pilgrim* foundered in the Bay of Biscay in February 1874. Another belongs to Emma, wife of Captain David Jones, who was lost in the 'wreck of the Royal Mail steamer *Berlin* off the Hook of Holland', February 1907. (See *England – Epsom*.)

Holyhead, Anglesey

114/244816

Dominating the centre of the cemetery is a memorial to the submarine HMS *Thetis*, which foundered during trials in Liverpool Bay on 1 June 1939 with the loss of 99 men. (See *England – Birkenhead, Heswall*.)

Elsewhere in the cemetery there are numerous memorials of maritime interest, including one to the 33 lost on the four-masted barque *Primrose Hill*, wrecked off South Stack in December 1900. Others commemorate John Hill, scalded to death during a boiler accident on the steam lifeboat *Duke of Northumberland* while returning from the Mersey to Holyhead in 1901, and W.H. Owen, aged 64, a greaser on the ferry *Scotia*, sunk during the Dunkirk evacuation.

An obelisk with the names of five pilots records they 'were drowned through the foundering of an open boat whilst nobly endeavouring to rescue during a terrific hurricane the crew of a vessel in distress', February 1905.

In St Seriol's churchyard one stone contains a reference to a casualty from the Irish Sea ferry *Leinster*, torpedoed on the morning of 10 October 1918 with the loss of 480 lives. Another stone remembers James Warren, who in 1869 had sailed from Glasgow 'in command of the SS *Greek* and has not been heard of since.'

Memorial at Holyhead cemetery to those lost from the barque Osseo.

One assumes that Eleanor Jones, who died on the Skerries aged 4 and is buried in St Cybi's churchyard, was the daughter of a

The Thetis *memorial in Holyhead cemetery.*

lighthouse keeper. In the church itself is a plaque to John Skinner who lost an arm, and later an eye, while serving with HMS *Phoenix* during the American War of Independence. For 33 years he was captain of the Royal Mail packet on this station until, at the age of 72, he was washed overboard from the *Escape* as she approached the harbour on 30 October 1832. An obelisk to his memory stands on the high ground to the east of the harbour.

Hubberston, Pembrokeshire
157/891062

A number of maritime graves can be seen in a very overgrown churchyard, while inside the church is the ship's crest of the minehunter HMS *Hubberston*. A small framed White Ensign has the names of those from her crew who took part in a sponsored cycle ride to the village.

Kerry, Montgomeryshire
136/147901

A huge memorial in the church records that Richard Jones, formerly a purser in the Royal Navy, died aged 65 in 1788.

Lamphey, Pembrokeshire
158/015005

An unknown American sailor lies in the churchyard. He came from the coastguard cutter *Tampa*, sunk by *UB-91* in St George's Channel in September 1918, when all 126 on board were lost.

Lawrenny, Pembrokeshire
158/012061

A trophy sailed for by the ladies of the Yacht Club is a living memorial to one of their members, Susan Penfold, killed in an accident in Cardiff in 1982. (See *Barry*.) Her great uncle, Lieutenant-Commander Arthur Driscoll, was first officer of the *Jervis Bay* when she encountered the *Admiral Scheer* in November 1940.

Little Newcastle, Pembrokeshire
157/980289

We are reminded by a stone on the village green that one of the world's most notorious pirates hailed from here – Bartholomew Roberts, better known as Black Bart. Born in 1682, he was captured by pirates off Annamabo and decided to throw in his lot with them. He raided ports and shipping from Newfoundland to Surinam, until, in February 1722, he was intercepted off West Africa by Captain Chaloner Ogle in the 50-gun *Swallow* and killed in a short but fierce fight off Cape Lopez. (See *England – Pontelands*.)

Llanallgo, Anglesey
114/502851

A memorial pillar behind the church was erected by public subscription to commemorate 140 of those lost on the *Royal Charter* in October 1859, who lie buried here. (See *Dulas*; *Moelfre*.)

Llanarthney, Carmarthenshire
159/541192

High above the Twyi Valley is Paxton's Tower, built by Sir William Paxton in 1810 and dedicated 'to the invincible Commander Viscount Nelson in commemoration of deeds most brilliantly achieved at the mouths of the Nile, before the walls of Copenhagen and the shores of Spain'. (See *England – Burnham Thorpe*.)

Llanasa, Flintshire
116/109816

A memorial in the church, and a grave outside, are reminders of the Point of Ayre lifeboat disaster of 4 January 1857. The crew of 13, having already saved 476 lives, were lost 'while nobly endeavouring to assist the crew of a vessel wrecked in Abergele Bay. This tablet was erected by a few admirers of their gallant and devoted conduct.'

Llandegfan, Anglesey
114/564744

From 1877 until 1920 the training and reformatory ship *Clio*, for boys aged 11 to 15, was moored in the Menai Straits near Bangor Pier. Casualties from the ship are buried in the churchyard, including James Hemet, aged 11, who fell from the rigging in August 1878, and John Healey, who died two years later aged 13.

Llandysul, Cardiganshire
146/418406

It is a great pleasure to come across a war memorial like that in the church, which in addition to the names of the fallen includes their home address, unit, and place and date of death. From the First World War come R.J. Evans of HMS *Vanguard* (see *Scotland – Lyness*); Brindley Rees of HMS *Norwood*; and J. Osborne, gunner on the *Madame Renee*, sunk off Scarborough in August 1919. Remembered from the Second World War are radio operator Leonard Ball of the *Shahdaza*, sunk in July 1944; Benjamin Stewart, who died on the *Coast Wings*; and Owen Thomas and Algwth Thomas, who were among the casualties when HMS *Charybdis* was sunk in 1943. (See *Castlemartin*.)

Llanenddwyn, Merionethshire
124/583234

A gravestone includes a reference to Cyril Lanman, lost when the Elder & Fyffes ship *Aracataca* was torpedoed in the North Atlantic in November 1940.

Llanengan, Caernarvonshire
123/294270

Friends at Abersoch erected a stone in 'proud and grateful memory of the Heroes resting here', washed ashore in October 1917 after the *Greldon* was torpedoed. Just two names are given: Edward Williams, the wireless operator, aged 17, and Harold McCormick.

Llanfairpwllgwyngyll, Anglesey
114/537711

Possibly the only place where a memorial to Nelson has its feet, as it were, in salt water. Here on the shore, with the Menai Straits

Standing on the shores of the Menai Straits at Llanfairpwllgwyngyll is a fine statue of Nelson.

lapping its base at high tide, stands a fine statue some 19 ft high, on a plinth and a square base with a walkway which give it a total height of 41 ft. It was unveiled in September 1873, and in addition to being a memorial to the hero it also serves as a landmark for mariners. (See *England – Burnham Thorpe*.)

Among the graves in the nearby churchyard is one to Captain Henry Hughes of the *Monk*, wrecked on Caernarvon Bar in January 1845, 'on which occasion he perished in his noble and partially successful exertions to save the lives of the crew and passengers.' (See *Aberdaron*.)

Llanfihangel Crucorney, Monmouthshire
161/325206

Hanging at the bar of the lovely old Skirrid Inn, reputed to be the oldest in Wales, is the bell of HMS *Royal Arthur*, the training camp which was once situated close by. The timbers in the dining room came from a man-of-war broken up at Bristol.

Llangennith, Glamorgan
159/428914

The small stone in the south-east corner of the churchyard marks the resting place of AB Christopher Greenfield, lost when the collier *Glanrhyd* was overwhelmed in January 1938. The names of seven others lost from the ship, whose grave is the sea, are also recorded. (See *Port Eynon*.)

Llangian, Caernarvonshire
123/295289

An ornate wall-monument to Captain Timothy Edwards tells how after a successful command of the 74-gun *Cornwall* in the West Indies he was 'carried off by a bilious fever' in July 1780, aged 49, 'before he had received those honours from his King and Country which were destined to be the reward of his gallant and faithful services.'

Llanhowell, Pembrokeshire
157/818274

The war memorial in the tiny church has just two names from the Second World War, one of whom, Tom Lamb, was with the Fishing Fleet, while Jack Lamb was in the Royal Navy.

Llanwrtyd, Breconshire
147/865477

A plaque in the church records that John

Lloyd, who died aged 70 in 1818, 'left his native parish at the age of sixteen without friends or interest, but by good conduct and perseverance acquired both'. It adds that his career included '32 years of active naval service and 12 voyages to India in the course of which he twice suffered shipwreck and a cruel imprisonment at the hands of Tippoo, Sultan of Mysore.'

Llanyre, Radnorshire
147/044623

The church includes a plaque to Lieutenant Martin Gibson Watt DSC, who lost his life on the destroyer HMS *Kandahar* on 21 December 1941 when she attempted to effect the rescue of the cruiser *Neptune*, mined off Tripoli, and was herself so badly damaged by another mine that she had to be sunk the following day.

Ludchurch, Pembrokeshire
158/141109

John Henry Martin, buried here in 1823, aged 70, was one of the last surviving officers to have sailed with Captain Cook on his third voyage round the world. At the Battle of Copenhagen he had commanded the bomb vessel HMS *Explosion*.

Manorbier, Pembrokeshire
158/065976

The collier *Satrap* foundered offshore on New Year's Eve 1915, without survivors. A plaque in the church is erected 'in affection-ate memory of the brave men who died while serving their Country and in recognition of the Christian treatment accorded to the departed, their relatives and the owners by the Vicar and Parishioners.'

Margam, Glamorgan
170/001003

A plaque records William Llewellyn, who 'was eminent as a surgeon in the Royal Navy for twenty years during the war' and who died in April 1840.

Merthyr Tydfil, Glamorgan
160/049058

At St Tydfil's Church there is a unique garden of remembrance which includes several plaques to the Royal Navy, including the Coastal Forces – the motor torpedo boats, motor gun boats, and motor launches, which played such a major part in coastal actions in all theatres of the Second World War. (See *England – Flushing*.)

Hanging in St David's Church is the White Ensign flown by HMS *Glamorgan* during the Falklands conflict, together with a framed history of the ship and a list of the 14 men killed when she was hit by an Exocet missile. (See *England – Egerton*.)

Milford Haven, Pembrokeshire
157/906056

On the Rath overlooking the waterway is the Fishermen's Memorial with the words: 'Thanks to them Milford Haven flourished.'

The Garden of Remembrance at Merthyr Tydfil. (Duncan Hill)

Alas, little else other than memories is left now to the days when the whole town revolved around the fishing industry, save for the names on the war memorial, graves in the cemetery, and several plaques in the Town Hall to those lost on the *Milford Viscount* (1950), *Richard Crofts* (1953), *Robert Limbrick* (1957), and the *Boston Heron* (1962). A plaque here also recalls the town's links with its adopted warship, HMS *Ardent*, sunk in the Falklands in 1982.

Also on the Rath stands a memorial to the Fast Minelayers Association, unveiled during the Victory in Europe celebrations of May 1995. Nearby is a monument 'erected by the Steam Trawler Owners and people of Ostend who were resident in this town during the Great War' in gratitude for the hospitality received during their exile from Belgium.'

Look for a fine oak seat on the quayside, inscribed with the words: 'In memory of Les Jones from his friends.' He was one of the great characters of the town, and the historian of its fishing fleet, though, alas, his work remained incomplete at his death in January 1993.

On a large boulder at the eastern edge of the cemetery is a plaque commemorating the tragedy of 25/26 April 1943, when Landing Craft Gun (Large) Numbers 15 and 16 were swamped in heavy seas at the entrance to Milford Haven, with the loss of 73 officers and men. Also listed are the six ratings from the sloop HMS *Rosemary* who gave their lives in a rescue attempt.

Moelfre, Anglesey
114/508871

Often known as the 'Golden Wreck', on account of the bullion she carried, the loss of the *Royal Charter* on 26 October 1859, during the final part of her passage home to Liverpool from Melbourne, was one which struck the heart of the nation. While off the eastern side of Anglesey and within just a few hours of safety she was overwhelmed in hurricane-force winds and wrecked just below where the memorial stands. The seas were tremendous, and despite the close proximity to the shore only 39 managed to reach it, and 459 lives were lost. (See *England – Liverpool*; *Dulas*; *Llanagllo*.)

Monmouth, Monmouthshire
162/528125

High on the Kymin, above the town which boasts a Nelson Museum, stands the Naval Temple, crowned with Britannia. This was built in 1801 to commemorate Nelson's victory at the Battle of the Nile in 1798. The names of naval heroes and the dates of their victories are recorded on plaques – Boscawen, Bridport, Cornwallis, Duncan, Gell, Hawke, Hood, Howe, Keith, Mitchell, Nelson, Parker, Rodney, St Vincent, Thompson, and Warren. The 'gentlemen and other inhabitants' had subscribed towards its construction, and Nelson himself paid a visit in August 1802, saying 'it was not only one of the most beautiful places he had ever seen, but, to the boast of Monmouth, the Temple was the only monument of the kind erected to the English Navy in the whole range of the Kingdom.' (See *England – Burnham Thorpe*.)

Montgomery, Montgomeryshire
137/224965

A memorial in the church recounts the details of the career of Rear-Admiral Charles

The Royal Charter *memorial, above the spot where the ship ran ashore near Moelfre.*

Thomas, who died aged 73 in 1853. He had served at Toulon, at the Glorious First of June, and later on the North American and West Indies Stations.

Mumbles, Glamorgan
159/616880

There have been three disasters involving lifeboats from the Mumbles Head station. In the first, in 1883, four crew were lost during the rescue of men from a German barque, and are remembered by a plaque and window in All Saints Church. Twenty years later six lifeboatmen were lost at the entrance to Port Talbot and are buried in the Oystermouth cemetery. Then in April 1947 all eight crew were lost on Sker Point during a gallant attempt to reach the *Santampa*. (See *Porthcawl*.)

Nefyn, Caernarvonshire
123/309406

The church, now a maritime museum, boasts a very fine weather vane in the shape of a schooner, some six feet in length.

Ships' masters remembered in Nefyn church-yard.

Newport, Monmouthshire
171/313882

Close to the Usk is a memorial to Commander J. 'Tubby' Linton VC, DSO, DSC, born just over a mile away, who while in command of the submarine *Turbulent*, sank 'one cruiser, one destroyer, one U-boat, twenty eight supply ships, some 100,000 tons in all, and destroyed three trains by gunfire.' He was lost with all his crew off Sardinia in March 1943. His eldest son died when the submarine *Affray* sank in the English Channel in 1951. In Cardiff Road the Merchant Navy Monument includes a bronze figure holding a sextant while surveying the horizon.

Newport, Pembrokeshire
145/058389

Among over 129 maritime graves in the churchyard are those of the children of Thomas Volk, master mariner – John, aged 16, lost with the brig *Hope* on a voyage from Llanelli to Limerick in 1856, and David, a channel pilot, lost off the Scilly Isles in 1874.

Newquay, Cardiganshire
145/385598

A grave just inside the church gate has an interesting inscription referring to an unknown sailor, to which has been subsequently added: 'It is now known that in this grave is buried Boatswain F. Stephens SS *Memphian* 8 October 1917.' She had been torpedoed north of the Arklow Lightship with 32 casualties. Another grave is that of David Jones, chief officer of the SS *Anking,* who was killed by pirates in the Gulf of Tonkin in 1928.

Newton, Glamorgan
170/836775

In February 1839 the brig *Charles*, bound for Gloucester from New Brunswick with a cargo of timber, was wrecked on the Scarweather Sands. Two boats put out and rescued the crew, then decided to return for salvage. When the weather deteriorated one reached safety, but the other, a coastguard boat, sank with the loss of six, including a father and two sons, all of whom are remembered in the churchyard.

Old Walls, Glamorgan
159/489918

A plaque records that George Tucker 'died a hero's death standing by his gun until the last' when his ship was sunk by enemy action off the south coast of Ireland, 12 May 1918.

Nearby, a plaque to those who gave their lives in the Second World War lists three names, two of whom died at sea: Hugh Jones, serving as a flight mechanic in the RAF on board HMS *Courageous* when she was torpedoed on 17 September 1939 with the loss of 515 lives; and Griffith Gwyn, lost when HMS *Venetia* was mined in the Thames estuary in October 1940.

Pembrey, Carmarthenshire
159/428012

The most famous memorial stone here is that to Lieutenant-Colonel Coquelin and his daughter Adeline, aged 12, lost when the *La Jeune Emma* was wrecked in November 1828 on Cefn Sidan Sands on a journey from Martinique: 'The above named Lady was Niece to Josephine, Consort of that renowned indivdual Napoleon Buonaparte.'

A large square tomb to George Bowser, who died in 1835, records that 'he was the first to discover the rare and most valuable properties of that part of Pembrey on which the harbours are situated.' Another refers to Joseph Emery, who 'died at sea from the effects of enemy submarine shell fire', 2

A memorial in Pembrey churchyard listing three shipwrecks.

January 1918. Among the shipwreck memorials is that to the brothers Rendal, the youngest aged 13, who lost their lives when the *Burry* was lost off the North Foreland in 1879.

Pembroke, Pembrokeshire
158/983015

The terrible disaster when HMS *Natal* blew up off Invergordon on 30 December 1915 is remembered here by a plaque to Richard Treweeks. (See *Scotland – Invergordon*.)

Pembroke Dock, Pembrokeshire
158/966032

Some years ago all the gravestones in the Upper Park Street cemetery were removed to the side walls and stacked, their bases concreted to prevent removal, without any serious attempt having been made to first record the inscriptions. Many would have been of naval or Royal Marine interest. Special attention was fortunately paid to the grave, originally within a railed-off enclosure, of Captain William Cumby, superintendent of the Royal Dockyard, a modern plaque now marking the site where this previously stood. (See *England – Heighington*.)

A plaque in St John's Church records that Lewis Davies was 'killed in an attack on pirates on the coast of Borneo' in 1868.

The bent propeller from a crashed Sunderland aircraft was dredged up by a Milford Haven trawler in 1986 and set up on a plinth in 1994 on the fiftieth anniversary of the Battle of the Atlantic.

Pennal, Merionethshire
135/699004

A plaque records a casualty from one of the great mysteries of the Second World War. What exactly happened when HMAS *Sydney* and the commerce raider *Komoran* sank each other off Western Australia in November 1941? Remembered here is one of the *Sydney*'s crew, Commander Edward Thruston DSC. Another Thruston died of measles at the Royal Naval College, Dartmouth in March 1926, while a naval ancestor, Charles Thruston, is remembered in an ornate wall-monument.

Pennally, Pembrokeshire
158/116992

The Cook memorial in the church includes a reference to Hugh, who is buried in St Martins-in-the-Fields. He had joined the Royal Navy in 1784 and, as first lieutenant of the *Agamemnon*, took part in Sir Robert Calder's action of July 1805, at Trafalgar in

October, and at St Domingo the following February. Later he was flag captain in the *Diomede* on the Jersey station.

Peterstone, Breconshire
160/089265

A plaque is in memory of Seabright Jones of HMS *Cassandra*, who died on 14 July 1920 'the result of exposure on active service.' The war memorial records that Lieutenant Eric Swire was lost on HMS *Queen Mary*. (See *England – Brooksby*.)

Port Dinorwic, Caernarvonshire
115/528678

Of the war memorial's 44 First World War names seven have maritime connections, as do 16 of the 19 from the Second World War, including three chief officers and a master mariner.

Port Eynon, Glamorgan
159/467854

Standing at the roadside corner of the church-yard is a figure of a lifeboatman, a tribute to Coxswain William Gibbs, Second Coxswain William Eynon, and crewman George Harry, all lost when the lifeboat *Janet* twice capsized while endeavouring to render assistance to the SS *Dunvegan* on 1 January 1916. The rest of the crew of 10 'after great suffering succeeding in landing the following morning.' Inside the church a plaque recalls the tragedy, and a communion rail is dedicated to their memory.

Elsewhere in the churchyard there are several other maritime memorials, including that to 'the memory of the eighteen mariners who perished in the wreck of the SS *Agnes Jack* of the Bacon Line on Port Eynon Point January 27th 1883 within sight of a large number of people on the shore who were powerless to render any aid'. Then follows a list of those lost which concludes: 'Oh! had there been a lifeboat there to breast the stormy main, These men might not have perished thus, Imploring help in vain.' The lifeboat station was opened the following year, but closed after the tragedy of 1916.

Porthcawl, Glamorgan
170/790795

On the night of 23 April 1947 the Mumbles lifeboat *Edward Prince of Wales* was launched to go to the aid of the 7,200-ton tanker *Samtampa*, which had encountered heavy weather on the last leg of her journey to Newport. During the attempt the lifeboat was overwhelmed and Coxswain William Gammon and his seven crew lost, as were the

Lifeboat memorial at Port Eynon.

38 on board the *Samtampa*. The lifeboat was thrown ashore on Sker Point, where in 1992 a memorial was unveiled at the very spot where she came to rest among the rocks. A memorial to the captain, officers and men of the *Samtampa* had been unveiled in the New Cemetery at Porthcawl two years after the tragedy. (See *Mumbles*.)

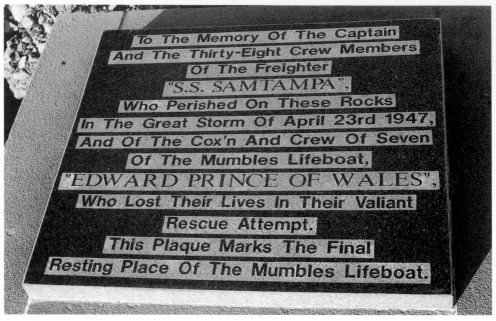

The Santampa *memorial at Sker Point, Porthcawl.*

Portmadoc, Caernarvonshire

124/565388

The open page in the memorial book when I called at St John's Church revealed the loss of Hugh Edwards, saved from the *Zent* when torpedoed in 1916, and from the *Aracataca* when she was sunk after fighting a submarine (for which action he was awarded the DSM), but drowned when chief officer of the *Reventazen* while trying to save crewmen's lives after the ship was sunk in the Gulf of Salonika in October 1918.

Pwllheli, Caernarvonshire

123/374352

A plaque records that Harry Humphreys met his death on the *Lusitania* 'when on his way home to fight for his Country.' (See *England – Barnston*.) Another lists three men drowned near Cromer Island on the coast of Denmark through the loss of the schooner *Janet* in November 1910.

Rhoscolyn, Anglesey

114/268757

In December 1920 the steamer *Timbo* was driven to anchor close offshore and the lifeboat *Ramon Cabrera* was launched to provide assistance. Later, as she sought shelter, two of the lifeboat's crew were swept overboard, and later a further three were lost when she was capsized by a breaking wave.

Some eight hours after they had set out the remaining eight crew brought the life-boat back to the shore. A memorial in the churchyard is a reminder of the sacrifice that day.

Rhoscrowther, Pembrokeshire

158/904022

A church plaque records that Midshipman Edward Skinner 'met with an untimely end near this spot in the year 1792' whilst serving on HMS *Iphigenia*.

Rhosneigr, Anglesey

114/320735

Outside the fire station a memorial records the efforts made just offshore in August 1941 to rescue the crew of an aircraft that crashed during a gale. All three crewmen were lost, as were no fewer than 11 of those who, in small boats, made valiant attempts to save them.

Rhossili, Glamorgan

159/417880

Close to the church gate is a Sailors' Corner, while inside is a plaque in memory of Edgar Evans, born just up the road at Middleton, who served in the Antarctic under Scott on both the *Discovery* and the *Terra Nova* expeditions. He was one of the five who reached the South Pole on 17 January 1912, to die a month later following a fall as they fought their way down the Beardmore Glacier on the

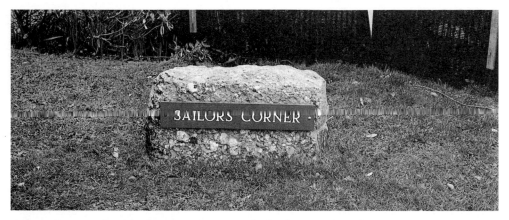

Sailors Corner, a burial place for seamen washed ashore at Rhossili.

fateful return march. (See *England – Portsmouth.*)

Rudbaxton, Pembrokeshire
157/960205

Remembered in the church is Lieutenant J. Warlow, who had served in the army of a native prince in the East Indies before he returned home 'for his health and entered the British Navy. His profession called him to the West Indies where he soon fell a sacrifice to the Yellow Fever on 28 January 1827.'

St Asaph, Flintshire
116/039743

A chorister of the Cathedral, Herbert Jones, is remembered there following his loss in the upsetting of a lifeboat off Douglas Head, Isle of Man, in October 1881.

St David's, Pembrokeshire
157/752257

The names of three lifeboatmen – John Stephens, aged 63, Henry Rowlands, aged 51, and James Price, aged 44 – lost when the lifeboat *Gem* was wrecked on The Bitches in Ramsey Sound during the rescue of the crew of the *Democrat*, are remembered on a fine memorial in the cemetery. They are also named in the Memorial Hall, as are those who survived. On a separate plaque is Ieuan Bateman, washed overboard when the lifeboat was rounding St Ann's Head to seek shelter in Milford Haven after going to the assistance of the trawler *Notre Dame de Fatima* in 1956.

St Dogmael's, Pembrokeshire
145/164456

Many mariners are remembered in the churchyard hard by the Abbey ruins. Many came safely home to port, but others, like Thomas McFadden, second officer on the *Framfield*, sunk by a mine near the Sunk Lightship in 1916, have no grave but the sea.

Skokholm Island, Pembrokeshire
157/741050

In February 1928 the barque *Alice Williams* ran aground at the entrance to South Haven. Part of her cargo of coal, and many of her timbers and items of equipment, were salvaged by the naturalist R.M. Lockley, who was setting up home on the island. Her figurehead, perhaps modelled on Alice, the wife of the first owner Henry Williams of Truro, was dragged from the sea. For many years it stood on the cliffs nearby, though recently the ravages of time have resulted in a replacement being set there.

Solva, Pembrokeshire
157/802242

A plaque on the side of the lifeboat shed records that the widow of Captain Charles Egerton gave the lifeboat in his memory. It was on station from 1869 to 1887 and a model can be seen in the National Trust shop in St David's. Close to the entrance to the lower car park are some metal stanchions from the old Smalls lighthouse, which had been replaced by oaken beams so that it would give a little in high winds.

Swansea, Glamorgan
159/639921

Swansea Jack, a large, flat-haired retriever gained huge publicity from 1931 onwards by rescuing people from drowning, mostly in the North Dock near to where he lived. It is said that 27 persons were saved and he was feted

Sea-front memorial to 'Swansea Jack'.

with honours including the canine VC, and guest appearances at Crufts and elsewhere. Alas, he died from the effects of rat poison in 1937, and was buried here in an oak coffin with much ceremony.

In St Mary's Church is an oak chair in memory of Petty Officer Edgar Evans, and the Captain Scott Society recently commissioned a fine bust of Evans for presentation to the city. St Helen's Primary School in Vincent Street, which Evans had attended, have a framed photograph of the school hero to inspire future pupils. (See *England – Portsmouth*.)

Tenby, Pembrokeshire

158/135004

Captain Bird Allen, who with many companions 'fell victims to the climate of the River Niger', died at Fernando Po in October 1841 while in command of HMS *Soudan*. The Niger expedition had been decimated by fever, both on the river and subsequently at sea.

On a wall close to the museum and ruined castle is a simple slate plaque commemorating a noteworthy local seaman, with a picture of a Tenby lugger and the words: 'Ivor Crockford 1911–1990'.

Twyn, Merionethshire

135/587008

On the war memorial plaque in the church porch occurs the name Sister Jane Roberts, lost on the hospital ship *Salta*, sunk by a mine off Le Havre in April 1917 with the loss of 86 lives.

Whitewell, Flintshire

117/495414

One of the great naval actions of the Second World War, and one of its heroes, is remembered here by a fine Welsh slate plaque with a detailed description of how Captain B.A. Warburton-Lee, while in command of the 2nd Destroyer Flotilla flying his flag in *Hardy*, sailed into Narvik fjord and sank two destroyers and nine other vessels. Unfortunately *Hardy*, also badly damaged, was run ashore, with Warburton-Lee dying of his wounds. His last signal was: 'Continue to engage the enemy.' He was posthumously awarded the Victoria Cross.

Winston Churchill's words, when recalling the action, neatly encapsulate much that has been written in this book:

'He and they left their mark on the enemy and in our naval records.'

Index of locations by county

Canford Magna
Chideock
Easton
Hamworthy
Langton Matravers
Lychett Minster
Lyme Regis
Minterne Magna
Netherbury
Osmington
Owermoigne
Pimperne
Portesham
Portland
Shaftesbury
Sherborne
South Perrot
Southwell
Studland
Swanage
Wareham
Whitchurch Canonicorum
Wool
Wyke Regis

County Durham
Durham
Hartlepool
Hebburn
Heighington
Jarrow
Norton
South Shields
Sunderland
Whitworth

Essex
Barking
Brightlingsea
Colchester
Dovercourt
Grays
Hornchurch
Mistley
St Osyth
Shoeburyness
Walton-on-the-Naze

Gloucestershire
Bristol
Cheltenham
Deerhurst
Down Ampney
Dursley
Dyrham
Fairford
Leckhampton
Painswick

Sharpness
Shirehampton
Slimbridge
Stow-on-the-Wold
Swindon
Tetbury
Tewkesbury
Thornbury
Woodchester

Greater London
Crystal Palace Park
Deptford
Dulwich
East Greenwich
Eltham
Forest Gate
Greenwich
Lower Edmonton
Manor Park
Putney Vale
Richmond
Upper Norwood

Hampshire
Alum Bay (Isle of Wight)
Basing
Beaulieu
Bishop's Sutton
Bishop's Waltham
Boldre
Bonchurch (Isle of Wight)
Bournemouth
Brading (Isle of Wight)
Bramley
Bramshaw
Brighstone (Isle of Wight)
Brook (Isle of Wight)
Burlesdon
Catherington
Culver Down (Isle of Wight)
Exbury
Fareham
Freshwater (Isle of Wight)
Gosport
Hamble
Hambledon
Highfield
Lee-on-Solent
Lymington
Marchwood
Martyr Worthy
Meonstoke
Micheldever
Newport (Isle of Wight)
North Stoneham
Old Alresford
Old Bonchurch (Isle of Wight)

Pear Tree Green
Porchester
Portsdown
Portsmouth
Romsey
Ryde (Isle of Wight)
St Helen's (Isle of Wight)
Sandown (Isle of Wight)
Shalfleet (Isle of Wight)
Southampton
South Harting
Southsea
Stubbington
Titchfield
Warblington
Warnford
Warsash
West Meon
Whippingham (Isle of Wight)
Widley
Winchester
Yarmouth (Isle of Wight)

Herefordshire
Canon Pyon
Hereford
Kington
Lyonshall
Ross on Wye
Stoke Prior
Wellington

Hertfordshire
Aldenham
Bayfordbury
Little Berkhamstead
St Albans

Kent
Addington
Bearsted
Betteshanger
Biddenden
Burntwick Island
Canterbury
Chatham
Chislehurst
Cliffs End
Deal
Dover
East Farleigh
Eastry
Ebony
Erith
Faversham
Folkestone
Gillingham
Gravesend

North Shields
Pontelands
South Charlton
Swarland
Tweedmouth
Tynemouth

Nottinghamshire
Beckingham
Bulwell
Nottingham

Oxfordshire
Aston Rowant
Bampton
Banbury
Oxford
Shipton-under-Wychwood
Waterperry

Rutland
Exton

Shropshire
Audlem
Bedstone
Dawley
Ludlow
Newport
Rushbury
Shrewsbury
Whitchurch

Somerset
Bath
Bathampton
Batheaston
Bishop's Lydeard
Bridgwater
Butleigh
Cricket St Thomas
East Coker
East Pennard
Frome
North Wootton
Somerton
Taunton
Wells
Wraxall
Yeovilton

Staffordshire
Bishop's Wood
Colwich
Endon Bank
Hanley
Lichfield
Stone

Walsall
West Bromwich
Weston under Lizard
Wolverhampton
Yoxall

Suffolk
Aldeburgh
Bury St Edmunds
Elevedon
Framlingham
Holbrook
Long Melford
Lowestoft
Nacton
Shotley
Southwold

Surrey
Bletchingley
Brookwood
Chiddingfold
Compton
Cranleigh
Crondall
East Clandon
Epsom
Farncombe
Farnham
Frimley
Godalming
Godstone
Guildford
Leatherhead
Morden
Petersham
Pirbright
Redhill
Reigate
Seale
Tatsfield
Thursley
Windlesham

Sussex
Angmering
Bosham
Brighton
Chichester
Eastbourne
Forest Row
Haslemere
Hove
Lancing
Newhaven
Parham
Playden
Racton

Rye
Rye Harbour
St Leonard's on Sea
Up Marden
Winchelsea
Worthing

Warwickshire
Arrow
Binton
Birmingham
Coventry
Kineton
Southam
Warwick

Westmorland
Grasmere
Kirkby Stephen
Martindale
Storrs

Wiltshire
Corsham
Fittleton
Highworth
Melksham
Pewsey
Salisbury

Worcestershire
Bredon
Upton on Severn
Whittington

Yorkshire
Bradford
Bridlington
Clayton West
Filey
Gilling West
Goole
Great Ayton
Guiseley
Hinderwell
Hull
Leconfield
Leeds
Marton-in-Cleveland
Naburn
Rawden
Redcar
Ripon
Scarborough
Selby
Sneaton
Wentworth Woodhouse
Westerdale

Lerwick
Otterswick
Whalsay

Sutherland
Kylesku
Tongue

West Lothian
Blackness
Port Edgar

Wigtownshire
Drummore
Stranraer
Wigtown

WALES

Anglesey
Amllwch
Church Bay
Dulas
Holyhead
Llanallgo
Llandegfan
Llanfairpwllgwyngyll
Moelfre
Plas Newydd
Rhoscolyn
Rhosneigr

Breconshire
Brecon
Llanwrtyd
Peterstone

Caernarvonshire
Aberdaron
Bangor
Caernarvon
Llanengan
Llangian
Nefyn
Port Dinorwic

Portmadoc
Pwllheli

Cardiganshire
Aberaeron
Aberporth
Aberystwyth
Borth
Cardigan
Henfynyw
Llandysul
Newquay

Carmarthenshire
Llanarthney
Pembrey

Denbighshire
Abergele

Flintshire
Llanasa
St Asaph
Whitewell

Glamorgan
Barry
Cardiff
Cowbridge
Llangennith
Margam
Merthyr Tydfil
Mumbles
Newton
Old Walls
Port Eynon
Porthcawl
Rhossili
Swansea

Merionethshire
Aberdyfi
Dolgellau
Llanenddwyn
Pennal
Twyn

Monmouthshire
Chepstow
Llanfihangel Crucorney
Monmouth
Newport

Montgomeryshire
Breidden Hill
Criggion
Kerry
Montgomery

Pembrokeshire
Amroth
Angle
Bosherston
Carregwasted Point
Castlemartin
Cilgerran
Fishguard
Granston
Haverfordwest
Hubberston
Lamphey
Lawrenny
Little Newcastle
Llanhowell
Ludchurch
Manorbier
Milford Haven
Newport
Pembroke
Pembroke Dock
Pennally
Rhoscrowther
Rudbaxton
St David's
St Dogmael's
Skokholm Island
Solva
Tenby

Radnorshire
Llanyre

Index of important persons

Coram, Thomas — London (Holborn Viaduct).

Cornwell, Jack, VC — Chester, Greater London (Manor Park & Richmond), and Hornchurch.

Cowan, Walter — Kineton.

Craddock, Christopher — Catherington, Gilling West, and York.

Crawford, Jack — Sunderland.

Cromie, Francis — Haverfordwest, Wales.

Crozier, Francis — Banbridge, Northern Ireland.

Crusoe, Robinson — East Coker and Hull.

Cumby, William — Heighington; Pembroke Dock, Wales.

Cumming, Arthur — Scropton.

Cunningham, Andrew — Bishop's Waltham and London (St Paul's Cathedral).

Dampier, William — East Coker.

Darling, Grace — Bamburgh, Hull, and Inner Farne.

Davison, Alexander — Felton and Swarland.

Defoe, Daniel — London (Bunhill Fields).

Denning, Norman — Micheldever.

Dibdin, Charles — London (Camden Town).

Dorling, Taprell — London (Tower Hill).

Douglas, James — Dartmouth and Plymouth.

Drake, Sir Francis — London (Westminster Abbey), Oxford, and Plymouth.

Drewry, George, VC — Greater London (Manor Park and Forest Gate).

Duncan, Adam — Dundee, Scotland.

Edgcumbe, John — Bath.

Esmonde, Eugene, VC — Gillingham.

Evans, Edgar — Portsmouth; Rhossili and Swansea, Wales.

Fisher, John — Kilverstone.

FitzRoy, Robert — Greater London (Upper Norwood).

Flinders, Mathew — Donnington and Lincoln.

Franklin, John — Gravesend, London (Waterloo Place and Westminster Abbey), and Spilsby.

Frohman, Charles — Marlow.

Fryatt, Charles — Dovercourt and London (Liverpool Street).

Gambier, James — Iver.

Glasfurd, C.E. — Bearsted.

Gower, Erasmus — Hambledon; Cilgerran, Wales.

Graville, John — Hull.

Greathead, Henry — South Shields.

Grenfell, Julian — Parkgate.

Grenville, Sir Richard — Bideford.

Hakluyt, Richard — Bristol.

Halahan, Henry — Chiddingfold.

Hammond, Andrew — Terrington St Clements.

Hampden, John — Prestwood.

Hardy, Thomas — London (Westminster Abbey) and Portesham.

Hargood, William — Bath.

Harland, Edward — Belfast.

Harris, Douglas — Wolverhampton.

Harrison, James — Wallasey.

Harvey, John — Eastry.

Hawke, Edward — North Stoneham.

Hichens, Robert — London (Hill Street); Penrhyn, Wales.

Hillary, William — Douglas, IOM.

Hobart, Augustus — Walton on the Wolds.

Hood, Alexander — Cricket St Thomas.

— Arthur — Netherbury.

— Horace — Brooksby.

— Samuel — Butleigh and South Perrot.

Hopwood, Ronald — Deerhurst.

Horton, Max — Liverpool.

Hoste, William — King's Lynn.

Howard, Charles — Reigate.

Howe, Richard — Melton Mowbray and London (St Paul's Cathedral).

Ismay, Thomas — Maryport and Thurstaston.

Jackson, George — London (St Paul's Cathedral).

Rae, John — Kirkwall.

Raleigh, Walter — London (Westminster and St Paul's Cathedral).

Ramsey, Bertram — Portsmouth.

Richardson, John — Grasmere.

Rigden, Weasel — Whitstable.

Roberts, Bartholomew — Little Newcastle, Wales.

Roddam, Robert — Ilderton.

Rodney, George — London (St Paul's Cathedral) and Old Alresford; Breidden Hill, Wales.

Rogers, Mary Anne — London (Aldersgate) and Southampton.

Rooke, George — Canterbury.

Ross, John — Stranraer, Scotland.

Sandford, Douglas, VC — Exeter.

Schermuly, Augustus — Morden.

Scott, Robert Falcon — Binton, Devonport, Exeter, and London (Waterloo Place); Glen Prosen, Scotland; Cardiff, Wales.

Selkirk, Alexander — Lower Largo, Scotland.

Sephton, Alfred, VC — Coventry and Wolverhampton.

Seppings, Robert — Taunton.

Seymour, George — Arrow.

— Hugh — Arrow.

Shackleton, Ernest — Eastbourne, Greater London (Dulwich), and London (South Kensington and Tower Hill).

Shaftoe, Robert — Whitworth.

Shelvocke, George — Greater London (Deptford).

Shovell, Cloudsley — Rochester and St Mary's.

Skinner, John — Holyhead, Wales.

Slater, Jim — South Shields.

Smeaton, John — London (Westminster Abbey).

Smith, John (died 1631) — London (Cheapside and Ludgate Hill).

— John (died 1912) — Hanley and Lichfield.

— William — London

Snook, S. — Iver.

Somers, George — Whitchurch Canonicorum.

Spearman, Alexander — Crediton.

Stevenson, George — London (Westmister Abbey).

— Robert — London (Westminster Abbey).

Stokes, John — Haverfordwest, Wales.

Sturdee, Doveton — Frimley.

Symington, William — Leadhills.

Tennant, William — Upton-on-Severn.

Tennyson, Alfred Lord — Freshwater.

Thomson, James — Edam, Scotland.

Thornburgh, Edward — Exeter.

Tisdall, Arthur, VC — Deal.

Tompion, Thomas — Northill.

Tovey, John — Langton Matravers.

Tryon, George — Bulwick.

Vancouver, George — King's Lynn and Petersham.

Van der Velde, Willem — London (Piccadilly).

Vernon, Edward — Nacton.

Vian, Phillip — London (St Paul's Cathedral).

Vince, George — Blandford.

Waghorn, Thomas — Chatham and Snodland.

Walker, William — Winchester.

Warburton-Lee, B., VC — Whitewell, Wales.

Warneford, Ronald, VC — Highworth and London (Brompton Cemetery).

Watt, James — Leeds and London (Westminster Abbey).

Webb, Mathew — Dawley.

Wemyss, Roslyn — West Wemyss, Scotland.

Whitshed, James — Iver.

Williams, William, VC — Chepstow, Wales.

Wintour, Charles — Brooksby and Clayton West.

Wishart, James — Leatherhead.

Woodget, Richard — Burnham Overy Staithe.

Wouldhave, William — South Shields.

Wylie, William — Porchester.

Index of vessels

Further reading

Albion, Robert Greenhalgh, *Naval and Maritime History*, David & Charles, revised edition 1973.
Bush, Captain Eric, *The Flowers of the Sea*, George Allen & Unwin, 1962
Colledge, J.J., *Ships of the Royal Navy: an Historical Index* (two volumes), David & Charles, 1969–72.
Corbett, Sir J.S. & Newbolt, Sir H., *History of the Great War – Naval Operations* (five volumes and maps), Longman, Green & Co., 1920–31.
Dictionary of National Biography.
Evans, A.S., *Beneath the Waves: A History of HM Submarine Losses 1904–1971*, William Kimber, 1986.
HMSO, *British Vessels Lost at Sea 1914–18*, Patrick Stephens, 1977.
HMSO, *British Vessels Lost at Sea 1939–45*, Patrick Stephens, 1977.
Haythornthwaite, Philip J., *The World War One Source Book*, Arms & Armour, 1992.
Hocking, Charles, *Dictionary of Disasters at Sea During the Age of Steam* (two volumes), Lloyd's Register of Shipping, 1969.
Manning, T.D. & Walker, C.F., *British Warship Names*, Putnam, 1959.
National Maritime Museum, *Catalogue of the Library: Volume II Parts one & two*, 1969.
Parker, Harry, *Naval Battles*, T.H. Parker, 1911.
Rohwer, J. & Hummelchen, G., *Chronology of the War at Sea 1939–1945* (two volumes), Ian Allan, 1972.
Roskill, S.W., *The War at Sea* (three volumes in four), HMSO, 1954–61.
Shrubb, R.E.A. & Sainsbury, A.B., *The Royal Navy Day by Day*, Centaur Press, 1979.
Warner, Oliver, *Battle Honours of the Royal Navy*, George Philip & Son, 1956.
Weightman, Alfred E., *Crests & Badges of H.M. Ships*, Gale & Polden, 1957.
Who Was Who.
Winton, John (Editor), *Freedom's Battle: The War at Sea 1939–1945*, Hutchinson, 1967.
Young, John, *A Dictionary of Ships of the Royal Navy of the Second World War*, Patrick Stephens, 1975.